CANTERBURY CATHEDRAL
AND ITS ROMANESQUE
SCULPTURE

DEBORAH KAHN

Canterbury Cathedral and Its Romanesque Sculpture

UNIVERSITY OF TEXAS PRESS, AUSTIN

International Standard Book Number 0–292–71137–9
Library of Congress Catalog Card Number 90–71955

First University of Texas Press Edition, 1991

Requests for permission to reproduce material
from this work should be sent to Permissions,
University of Texas Press, Box 7819, Austin, TX 7813-7819.

*The University of Texas Press
wishes to acknowledge a grant from
the Andrew W. Mellon Foundation
which has assisted the publication
of this edition for the Americas.*

Originating Publisher HARVEY MILLER PUBLISHERS · 20 Marryat Road · London SW19 5BD · England

Contents

Preface   page 7

Introduction   13

I. Archbishop Lanfranc's Cathedral   27

II. Archbishop Anselm's Crypt and Choir   35

III. Sculpture under Archbishop Theobald   95

IV. Sculpture after the Death of Becket   139

Epilogue   172

Appendix I: The Infirmary Complex   173

Appendix II: Twelfth-century Carved Images

        of Becket at Canterbury   180

Notes to the Text   183

List of Archbishops and Priors   205

Map   206

Abbreviations   207

Bibliography   209

List of Illustrations   219

Index   225

To David

Preface

ROMANESQUE SCULPTURE in England has long been regarded as inferior to that of the Continent. Responsibility for this is in large measure due to the extraordinary success (if one may call it that) of Henry VIII's Dissolution of the monasteries, with its accompanying destruction of carved decoration, and the subsequent birth of Anglicanism in England. The arts in the service of the church became less important than in the countries which remained Catholic, and the reform in England was far more wide-ranging in terms of destruction than it was in Protestant Germany. It was also to be consolidated by a second wave of destruction by the Puritans in the seventeenth century. However, recent scholarship has brought about a profound re-evaluation of Romanesque sculpture in England, and along with English architecture, painting, ivory carving and metalwork, it has come to be counted among the greatest achievements of the Romanesque period.

The Cathedral Priory of Christ Church, Canterbury holds an eminent position in the development of Romanesque sculpture. Christ Church was after all the primacy of all England, and thus it had a status that could not be rivalled. The foundation of the cathedral by St Augustine soon after his arrival in England in 597 is a cardinal event in European history: it marked the true starting point of Roman Christianity in Britain, which finally triumphed over the Celtic church that had been established in the North of England. There is no other site in England where the full sequence of sculptural styles of the eleventh and twelfth centuries can be followed so continuously, and yet no comprehensive study of this sculpture at Canterbury exists. It is therefore of considerable importance to examine its characteristics, its sources and its influence, to assess the many changes in fashion, consider its international links and its responsiveness to developments on the Continent. At no other English cathedral is the range of carving from this period of such consistently high quality, but even so only a small percentage of what once existed has survived. To piece together the story of its development is a work of detection.

The time span covered in this book is brief — just over one hundred years, from 1066 to about 1180 — but it is a period of many vicissitudes and powerful growth. The great architectural campaigns and their accompanying sculpture at Canterbury Cathedral fall into four distinctive phases. These phases coincide roughly with the terms of four archbishops, and the book has been divided accordingly. But it should be borne in mind that artistic styles sometimes bridge these chronological divisions, and similarly that the terminology of Romanesque and Gothic are intended as useful labels not as watertight divisions of style.

The first chapter examines the efforts of Archbishop Lanfranc's craftsmen in the new Anglo-Norman church and monastic buildings, erected in the wake of the Norman Conquest and after the fire of 1067. The sculptural decoration at this stage is modest; nevertheless, the church is of great interest as a straightforward transposition of a Norman building onto English soil. The next chapter turns to Archbishop Anselm's magnificent crypt and choir, which bears an abundance of sculpture of the highest standard, including not only the justly famous capitals in the crypt but also those of the external choir arcade. The latter have only recently been cleaned and studied at close range, and they are examined here in depth for the first time. The third chapter is concerned with the enlargement of the monastery under Archbishop Theobald. This was an enormous undertaking, and the sculpture is impressive mainly by virtue of its sheer output. But the buildings also reveal some remarkable facts about the origins of the masons and workshop techniques in a period when there are few documents to answer such questions. The final chapter spans the most momentous events in the cathedral's history. Archbishop Thomas Becket was murdered in his church by Henry II's knights on 29 December 1170. He was canonized in 1173, and in the following year fire gutted the cathedral. In this chapter, the introduction of the Gothic style and its effects on longstanding local traditions in sculpture are the main focus. The magnificent sculptures from the choir screen, which have not previously received careful study, are also treated in detail.

This book makes considerable use of the literary sources, for Christ Church had a well established biographical and historiographical tradition. The two best known chroniclers of Christ Church were Eadmer and Gervase. Their writing was moulded by their loyalty to the convent, and while this may distort the historical evidence, it adds greatly to the vividness of the architectural descriptions. Eadmer (*c.*1060-*c.*1144) was precentor (or cantor) at the cathedral, a member of Anselm's household and keeper of the archbishop's relics and chapel. His two principal works are the *Life of St Anselm*, a biography of the saintly archbishop, and the *Historia Novorum in Anglia*, a history of events in England from 960 to 1122. Gervase (*c.*1141-*c.*1210) became a monk at Christ Church in 1163, and between 1193 and 1197 he was sacrist at the cathedral. His most ambitious works were the *Chronica*, a history of Christ Church set in its wider context, a smaller chronicle known as the *Gesta Regum*, and the *Actus Archiepiscoporum Cantuariensium*, a history of the archbishops of Canterbury.

Both authors offer precise information about the appearance of the cathedral in its various forms. Eadmer, whose obsession was with relics and their location in the church, inadvertently provides many details about the arrangement of the Anglo-Saxon structure, Lanfranc's church, and Anselm's new choir. Gervase, writing a little later, brings a complete eyewitness record of the rebuilding of the choir after its destruction by fire in 1174, in his *Tractatus de Combustione et Reparatione Cantuariensis Ecclesiae*.

He also gives a brief account of Lanfranc's church (which he never saw) and a comparison between Anselm's choir and the new one which encapsulates some of the fundamental differences between Romanesque and Gothic architecture. He writes, for example: 'The pillars of the old and new work were alike in form and thickness but different in length. For the new pillars were elongated by almost twelve feet...'.[1] He notes that ribbed vaults had replaced the previous stone vaults and painted wood roofs and that the new choir was altogether taller, lighter and more highly decorated than the old. The accuracy of his observations in passages such as this, as well as his detailed discussion of the rebuilding, make him a unique and invaluable source.

There are of course other major historical works, not least the ten biographies of Thomas Becket that appeared at the end of the twelfth century. Different types of records further enhance our knowledge, such as the valuable rental lists of cathedral property pieced together and analyzed by the late William Urry. There is also a rich tradition of local antiquarian scholarship among writers like William Somner, born in Canterbury in 1598 and William Gostling, born in the city in 1696. An institution as important as Canterbury Cathedral has obviously attracted many authors over the centuries, and the fine recent biographies of the Anglo-Norman archbishops provide a useful context for the study of the building, although they shed little direct light on its architectural form or decoration.

But the building itself has not received short shrift. The nineteenth-century scholar, Reverend Robert Willis produced two pivotal architectural studies: one on the cathedral church, the other on the monastic buildings. Since then, the work of more recent architectural historians and archaeologists has considerably added to our knowledge of the buildings. The Canterbury Archaeological Trust continues to make startling discoveries by excavating in the precious time before each new car park or shopping precinct rises in the town. The manuscripts produced both at Christ Church and at the nearby abbey of St Augustine's have also been studied intensively, by C.R. Dodwell in the 1950s and more recently by T.A. Heslop and A. Lawrence. Moreover, other artistic productions, notably stained-glass, have received the attention they deserve, in this case thanks to the work of M.H. Caviness.

As far as sculpture itself is concerned, I owe my most profound thanks to the pioneering work of George Zarnecki. My debt to him is enormous and extends far beyond his learned volumes and articles. Without his guidance, careful reading of my text and encouragement, this book could never have been written. For this I am grateful beyond words.

It gives me great pleasure to record my thanks to several of my other friends. I had the benefit of the learned counsel of Eliane Vergnolle, Jacques Henriet and Maylis Baylé who helped me particularly with the French material. Caroline Barron and Gervase Rosser saved me from many errors which the art historian who strays into the field of history is likely to

9

commit. Many others helped me, but I am especially grateful to T.A. Heslop, Christopher Hewat, Peter Kidson, Neil Stratford, Paul Williamson and William Wixom for their knowledgeable suggestions and generous discussion. My visits to the site were facilitated by Tim Tatton-Brown, who was not only liberal with his time but also shared his recent archaeological discoveries and views on the buildings. I was also assisted by many members of the Chapter and staff at Canterbury, notably the then Dean, Victor de Waal, the cathedral treasurer, Canon de Sausmarez and the architect, Peter Marsh.

The writing of this book was carried out in the Metropolitan Museum of Art where I was the fortunate recipient of a Mellon research grant, and in the Society of Antiquaries of London. The kindness of the librarians of these two institutions, together with that of the entire Medieval Department at the Metropolitan Museum of Art in New York City was enormous and leaves me greatly in their debt.

The inclusion of colour plates was made possible in part by grants from the British Academy and the Marc Fitch Fund. I am most grateful to them for their generous support of this project. The intelligent editing and attention to the plates by Elly Miller and Clare Reynolds has contributed greatly to the book, and is much appreciated. My profound thanks are also due to my parents who not only saw me through my studies but actually first introduced me to Canterbury Cathedral many years ago. Finally I wish to thank David Freedberg for his enduring patience and valiant reading of the manuscript. If nothing else, I hope he is surprised by how much the iconoclasts missed at Canterbury.

The Author and Publishers wish to thank all those who have made photographs available for this book and given their permission for publication. In particular we wish to thank Professor George Zarnecki, the staff of the Conway Library – especially Ms Constance Hill, Mr Roger Musgrave, Mr John Bowen, The Canterbury Royal Archaeological Museum and Professor Reginald Dodwell.

CANTERBURY CATHEDRAL

Alexander episcopus seruus seruorum dei· Lanfranco utriusq; sapientie gra referto salute & apostolicam benedictione. ...

Hunc librum dato pretio emptum ego LANFRANCVS archieps de beccensi cenobio in angliam terram deferri feci & ecclesie xpi dedi. Siqs eum de iure prefate ecclesie abstulerit. anathema sit.

Clemens eps seruus seruorum dei Lanfranco cantuarbariensi archiepo. salute & apostolicam benedictione. ...

Clemens eps seruus seruorum dei LANFRANCO cantuarbariensi archiepo sicut bono confratri salute & apostolicam benedictione· ...

1. Last page of the 11th-century manuscript in Cambridge, Trinity College, MS B.16.44, p.405,
where it is stated that 'I Lanfranc archbishop bought this book and had it brought from Bec
and presented it to the church of Christ'. Lanfranc seems to have used this book as his authority,
and his quotations from canon law were probably taken from it.

Introduction

Background

THE STORY BEGINS with Lanfranc, the first Norman appointment as archbishop at Canterbury following the Norman Conquest (ill. 2). When Lanfranc came to Canterbury in 1070, the cathedral fabric was in a damaged state after the fire of 1067 but the first shock of the Conquest had passed. The Anglo-Saxon archbishop Stigand, who had held the see since 1052, was deposed in 1069 and the primacy of all England became vacant.

Italian by birth, Lanfranc had been prior of the great abbey at Bec in the Duchy of Normandy. In 1063 Duke William moved Lanfranc into the position of abbot of his new foundation at Saint-Etienne at Caen (ill. 18), and he proved an effective figure there in the crucial years during which the abbey was established and built anew. A distinguished scholar, theologian and churchman of wide reputation, Lanfranc would probably have preferred to remain in retirement from the world. But when seeking a new archbishop of Canterbury, William clearly saw the need for a vigorous reformer and administrator with whom he would be able to work in close co-operation, and in 1070 he shrewdly persuaded his friend Lanfranc to fill the vacancy. Together, these two powerful men did much to reshape the English Church according to the standards then current in Normandy. At Christ Church in particular the Normanization of the monastic community was hastened by the introduction of the monks from Bec and Caen who had accompanied Lanfranc to his new see.

As a result of his work at Bec and Caen, Lanfranc had gained a good practical sense as an administrator when it came to new buildings. At Canterbury he put these skills to use when he constructed the new Anglo-Norman church and monastic buildings to replace those destroyed by fire in 1067. Lanfranc's new church at Canterbury can be understood in terms of the general policy to use buildings as a means to help secure Norman dominance. With hindsight it is easy to forget that in the 1060s the Normans were by no means certain that they would be able to keep the English population under their control, and building was an effective tool to that end.[1] In the decades after the Conquest, encouraged by the enormous wealth which the recently conquered realm of England had begun to yield, the Anglo-Norman church undertook a prodigious amount of building. Many of these new churches were on a scale of unprecedented grandeur. In fact, the nave of Lanfranc's church at Canterbury was so large that the length and width was exactly repeated when it was replaced, roughly three hundred years later, by the fourteenth-century nave that we see today.[2]

As archbishop, Lanfranc's aims were wide-ranging. The renewal and promotion of canon law was of special concern to him as a means of raising the level of ecclesiastical discipline and organization in the English Church, and a version of the collection of councils and papal decretals that he used was copied in almost every English cathedral library. Indeed, the original volume which Lanfranc bought from Bec and gave to Christ Church still survives (ill. 1). Lanfranc's training in law and logic greatly benefited his new cathedral priory. The most celebrated instance of this came in the aftermath of Archbishop Stigand's fall. Many of the estates of the cathedral had been alienated during Stigand's archiepiscopacy, and to recover them Lanfranc was obliged to prove title of law, which he did successfully at the Trial of Penenden Heath in 1072.[3]

On a national level, Lanfranc strove to assert the rights of Canterbury over York, above all in 1072 when Archbishop Thomas of York was required to make a profession of obedience to Lanfranc and his successors. The cause of the dispute between Canterbury and York extended back over five hundred years to the instructions which Pope Gregory I had issued to St Augustine, the first archbishop of Canterbury. St Augustine had seen to it that England was partitioned into two provinces with archiepiscopal sees in London (for which Canterbury was substituted) and York. This scheme proved unsatisfactory, since York never succeeded in matching Canterbury, and as a result the English Church remained unequally divided. Moreover, there was a repeated claim by Christ Church that the wide control which St Augustine had exercized over the whole British Church, and the acceptance of his position as special envoy to the pope, should be passed to the cathedral priory.[4]

While Lanfranc and William the Conqueror were at the helm, there was a firm alliance between Church and State, but this soon waned. After the death of Lanfranc in 1089, the archbishopric was kept vacant by the Conqueror's successor William Rufus, who consistently used the English Church for his own purposes. Canterbury Cathedral was no exception. It was only when the king fell seriously ill in 1093 that, in an attempt to ward off death, he promised reform and allowed the primacy at Canterbury to be filled. The choice fell once more on a prior of Bec, this time Anselm (ill. 3).

In certain respects, Anselm's life paralleled Lanfranc's. He too had been raised south of the Alps, and he succeeded Lanfranc as prior of Bec in 1063 (becoming abbot in 1078). Like Lanfranc, he was a scholar of great reputation and a monk of profound integrity and sanctity, who would probably have preferred a life of quiet devotion and scholarly pursuits. But when he arrived in England, his position instantly brought him into the limelight and he became an important figure in many of the central controversies of the day.

Unlike Lanfranc, whose first allegiance had been to the king, Anselm insisted that his loyalty belonged to the pope. The question of obedience was of primary importance to him. This stance, together with conflict over the issue of feudal obligations and Anselm's demand for the restitution of certain Church property, led to a dispute with William Rufus and eventually Anselm was forced into exile. Much of this first period of exile was spent in Rome, where Anselm was received with every honour. Indeed, it was only Anselm's intervention that saved William Rufus from excommunication. In the event this proved unnecessary, for William Rufus was killed in a hunting accident in 1100; and soon after assuming the throne, King Henry I called Anselm back from his exile in Italy. But a new dispute with the Crown ensued almost immediately. Anselm not only refused to consecrate Henry's chancellor, William Giffard, as bishop of Winchester, but declined to do homage to the new king. This forced Anselm into a second, more protracted exile, from 1101 until 1107, until a compromise was finally reached. Henry gave up the right of episcopal and abbatial investiture, while the bishops agreed to continue to do homage to the king and to provide lay fees.

In addition to his efforts to demonstrate his independence from the monarchy, Anselm was determined to strengthen the authority of the cathedral priory in the battle for primacy with York. He pressed his cathedral's claims at every available opportunity in Rome, until in 1103 Pope Paschal II finally intervened in Canterbury's favour. With such long absences and intense political concerns as these, it is hard to imagine where Anselm found the energy to engage in any other pursuits. Yet he remained a productive author, and works such as his treatise *Cur Deus Homo* influenced many generations of medieval theologians.

Anselm was also engaged on an important architectural project during this period: the construction of an enormous new crypt and choir that nearly doubled the size of Lanfranc's church (ills. 31-32). This work was accompanied by a burst of artistic activity. A new atmosphere was emerging at Christ Church. The disruption caused by the Norman Conquest had diminished, and the monks from Bec and Caen were absorbed into the community. The cults of many of the Anglo-Saxon saints suppressed by Lanfranc were revived, and the deployment of local motifs was encouraged. Since there was little earlier carving to draw on, sculptors turned for models to the illuminated initials produced in their own scriptorium. During this period the community was allowed the freedom to rediscover its own identity, and under the influence of Anselm's political and scholarly achievements it began to reawaken to its own importance a development made manifest in contemporary artistic production.

Anselm died in 1109. The esteem in which he was held at Christ Church and in the medieval world at large is made clear by his cult as a saint.[5] Anselm was succeeded by Ralph d'Escures (1114-1122), former bishop of Rochester and he in turn by William de Corbeil (1123-1136), a regular canon and former prior of the Austin canons of St Osyth in Essex. Neither of these two men had either the intellectual or the international stature of their two predecessors. Nevertheless, the style of the sculpture found at Christ Church suggests that work on the rebuilding of the choir initiated by Anselm continued almost until the time of the dedication ceremony, which was performed by Archbishop William in May 1130.

2. Pen and ink drawing of Archbishop Lanfranc,
Oxford, Bodleian Library 569 (S.C.2311) f.1.

3. Initial, produced at Jumièges probably by Hugo Pictor,
showing Archbishop Anselm seated on a throne, Rouen, MS 539, f.59

4. Seal of Theobald, Archbishop
of Canterbury (1139-1161)

5. The gabled end of a tomb showing an archbishop,
presumably Thomas Becket.

It is interesting to note the changes manifested in the liturgical headpieces of the four archbishops on this page.
Both Lanfranc and Anselm have simple tonsures. Theobald wears a double peaked mitre. Becket's mitre has a single peak.
The later form came into use towards the end of the twelfth century and has remained standard ever since.

With Archbishop William's successor Theobald, consecrated in 1139, the high intellectual standard and prominent political position of the archbishop himself was reasserted (ill. 4). Like his two distinguished predecessors Lanfranc and Anselm, Theobald came from the community at Bec in Normandy, where he had first been a monk and in 1137 had become abbot. Archbishop Theobald was among the most cultivated figures of his day. He was deeply involved in church affairs outside England and made frequent journeys to France and Italy. At home he established one of the most learned households of the time, which attracted such eminent intellectuals as Master Vacarius and John of Salisbury. The cosmopolitan atmosphere fostered at Canterbury by Archbishop Theobald is reflected in the enlargement of the church and monastery, and its modernity emerges convincingly in the installation of a vast new water system (ill. 154, Colour Pl. VII), a work of great engineering skill, sophistication and ingenuity.

Considering the ambitious scale of the campaign of rebuilding the cathedral in the third quarter of the twelfth century, it is hardly surprising to find several contiguous sculptural styles, probably representative of different workshops or at least of the various trainings of individual sculptors. The style and motifs initiated during Anselm's archiepiscopacy had taken firm root and later generations of sculptors continued to draw on this. But sculpture of the third quarter of the twelfth century was nourished by an abundance of new ideas from abroad. Awareness of developments in Flanders and North-eastern France are undeniable in some carvings of this phase. Another distinctive stylistic group of sculptures reveals a thorough knowledge of sculpture in Lower Normandy. By now the artistic production of Christ Church showed signs of full participation in many developments on the Continent, as one would expect from England's merger with Normandy, Maine, Anjou, Poitou, Angoulême and Gascony into a single political unit, the so-called Angevin Empire, ruled by Henry II (Map, p. 206). That Normandy again proved an important source of architectural and sculptural designs, possibly even of masons, may be rooted in the fact that throughout the Romanesque period, the main building stone in use at Canterbury Cathedral was imported from the quarries of Caen. In terms of the future development of art and architecture at Christ Church the cosmopolitan links with Normandy, Northern France and Flanders during this period had ramifications of vast importance.

Thomas Becket succeeded Theobald as archbishop, and curiously it was Becket's death even more than his life that brought Canterbury to the centre of the European stage (ill. 5). In electing his own chancellor as archbishop of Canterbury, Henry II believed that he had installed a devoted supporter, and initially his assessment of Becket's loyalties was probably correct. Indeed, the secular nature of the appointment is apparent from the fact that Becket only became a priest one day before his installation as archbishop in 1162. But shortly after Becket was consecrated archbishop, the once warm relations between the two men began to cool. The king brought matters to a head in January 1164, at the Council of

Clarendon, when he issued a list of sixteen written articles reasserting certain of the customs of the kingdom as they had stood in the time of his grandfather, Henry I. One important issue concerned the extent of the jurisdiction of the secular courts. Henry insisted that a clerk who had committed a felony should first be taken before the king's justice for breach of the king's peace. If convicted, he ought no longer to be protected by the Church. He should then be returned to and sentenced by the king's court. Many bishops sided with the king, but Becket opposed this policy on the grounds that a man should not be tried twice for the same offence.[6] Other issues, including episcopal elections, fuelled the disagreement between the two men. Becket would not give way to the king's will. Instead, on 8 October 1164, he fled to the archiepiscopal city of Sens, where Pope Alexander III was also in exile. Though reconciled briefly with King Henry II in Normandy, Becket's conduct upon his return to England in 1170 sent the king into a new rage. The king's feelings of anger and impotency in reaction to Becket's behaviour seems to have provoked four of his knights (Reginald FitzUrse, William de Tracy, Hugh de Morville and Richard Brito) to cross the Channel to England in pursuit of Becket. On 29 December they murdered the archbishop in the north transept of his own cathedral, as he stood between the altars of the Virgin Mary and St Benedict.

The news of Becket's death spread rapidly and shocked the entire medieval world. Three years later he was canonized, the same year that Henry made peace with the Church. As the relics began to perform miracles and the number of pilgrims began to grow to large crowds, the monks gradually came to recognize the implications of the nascent cult and its financial benefits for their community. The following year, in 1174, fire gutted the cathedral choir. Rebuilding began almost immediately, with the Becket tomb as the focal point.

The artistic contacts already established with Normandy and Northern France make the monks' decision to employ not an English, but a French architect to rebuild the choir less aberrant than it might at first appear. Artistic interchange with the Continent also sheds light on the beautiful sculptures from the cathedral's late twelfth-century choir screen (ill. 6), which were inspired in particular by contemporary metalwork. And yet, although conversant with a wide range of styles in various media, this last phase of Romanesque sculpture at Christ Church still maintains a firm allegiance to earlier artistic traditions.

6. Fragment presumably from the choir screen, c.1180, in Canterbury Cathedral.

The Community

The earliest Anglo-Norman archbishops were abbots *de facto* as well as *de jure*, living a common life with the monks in the cloister. The highest privilege of the monks was their right to elect the archbishop, who was their abbot.[7] In return, the monks were obliged to recognize the authority of their titular abbot. Despite the fact that the endowments and lands of the archbishop and monks were separate, their lives were thus closely intertwined. Lanfranc was sympathetic to the organization of Canterbury Cathedral as a Benedictine monastery, for as a monk himself he looked to the monastic order as the chief instrument of reform. Canterbury was by no means the only English cathedral monastery. At the time of the Conquest there were three others — at Sherborne, Winchester and Worcester. The fifty years that followed the Conquest brought about a considerable extension of monastic influence in England's cathedrals, with their number reaching nine.

Although the archbishop had ultimate authority and control over the monastery of Christ Church, the general administrative burden was subdivided between various other subordinate officials. The upkeep of the buildings themselves was normally the prior's responsibility. In the Romanesque period at Christ Church there were three priors of particular note as far as art and architecture were concerned: Prior Ernulf (1096-1107), Prior Conrad (1108/9-1126) and Prior Wibert (1152/3-1167). Each of these men played a major part in new building work on the cathedral or monastic buildings, although at Christ Church there is evidence that the archbishops participated as well, at least financially.

There can be little question that Christ Church was able to afford whatever new building and sculpture was required. The Domesday Book (compiled in 1086) estimated the income of Christ Church to be one of the highest of any religious house in the country. A local Kentish assessment list compiled in the interval between the Conquest and the Domesday Book confirms that the archbishop was also enormously wealthy. In Kent alone he held 325 sulungs, at a time when 2 sulungs made up a knight's fief.[8] Thus we can assume that the monks of Christ Church were able to engage the services of whatever sculptors they chose. The surviving carving suggests that they were very discriminating patrons.

Other Major Local Monuments

Canterbury Cathedral was of course not the only major building in the region, and its artistic relationship with neighbouring churches was often crucial to the development of its sculpture. The cathedral church stands within the walls of the medieval town, while just on the outskirts is its

7. The south doorway (c.1180) of the parish church of St Nicholas, Barfreston showing Christ surrounded by angels, a king and a queen, Labours of the Months, Signs of the Zodiac, musicians, wrestlers and other fanciful figures. At the apex of the inner archivolt is the figure of a bishop, possibly Becket.

nearest neighbour, St Augustine's Abbey.[9] The existence of two large monasteries in such close proximity often gave rise to competition and bitter feuding. The abbey contained not only the body of St Augustine (interred in the north porch in 613) and various royal burials, but also the mortal remains of the first ten archbishops of the cathedral. The monks of Christ Church were jealous of this not only because of prestige but also because of the offerings of visitors. In addition, there were bitter quarrels concerning the archbishop's jurisdiction over the abbey, and its privileges. The venerable traditions of the great abbey vied with those of the cathedral and so did its income.[10] But the rivalry between the two houses did not inhibit artistic interchange, and it is not always possible to be certain which may have initiated a new style.

The other important local cathedral monastery, Rochester, came under the special influence and tutelage of Christ Church.[11] Rochester was directly dependent on Christ Church and functioned as a sort of satellite community. It is not suprising then to find Canterbury's artistic development constantly reflected at Rochester (ill. 9).

The other major monuments in the region have perished. For example, only one capital and a few architectural fragments remain from the royal abbey at Faversham, founded by King Stephen in 1148 as his family mausoleum (ill. 8).[12] Fortunately there are more surviving parish churches from the period. Those at Patrixbourne (carved *c*.1170, ill. 10) and Barfreston (carved *c*.1180, ill. 7) are virtually intact. These small buildings, to some degree rural reflections of Christ Church, provide vital clues of lost sculpture at the metropolitan see. But the influence of the sculpture of Christ Church extended far beyond the local area. Reading Abbey, Worcester Cathedral and Oakham Castle (Rutland) are but a few of the far-flung buildings for which sculpture at Canterbury provided inspiration.

20

8. This capital (c.1150) of Purbeck marble
is one of the few surviving carved fragments
from the large and important royal abbey
which King Stephen and Queen Matilda founded
at Faversham not far from Canterbury.

9 (below). The west doorway of Rochester Cathedral (c.1165).
Of special interest is the tympanum
carved with Christ in Majesty and supported by
a lintel with the Apostles. These features together with
two column figures of a king and a queen
are based on the gothic portals of the Ile-de-France.

10 (right). The south doorway of St Mary's church,
Patrixbourne (c.1170). Like the tympanum at Rochester,
this too is carved with Christ in Majesty. The niche in
the gabled head contained the sculpted relief
of an Agnus Dei which has been defaced.

Regional Styles

The style of eleventh- and twelfth-century sculpture varied considerably from region to region and underwent constant change as time went on. The regional differences in carving depended largely on the existence of available models. In York, the chief centre of Viking Danelaw, Scandinavian influence was a powerful contributory factor in the formation of the Romanesque style.[13] At Canterbury, on the other hand, the effect of the Viking raids and settlement played only a marginal role in the artistic development of the region. Even though Kent was incorporated into the relatively stable kingdom of the Danish king Cnut (1016-1035), Scandinavian art had relatively little lasting impact on Canterbury productions.

By contrast, the South-east of England was profoundly affected by the Roman occupation, not least by the important legacy of Roman architecture. The cathedral itself was actually erected on the site of a Roman building.[14] While the imprint of Roman architecture is hard to ignore in Italy or in the South of France, its importance is more easily overlooked in South-east England. And yet, visible evidence of a strong Roman presence in Kent remained for centuries and was still apparent in the twelfth century. The Roman theatre is the largest (it held an audience of 7,000), and most magnificent classical building yet uncovered in the town of Canterbury itself, and part of it survived until the twelfth century. Some idea of the grandeur that Roman architecture achieved in the region may be drawn from the triumphal monument at Richborough only a short distance from Canterbury, which consisted of a large marble cross-shaped structure, decked with life-sized bronze statues.[15]

Another important factor in the creation of the regional style was Canterbury's geographic position close to the Continent. The Channel served as a unifying rather than a divisive element: it made travel easier, and facilitated the frequent journeys English churchmen made to the Continent, especially to Rome. It also eased the problems of trade. Where heavy or bulky loads were involved, water transport was far preferable to transport over land, and this partially explains why most of the stone used for building the Romanesque cathedral was imported from quarries across the Channel, near Caen. The Channel was a decisive element too in the success of the wool trade between England and Flanders, and these commercial links account for many of the artistic connections between the regions. Because its geographical location is near the northern coast of France and Flanders, Canterbury Cathedral was able to feel and absorb the artistic currents of the time better than other English houses. European culture provided a constant source of fertilization, and the art and architecture at Christ Church shows itself to have been responsive to it.

11. A detail of Eve hiding from the Lord in the Garden of Eden, (c.1000) in one of the many important Anglo-Saxon manuscripts produced at Christ Church. Oxford, Bodleian Library, MS Junius 11, p.41.

Inter-relation of the Arts

Sculpture did not develop in isolation from other arts. The dependence of sculptural motifs on manuscript illumination in the late eleventh century is particularly striking, and it is helpful to look briefly at the development of the library at Christ Church, particularly the additions made by Lanfranc. The foundations of the extensive library, among the richest in England, date back to the time of St Augustine's sixth-century mission to Southern England.[16] His successors continued to enrich it with gifts of manuscripts so that the cathedral became a repository of an extraordinary range of ancient texts and works of art. Its manuscripts were copied and imitated throughout the ages, from the great eighth-century Codex Aureus onwards. In the tenth century St Dunstan added to the cathedral library by importing books from France and Flanders. This was also the period of a series of sophisticated line-drawings at Christ Church, including the richly illustrated poems of Caedmon (ill. 11). Towards the end of the tenth century a series of magnificent psalters, such as the Eadui (ill. 13) and Harley Psalters, and many lavish gospel books, like the Arenberg Gospels (ill. 12) and Grimbald Gospels, were also produced at Christ Church.

12 (left). St Luke from the Arenberg Gospels (c.990) produced at Christ Church. New York, Pierpont Morgan Library, M 869, f.83v.

13 (right). St John from the Eadui Psalter (c.1020) produced at Christ Church. Hanover, Kestner Museum WM XXIa 36, f.147v.

23

14. The Gloucester Candlestick was commissioned between 1107 and 1113 by Abbot Peter for the Benedictine Abbey of St Peter's, now Cathedral, at Gloucester. Close stylistic comparisons with manuscript illuminations suggest that it was made at Canterbury. London, Victoria and Albert Museum.

15 (right). One of a pair of pierced bookcovers made of whalebone c.1100, which can be attributed to Canterbury. (Compare the leaf forms with those of the capital from the Cathedral crypt shown in ill.109). London, Victoria and Albert Museum.

After the Norman Conquest, one of Lanfranc's first concerns was to bring English service books into line with those used abroad, and he may also have had to replace texts lost in the fire of 1067.[17] This called for new manuscripts. In addition to the works of the Church Fathers and other standard commentaries, Lanfranc was interested in a wide range of theological and legal texts, some of which he purchased from Normandy while others he had made in the scriptorium at Christ Church. Lanfranc was consistently concerned to preserve the accuracy of texts, first at Bec, then at Canterbury, so it is not surprising to discover well-trained scribes from Normandy working for him at Christ Church. Moreover, a twelfth-century obituary records that Lanfranc, 'bestowed upon the church the special ornament of a valuable library, and many of the books which it contained were corrected with his own hand'.[18]

A few of these early Romanesque manuscripts have decorated initials, but the full-page illuminations of the Anglo-Saxon manuscripts vanished completely at this time. The shift of emphasis in illumination had important consequences. In the period following the Norman Conquest the initial became the main focus of decoration. From the 1070s until the 1120s, an endless variety of decorated letters were produced which manifest an

24

unconstrained and imaginative spirit, unrivalled elsewhere in Europe at that date. But artists soon reverted to full-page miniatures too, and some splendid twelfth-century manuscripts were illuminated at the cathedral.

It was not only the scriptorium at Canterbury which turned out works of art of the highest quality. Some major masterpieces of twelfth-century metalwork, notably the Gloucester candlestick (ill. 14), were probably produced there.[19] Many splendid ivories were also carved at Canterbury; a pair of ivory bookcovers now in the Victoria and Albert Museum have long been recognized as Canterbury works (ill. 15). Further testimony to the importance of Christ Church as an artistic centre appears in the magnificent twelfth-century stained-glass windows and the wall-paintings, once splendid, but now reduced to a few precious vestiges. There were certainly embroideries and wall-hangings, and all the evidence indicates that the Bayeux Tapestry itself is a Canterbury work (ill. 16).[20]

However, the bulk of furnishings, liturgical objects, reliquaries, crucifixes, statues, panel paintings and so many other works of art have vanished forever. Some of these would have been produced by monks, but since Canterbury was a considerable town one must also assume that there were many skilled lay craftsmen. Indeed, twelfth-century rental lists record not only textile workers and artisans, but goldsmiths among the town's most prominent citizens.[21]

From the rebuilding of the Christ Church after the Norman Conquest to the years following the murder of Thomas Becket the evolution of sculpture at Canterbury Cathedral was inspired repeatedly by stimuli from the neighbouring territories of Normandy, Flanders and Northern France. Yet despite this, Canterbury never lost the thread of its own powerful artistic tradition. A continual interplay of these two strains characterizes the history of eleventh- and twelfth-century sculpture at Canterbury, and it resulted in creations of great originality and importance. Although much has been destroyed, a great deal has also been saved. The magnificent Romanesque crypt and extensive monastic buildings are but two highlights. There is also the spectacular choir rebuilt after the fire of 1174 (ill. 122). Its grandeur and beauty are still supremely evident, but we can only gain the full measure of its achievement if we consider what went before.

16. A detail from the Bayeux Tapestry showing two important scenes. At the right the funeral bier of Edward the Confessor is carried in procession to Westminster Abbey. Simultaneously, at the left, a small skirted figure teetering on a ladder, places a cock-shaped finial on the abbey roof — the finishing touch to the building which Edward himself had started.

West Elevation.

North Elevation.

17. *Watercolour by J.C. Buckler showing the elevation of the north-west tower of Canterbury Cathedral as it stood in 1832. London, Society of Antiquaries.*

I. Archbishop Lanfranc's Cathedral

WHEN THE ANGLO-SAXON CATHEDRAL at Canterbury was burnt down in 1067 the chronicler Eadmer, who was brought up at Christ Church and eventually became a monk there, was only a boy. Despite his youth, he retained a vivid memory of the cathedral and the events connected with it. He described the fire some fifty years later, attributing it to the 'carelessness of some individuals', which suggests that it was not entirely accidental but rather that it was part of the calculated Norman policy to eradicate the Anglo-Saxon past.[1]

The destruction of the metropolitan cathedral of England was followed in 1069 by the deposition of its Anglo-Saxon archbishop Stigand. In the next year, Lanfranc left his position as abbot of Saint-Etienne at Caen to become archbishop of Canterbury. This appointment led to the drastic reorganization of the English Church along the lines of the Norman model. Lanfranc produced a set of written Constitutions to regulate monastic life and liturgy in the house under his care, and the model was soon adopted in monasteries all over the country.[2] In this way Lanfranc made Christ Church a centre of influence in spiritual matters, but it also set the standard in the area of artistic production. The ruinous state of the cathedral presented an opportunity to replace the outmoded Anglo-Saxon building with a new one in the early Romanesque style that was already well-established in Normandy. Lanfranc introduced the Romanesque style to Christ Church, and his well-designed buildings were part of a sophisticated monastic organization. Individual buildings that had outlived their usefulness were replaced by larger structures, but the actual layout introduced by Lanfranc proved excellent and has never been substantially altered.

The first Romanesque building in England was, of course, King Edward the Confessor's Westminster Abbey, probably begun in the 1050s. But it was only in the 1070s, following the example of Canterbury Cathedral that the new style gained momentum in England.

Lanfranc arrived at Christ Church with a few Norman monks and, as Eadmer puts it, 'postponing all thought of providing for his own convenience, he set urgently to work and completed the building and dwellings needed for the use of the monks'. We do not know exactly when he started to build the new church, only that he completed it in seven years.[3] Most writers assume that the work was already in hand by 1070, but since Lanfranc had only arrived at Canterbury on the 15th of August that year and was consecrated on the 29th of that month,[4] it is unlikely that any serious work could have started before 1071.

In the later stages of work Lanfranc was helped by his prior Henry, whom he appointed around 1076. But the man who most likely had a hand

18. West front of Saint-Etienne at Caen with its massive towers and restrained decoration — the type of façade from which the former 11th-century façade at Canterbury derived.

in the design and building of the new cathedral was Gundulf, brought to Christ Church by Lanfranc in 1070. He was probably also an Italian and a relative of Anselm, Lanfranc's successor as archbishop. A former sacrist at Bec, prior at Saint-Etienne at Caen and a future bishop of Rochester, he was an able organizer and an expert builder.[5]

Even though Saint-Etienne in Caen was not consecrated until 1077, it is probable that both Lanfranc and Gundulf had a very detailed knowledge of this church (ill. 18). They must also have been familiar with the design of the other ducal foundation at Caen, La Trinité, started in around 1060 and dedicated in 1066.[6] It is not suprising, therefore, that the cathedral at Canterbury shows striking similarities with the two churches in Caen, especially Saint-Etienne. As at Saint-Etienne, the nave of Lanfranc's cathedral consisted of nine bays, and the westernmost bay was flanked by twin towers. There was a large crossing tower, and a transept with single apsidal chapels in each of the east walls. The eastern part of Lanfranc's cathedral was replaced in the late eleventh century, but excavations in the late nineteenth century revealed that Lanfranc's choir had two bays only and probably terminated in an apse. The choir aisles also had apses.[7] A small crypt existed under the main choir, and was presumably entered by steps from the aisles. In this respect, Canterbury followed the model of La Trinité at Caen, where the crypt is confined to the eastern part of the presbytery.[8]

The extreme west end of Lanfranc's crypt survives. It has three aisles formed by two rows of columns supporting vaults. The four remaining capitals against the west wall of the crypt are all of cushion form, set on round or octagonal shafts (ill. 20). These cushion capitals are not carved,

19. Detail of watercolour by Buckler showing the cushion capitals of Lanfranc's western tower.

28

but their form alone raises interesting problems. Much of the Romanesque fabric survives beneath the Gothic masonry, including substantial parts of both western towers, which can still be seen from above the vaults of the aisles. The remnant of the north-west tower includes a plain cushion capital. A detailed watercolour of 1832, by J. C. Buckler shows a view of this tower with cushion capitals throughout (ills. 17, 19). The same capital form was used for the central crossing piers, for when the later masonry of one of these was cut back, a cushion capital was revealed.[9]

Thus every surviving capital in Lanfranc's church is of cushion form. This is important. From Eadmer's description it appears that the old church was not pulled down at once, and the western half was retained for the time being. According to Eadmer, Lanfranc commanded that 'the bodies of the saints, which were buried in the eastern part of the church, should be removed to the western part, where the oratory of the blessed Virgin Mary stood'. Eadmer continues, 'But in the course of time, as the new work of the commenced church proceeded, it became necessary to take down the remainder of the old work, where the bodies of the saints just mentioned were deposited'.[10] This shows that building was carried out, as so often in the Middle Ages, from east to west, in order to cause as little disruption as possible to services. Thus we may conclude that the use of cushion capitals in Lanfranc's church spans the entire period of construction: those in the crypt belong to the first phase, those of the central tower to the middle years, and those of the western towers to the final stages of construction. In a major building erected in the short period of seven years, the ease and speed with which cushion capitals could be

20. The west wall of Archbishop Lanfranc's crypt with its original cushion capitals and both round and octagonal shafts, c.1071.

21

22

21-24. Four columns from the dark entry passage of Lanfranc's church, c.1080. Although each shaft is enriched with a different geometric motif, the capitals are uniformly of the simple block form.

produced evidently made them an economic and convenient form. Church interiors were usually brightly painted at this period, and the cushion-shaped capital was easy enough to decorate in a pleasing way with simple polychrome motifs.

The origins of the cushion capital have been traced to the Byzantine world. From there it passed, in a modified form, to Italy, the German Empire, Flanders, Scandinavia and England, although just when and how it reached England remains an open question. It has been suggested that this simple but functional form of capital, derived from wooden architecture.[11] Perhaps there were Anglo-Saxon examples in wood, perhaps indeed in stone, but the lack of tangible evidence makes it impossible to draw a satisfactory conclusion. Nor was the type used in the duchy of Normandy during the early Romanesque period. Thus it is unlikely that the cushion capital existed as a standard type in Anglo-Saxon England or that it came to England from Normandy.[12]

Even more striking than the dominance of the cushion capital form in Lanfranc's cathedral is the complete absence of the simplified Corinthian capital with volutes. This was the most prominent type of capital used in Normandy during the second half of the eleventh century and moreover

30

it was employed throughout England during the last quarter of the century.[13] Besides the cushion form, the only other capital type for which there is any evidence in Lanfranc's church is the block form. These rudimentary capitals survive in the 'dark entry', the passage between the dormitory and the chapter house (ills. 21-24), and like the cushion capitals of Lanfranc's church they are uncarved, although they were presumably painted. Similar examples were used in the contemporary crypt at Rochester Cathedral and (albeit as bases), in the crypt of La Trinité at Caen.

We know a little about the internal aspect of Lanfranc's church. On the gallery of the south transept there was an organ; a gilded corona and a spectacular circular chandelier are mentioned; and so too is the screen and the great cross above it, with its two cherubim and the images of the Virgin and St John (presumably carved in wood and painted).[14] Thus, despite the fact that the documents are silent on the nature of the mural paintings, stained glass and wall-hangings, we have some idea of how very splendid the interior of Lanfranc's church must have been.

Since the number of monks had rapidly increased, the accomodation built by Lanfranc immediately upon his arrival at Canterbury soon became inadequate and, as Eadmer observes, their replacements 'excelled them greatly, both in beauty and magnitude'.[15] The new buildings included cloisters, cellarer's offices, a refectory, dormitories and many other buildings, which were completely enclosed by a wall. In Anglo-Saxon times, walls were not used around the monastic precinct, and this enclosing wall was the first of its kind in England. After the construction of this wall at Canterbury, however, they became a standard feature of monasteries throughout England.

The most substantial visible remains of any of Lanfranc's monastic buildings are those of the great dormitory.[16] The bases and the other remnants of decorated columns from the ground floor of the hall as well as the semi-column responds of the 'dark entry' also survive. These sturdy columns are decorated with various geometric motifs including incised chevron, spiral and lozenge, carved in raised relief (ills. 21-24). Columns carved with spiral decoration exist in the Anglo-Saxon crypt at St Wystan, Repton (Derbyshire), but those of the dormitory at Canterbury are the earliest carved columns in post-Conquest England. As such, they are the rudimentary forerunners of the majestic piers of Durham Cathedral.[17] They also led the way for the many and diversely decorated shafts which followed later in the eleventh and twelfth centuries at Canterbury itself.

The lozenge, spiral and chevron patterns on these shafts are the only attempt at carving that remain from Lanfranc's cathedral, so the discovery in the town of Canterbury in 1985 of a group of five carved panels of around 1080-1090 is of great interest (ills. 25-29). Although the original use of these pieces is uncertain, it seems likely that they came from the cathedral or its precinct.[18] The carving, with its silhouette-like forms of dragons and dogs surrounded by raised frames, is conceived entirely in two dimensions: there is no attempt at modelling. The type of confronted grotesques

23

24

25

26

27

28

carved on these four rectangular and one rhomboid-shaped stones recall those parts of the Bayeux Tapestry where paired animals are framed by the embroidered stitching of rhomboid shape (ill. 30) — significant similarities considering that the Tapestry was in all probability produced at Canterbury between 1067 and 1082.[19]

After the upheaval of the Conquest, new buildings were urgently needed to facilitate the smooth running of monastic life. The rapidity with which these buildings were erected left little time for refinements such as sculpture. Lanfranc's approach was largely utilitarian, and carving did not play an important role in the first Anglo-Norman cathedral at Canterbury. The same attitude towards decoration is evident in the manuscripts produced at Christ Church in the wake of the Conquest. Important texts were copied in clear Norman script, although decoration did play a small role in the interests of the efficient reproduction of the texts themselves.[20] The earlier traditions that existed at Canterbury were of little interest to Lanfranc.[21] But the suppression of the cathedral's past artistic traditions was only temporary. Under the next archbishop, Anselm, artistic life at Christ Church was to be regenerated and given free rein.

29

25-29. These five reliefs carved with foliage and grotesques are virtually the only surviving sculptures in Canterbury earlier than the capitals in the Cathedral crypt. On stylistic grounds they are probably roughly contemporary with the Bayeux Tapestry.

33

30 (left). Detail from the border of the Bayeux Tapestry. Like ill.27, this shows two confronted grotesques enclosed by diagonal frames.

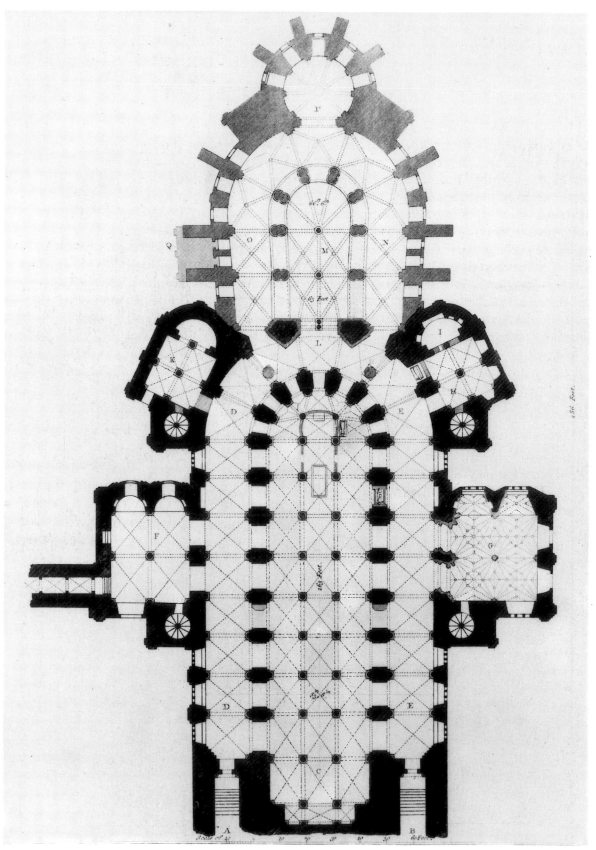

*Plan of the crypt. Black indicates the eleventh century crypt plan,
grey the eastern extension added after the fire of 1174*
H = *St. Gabriel's Chapel*   **K** = *The Holy Innocents' Chapel*

II. Archbishop Anselm's Crypt and Choir

BY CONTRAST with the sparse remains of Lanfranc's period, the evidence for sculptural activity at Canterbury under Archbishop Anselm is rich and abundant. When Anselm arrived at Christ Church in 1093 to become the second archbishop since the Norman Conquest, he found the buildings in good order and the monastic community well organized, maintaining the discipline outlined in Lanfranc's Constitutions.[1] Soon after his consecration, the decision was taken to double the size of Lanfranc's church by extending the east end and providing it with a much bigger crypt and choir (plan on facing page). Anselm clearly endorsed the plan to build, since in 1096 he made a gift of 'the revenues of his town at Peckham for seven years, the whole of which were expended upon the new work'.[2] It had taken seven years to complete Lanfranc's church at Canterbury, and perhaps Anselm had this in mind when he made his bequest.

It is not difficult to understand the need to enlarge Lanfranc's church: its presbytery had only two bays and a small crypt underneath.[3] With such a short choir, space and altars were at a premium for a community whose population had been rapidly increasing since the end of Lanfranc's term. Around 1080, according to Eadmer, there were some sixty monks, and at the time of Lanfranc's death in 1089 the chronicler Gervase puts the number at one hundred. The peak was probably reached by about 1120, when there were between one hundred and forty and one hundred and fifty monks.[4]

A very important factor in the decision to enlarge the crypt and choir was probably the need to provide space for newly flourishing devotions to old saints. In the wake of the Conquest the Normans had adopted a generally sceptical attitude towards the validity of many Anglo-Saxon saints. Like all other major English churches, Canterbury possessed the relics of numerous holy persons, but there were few written records to describe who they were or to vouch for the pureness of their relics. Two monks at Christ Church, however, embraced the old cults with special enthusiasm. The chronicler Osbern wrote the *Miracles of St Dunstan* and *Lives* of St Dunstan, St Elphege and St Oda in an attempt to reinstate the saints. Eadmer also produced hagiographies, including one on St Bregwin and one on St Dunstan with the intention of giving credence and respectability to their cults at Canterbury.[5]

Archbishop Lanfranc had remained ambivalent about the legitimacy of many English cults, and Eadmer quotes his comment to Anselm, 'These Englishmen among whom we are living, have set up for themselves certain saints whom they revere. But sometimes when I turn over in my mind their own accounts of who they were, I cannot help having doubts about the quality of their sanctity'.[6] This explains why Lanfranc did not allow a place for St Dunstan in the Calendar, and why the Feast of St Elphege was relegated to a place with those of secondary importance. Nor were the relics of St Dunstan and St Elphege given positions of importance in Lanfranc's church.[7] But the efforts of Osbern and Eadmer eventually succeeded, and under Anselm these saints rose in reputation. When the choir was extended, their relics were given places of honour on either side of the high altar.[8]

The greater freedom from archiepiscopal control enjoyed by the community under Anselm also allowed the gradual restoration of many of the old customs temporarily suppressed by Lanfranc. Anselm was sympathetic to Anglo-Saxon traditions and probably had personal contact with monks who well remembered pre-Conquest customs such as the Feast of the Immaculate Conception of the Virgin. Although the feast was not introduced at Christ Church until after Anselm's death, Marian devotions must have existed there, since the main altar and the entire new crypt were dedicated to the Virgin. Indeed, Anselm himself acquired a precious relic: some of the Virgin's hair.[9]

The vastly greater spaciousness of the new crypt and choir amply met the needs created by the resurgence of the cults of Anglo-Saxon saints. It also permitted the monks' choir to be moved east of the crossing tower. The decision to enlarge the choir was made, therefore, not only in response to the growing number of monks, but also because Anselm allowed the rich and varied local culture to flourish again after its suppression under Lanfranc. In this new atmosphere at Christ Church the community began to reawaken to its own traditions and importance.

Anselm certainly contributed a great deal to the enlargement of the cathedral, but the main administrative burden fell to the prior. In 1096, the very year that Anselm made his generous gift towards the rebuilding of the church, Lanfranc's prior Henry was replaced by Ernulf, a former monk of Beauvais. Ernulf was a learned man and a consistently capable organizer and builder, as he demonstrated first as prior at Canterbury, then as abbot of Peterborough and finally as bishop of Rochester.[10] It is recorded that 'he died in 1124, at the age of eighty-four leaving many monuments to his virtue'.[11] Ernulf's work on the eastern extension at Christ Church was continued by his successor Conrad, who served as prior from 1108/9 to 1126 and who is credited with decorating the choir 'with excellent paintings and furnishing it with precious ornaments' as well as the addition of 'five large bells that required the labours of sixty-three men to ring them and a cope woven in gold thread, with one hundred and forty little silver bells interspersed with precious stones'.[12]

Prior Conrad's work on the choir continued after Anselm's death in 1109 and well into the archiepiscopacy of Ralph d'Escures (1114-1122).[13] The style of the latest capitals of this campaign on the choir, those of the decorative arcade on the outside of the structure (c.1120), indicate that work must have been drawing to a close by this time. The dedication of

36

the new choir took place only in 1130, on 4 May, during the archiepiscopacy of Ralph's successor, William de Corbeil (1123-1136).[14] The ceremony was performed by William de Corbeil before a distinguished gathering which included King Henry I, Queen Matilda, her brother King David I of Scotland and thirteen English and Norman bishops.[15]

All this suggests that the first planning stages for the eastern extension must date back to 1093, when Anselm arrived; by 1107 the major building work must have been well advanced, since it was in that year that Conrad began to attend to the decoration and furnishing. But, as we shall see in more detail below, the sculptural evidence itself would indicate that the building of the choir was not finished until the 1120s.

Alas, the choir was gutted by fire in 1174, but a description by the twelfth-century chronicler William of Malmesbury suggests it must have been stunning:

'Nothing like it could be seen in England, either for the brilliancy of its glass windows, the beauty of its marble pavements, or the many coloured pictures which led the wandering eye to the very summit of the ceiling'.[16]

That this was not merely twelfth-century rhetoric is evident from the magnificent crypt which stands today. It is among the chief glories of the Romanesque period. Not only does the crypt itself survive virtually complete, but it is filled with an extraordinary range of contemporary carved capitals. There are few other sites in Europe where Romanesque sculpture of such originality and beauty can be studied to such advantage.

The Crypt

The general plan of the crypt (see plan on p. 34) follows that of the outer walls of the choir above, with a transept (each arm with two apses) and an ambulatory off which are set a pair of canted radiating chapels (Holy Innocents to the north, ill. 39; St Gabriel to the south, Colour Pl. I). The original termination of the ambulatory, a chapel dedicated to St Augustine, was replaced in the twelfth century when William the Englishman built a new addition to support the Trinity chapel and the Jesus chapel above.[17]

The crypt is approached from the west, down one of two stairways flanking the base of the crossing tower. From these dim stair passages there opens a spacious vista of columns and capitals, lit by large aisle windows (ills. 31, 32). Thus the interior is relatively well-lit — an unusual feature due to the fact that the Canterbury crypt is not fully subterranean.

The nave and aisles of the crypt are partitioned by short, rectangular piers with responds north and south; the central area is subdivided by two rows of columns which separate it into a nave with flanking aisles. It is groin-vaulted throughout with the transverse ribs supported by the responds. This system extends to the transepts, which have one free standing column, and into the chapels of St Gabriel and the Holy Innocents, which have two.[18] The general impression is of a clearly defined interior which conveys a sense of solidity and order.

The vast size of the crypt sets it apart from all other Romanesque crypts in England and Normandy. Only the churches of the Rhineland had such large crypts, notably the Imperial cathedral of Speyer and St Maria im Kapitol in Cologne. Although these German examples lack ambulatories, their monumental scale and impressive spaciousness recall the crypt at Canterbury. Furthermore, the canted chapels in the crypt at St Maria im Kapitol find echoes at Canterbury in the angled chapels of St Gabriel and Holy Innocents.[19]

A precedent for the plan of the crypt exists much closer to hand: at St Augustine's Abbey, just beyond the city walls. The eastern part of St Augustine's was complete by the time that work began on Anselm's choir. Abbot Scotland of St Augustine's (formerly of Mont-Saint-Michel), had already begun rebuilding around 1070; by his death in 1087, work had reached the third bay of the nave, west of the crossing tower. Beneath the eastern arm (an apsidal presbytery with a surrounding ambulatory) lay

an extensive crypt. The formula for the crypt at St Augustine's can in turn be traced to experiments in Normandy, made in the wake of the construction of the metropolitan cathedral at Rouen.[20]

As in Lanfranc's church, construction of the crypt followed the order which was regarded as practical: from east to west. The structure of Anselm's crypt makes it clear that it was built in the normal way. The vaults of the four easternmost bays are made of rubble covered in plaster, while those of the west show an advance in technique, being made from ashlar blocks. It is evident that Lanfranc's choir and its crypt were left untouched for as long as possible while building was carried on further east. Only at the last moment was the earlier choir dismantled and the junction of the new choir and the old crossing achieved; it was probably for fear of disturbing the stability of the crossing piers and their foundations that the west wall of Lanfranc's crypt was retained.

The main space of the crypt is divided by two rows of columns into

32. General view of the crypt looking north-west. The carved capitals with plain shafts alternate with plain capitals and carved shafts in the centre of the crypt, while all the capitals of the outer walls are of plain, uncarved cushion form.

39

three groin-vaulted bays, each 12 feet wide (ill. 32). The length of each bay is 14 feet, that is to say of each of the seven bays, starting from the east. There is no doubt that it was originally intended to have ten bays of equal length, for there is room for precisely that number. But it is apparent that when the new work approached Lanfranc's choir and crypt, the old structure was not entirely demolished as originally intended, and the western wall of the crypt was retained. On demolishing the old crypt, the space between the seventh bay of the new crypt and the west wall of the old was not taken by three bays, to conform with the original design. Instead, the width of the old crypt was retained in the first seven and a half feet from the west wall, and this space was divided into three small bays, the remainder being taken by two bays, three feet longer than those to the east. These changes in the original plan were surely caused by fear of disturbing the foundations of the crossing and the tower above, and by the urgent need to complete the crypt in order to provide abutment for the old tower. The unfinished carving of two capitals, one impost and three bases strongly suggests that, at this stage of work, finer details were sacrificed for the sake of speed and the security of the building (ills. 33-38).

Unfinished architectural sculpture is relatively common in Romanesque buildings. But in the case of the crypt capitals at Christ Church, the issue has acquired a special importance for the chronology of the building. At first scholars concluded from the unfinished pieces that the capitals were carved *in situ*, and therefore that the date of the sculpture was not necessarily tied to the chronology of the building. But there is a forceful case to be made for the capitals having been carved *avant la pose* and installed before the carving was finished.[21] Watertight evidence of this exists in the shafts and capitals of the external choir arcade (see p. 82), but in the case of the crypt the tooling indicates that the blocks were worked from various angles, which would have been very difficult to achieve had the carving been done *in situ*. Moreover, despite the fact that the crypt is bright, far better light for detailed carving would have existed in the masons' lodge. This suggests that the sculpture was being carved and then set as building progressed, so it must be contemporary with the late eleventh-century crypt. The only viable explanation for the unfinished carving is the pressure to complete the church quickly.

The progress of building from east to west means that the earliest surviving sculpture is in the two easternmost side chapels, those of St Gabriel and of the Holy Innocents, the central apse of the crypt having been rebuilt to support the new choir after the fire of 1174. In both cases, there are two free-standing columns supporting the vaulting, and these, as well as the capitals above them, are sumptuously carved. The columns are enriched with spirals, scales and zigzags. The capitals, like the majority in the crypt, are cushion-shaped (ill. 39 and Colour Pl. I).

Cushion capitals had already been used in the earlier cathedral built by Lanfranc at Canterbury (ill. 20), although they have not been found in any building in Normandy of the period. They were probably newly intro-

33 (right). Although the column illustrated here has been completed, the capital has not. The foliage stalks of the main face already have fluting and beading. The right hand side has not progressed beyond the stage of being blocked out.

34

34-35. Details of the unfinished cushion capital in ill. 33.

35

36. Unfinished crypt impost.

37. Crypt capital with unfinished scallop ornament.
The intention presumably was to decorate the capital
with a scallop motif as can be seen from the incised
cusped shapes.

38. Shaft with cushion capital
and moulded base. The base has
additional foliage suggesting the artist
changed his mind in the middle of work.

duced to England from Germany and the County of Flanders, where they had been popular since the late tenth century.[22] However, what is new and exciting in Anselm's crypt is not so much the appearance of this capital type as the fact that they are not merely painted, but carved. By the 1060s, the practice of carving cushion capitals was firmly established in Germany. The fact that the German examples pre-date Italian ones like San Abondio, Como and Santa Maria d'Aurona, Milan by some twenty years is probably merely an accident of survival.[23]

Several important comparisons have been drawn between the carved cushion capitals of Lombardy and those in the eastern area of the cathedral crypt. At San Abondio there are cushion capitals with grotesques and foliage (ill. 41). One, with a dragon and twisted tail contained in a shield, presents a convincing comparison with that in the Innocents chapel (ill. 40). Yet despite these close similarities it is unlikely that the carved cushion capitals of the crypt are solely dependent on Lombard precedents as some have claimed.[24] A glance in the direction of Germany reveals that the issue is considerably more complex than this. The chapter house at Bad Hersfeld in Hesse has similar capitals (ill. 42). Here too are crouched dragons contained within rope moulded, cushion-shaped shields, and these display a strong affinity with the carved cushion capitals in the Innocents chapel.

39. The Holy Innocents' Chapel.

40

41

40. Cushion capital, carved with
a winged dragon and twisted tail,
in the Holy Innocents' Chapel.
The design of this capital is very
similar to roughly contemporary
examples in Germany and Italy
(see ills.41, 42).

41 (above right). Capital with
dragon in the choir
of Sant' Abondio, Como.

42. Capital with dragon from the
chapter house at Hersfeld Abbey.

43. Cushion capital with a double-bodied lion in St Gabriel's Chapel. Similar motifs are found (ills.44-46) in German, English and Norman examples.

44. Initial D with a double-bodied lion in London, BL, Royal MS 5.B.XV, f.3.

The cushion capitals with two branches of foliage linked by a central clasp at St Emmeram in Regensburg recall those in the Innocents chapel in the crypt.[25] And since this motif also occurs in illuminated initials, we are reminded that manuscripts were often the primary vehicle for the dispersal of important sculptural motifs.[26] One last comparison with sculpture in Germany deserves attention. A carved capital in the crypt at St Margarethe, Weissendorf in Bavaria, has a grotesque with a single, central head and two flanking bodies which is very close to a capital in St Gabriel's chapel (ills. 43, 45). And once again, the most likely explanation for the appearance of this particular motif in such widely separated and unaffiliated centres must be that it was so common in contemporary illuminations. For in-

45. Cushion capital with a double-bodied grotesque in the choir of St. Margarethe, Weissendorf (Bavaria).

46. Initial O containing a double-bodied lion in Rouen, Bibl. Mun., MS A.85, f.36v.

stance, a manuscript initial from St Augustine's Abbey has an identical creature, who also appears in a manuscript produced in Normandy (ills. 44, 46).[27]

Canterbury manuscripts up to about 1130 show a clear awareness of Rhenish and Flemish artistic developments, so by the late eleventh century, when cushion capitals featured regularly in England, Germany and Flanders, it is no longer necessary to argue that the use of the same motif on the same type of capital implies direct emulation. The similarities appear rather to result from parallel paths of development: cushion capitals were common and these were decorated with motifs then current in the manuscripts on both sides of the Channel.[28]

47. Capital in the crypt based on the Corinthian type.

48. Capital based on the Corinthian type where forms are abstracted and made into two dimensional geometric shapes.

49. Free-standing capital in the crypt based on the Corinthian type.

50. This is by far the most awkward of the crypt capitals. It shows the uncomfortable merger of elements of the Corinthian and cushion forms. The clumsy appearance of this capital may reflect the craftsman's attempt to carve an unfamiliar form.

Although there were no volute capitals in Lanfranc's church they do make a small showing in Anselm's crypt, where there are four examples (ills. 47-50). These are of the same basic type as were employed elsewhere in the last quarter of the eleventh century (for instance, at York Minster, Richmond Castle in North Yorkshire, Colchester Castle, St John's chapel in the Tower of London, Lincoln Cathedral and Stogersey in Somerset). The frequency with which such capitals occurred in England increased after the Conquest, but some important earlier examples do exist, notably those from St Augustine's Abbey.[29]

Two of the volute capitals in the crypt are based on the Corinthian formula: one, a respond capital, has a tall 'ruff' of leaves on the lower capital with knob-like angle volutes and helices carved in low relief above (ill. 47). Its typological mate, a free-standing capital is divided into three horizontal registers, with a double 'ruff' and knob-like volutes and helices in low relief on the upper register (ill. 49).[30] The structures of the other two examples are more unusual. One is an abstract version of the volute capital type. It has knob-like volutes, but the leaves have been stretched to fill the whole height of the capital and they are entirely schematic, applied like cut-outs (ill. 48). The last example is half buried in the apse wall of the Huguenot chapel (ill. 50). The carving of this seems clumsy compared with the other crypt capitals. The upper part is cushion-shaped; a row of acanthus leaves around the lower register makes a tentative attempt to merge the volute and cushion forms. The hesitant application of leaves to this capital suggests that it was carved by one unfamiliar with the volute form — indeed, perhaps, unfamiliar with carving at all. If the crypt sculpture was installed starting from the east and moving to the west then this example, as the easternmost of all the volute capitals, was probably the first one to be produced in the crypt. The awkward merger of forms evident here suggests the possibility that the volute form represents an entirely new departure for the craftsman.

Seven of the most interesting carved capitals are block-shaped (ills. 57, 60, 62-63, 66, 70, 77, 81-82, 92-95). Like the cushion capital, the block form was ultimately derived from Byzantium and it later appeared, via Italy, in Ottonian Germany.[31] In the first half of the eleventh century it was adopted elsewhere in Europe, from the powerful Norman abbey at Bernay to the humble parish church at Bibury in Gloucestershire.[32] Yet despite such widespread use of the block form, there are no sculptures at Canterbury itself that anticipate these revolutionary carved capitals. But there are numerous manuscript illuminations that do. In order to gain a clearer knowledge of the sophisticated motifs that adorn the block and cushion capitals in the crypt, it is necessary to turn to their source — the cathedral's manuscript collection.

A large number of late eleventh- and early twelfth-century manuscripts with richly decorated initials have survived from Canterbury. These show that from about 1070 until 1120 the field of manuscript illumination in England was led by developments at Christ Church and St Augustine's

51. *Cushion capital in the crypt carved with foliage joined by a clasp.*

52. *Cushion capital in the crypt with animal head clasp and foliage.*

Abbey. In the climate that Anselm fostered at Christ Church, it is hardly surprising to find that artists looked not to the Continent for models but to the Anglo-Saxon manuscripts in their possession and, more important still, that they relied on their own inventive powers. There is abundant and compelling evidence that the imaginative and dynamic local initial style inspired the decoration of the sculpture of this period.[33]

Some of the examples which suggest the closest dependence of Canterbury sculpture on local manuscript illumination are to be found in the foliage motifs of the crypt, and here the clearest proof may be seen in the accompanying illustrations. For instance, one capital has two veined stalks joined by a double clasp; these stalks bow into graceful curved forms which terminate in springy trefoil leaves, just as in an initial B in an edition of St Augustine's *Commentary on the Psalms* which was produced in Lanfranc's scriptorium (ills. 51, 53). In another copy of this text, again produced at Christ Church, the clasp, in the form of an animal head, and the tapering leaves that surround it are also similar to another face of the same capital (ills. 52, 54). In another instance, the beaded scrolls looping together on the central faces of one of the block capitals have virtually the same calligraphic pattern as initials in the Priscian *Grammar* from St Augustine's Abbey of around 1067-1080 (ills. 57, 58). Similar, uncluttered vegetal compositions with coiled stalks and shell-shaped leaves are characteristic of other manuscripts too, notably the *Passionale* from St Augustine's Abbey.

53. (above) *Initial B with foliage joined by a clasp, in Cambridge, Trinity College, MS B.5.28, f.45v.*

54. (below) *Initial D with animal head clasp and foliage, in Cambridge, Trinity College, MS B.4.26, f.2.*

55. Cushion capital in the Innocents' Chapel with 'Winchester acanthus foliage' showing that artists drew not only on contemporary illuminations for inspiration but also on those produced by earlier generations.

56. Initial I with 'Winchester acanthus'. Durham Cathedral Library, MS A.II.4, f.36v.

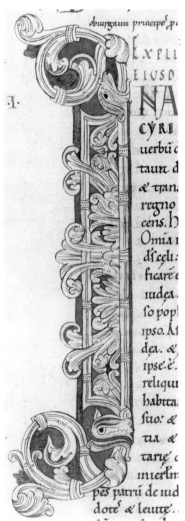

Two of the most beautifully designed foliage capitals in the crypt are based on Anglo-Saxon motifs. This type of foliage emerged during the late tenth century at centres across England like Ely, Glastonbury, Winchester and Canterbury. Characteristic of the style, which is ultimately derived from Carolingian sources, is the lush acanthus-leaf and scroll foliage that decorates the borders of many Anglo-Saxon illuminations. This foliage, the so-called 'Winchester School' acanthus, was copied on the two free-standing cushion capitals in the Holy Innocents chapel (ills. 39, 55, 104, 109). The capitals vary in detail — one has feathery leaves, the other (on the west face beaded, on the east face plain) has leaves with a firmer contour — but the concept of the design and the forms of the springy branches and tapering leaves is similar. It seems unlikely that the artists were consciously reviving Anglo-Saxon designs: rather this is a further indication of the important role that manuscripts played in inspiring the designs of the crypt capitals (ills. 55, 56).[34]

The borrowing and reinterpretation of motifs current in Canterbury manuscripts so evident on the foliage capitals is equally characteristic of the figural capitals. The north and west sides of a capital in St Gabriel's chapel are carved with goats, dogs, winged grotesques and a unicorn, playing musical instruments (ills. 66, 70). The general scheme recalls Canterbury initials where animals stand on their hind legs and play harps, viols and horns (ills. 67-69, 71-72). Some of the individual figures are replicas of the grotesques used in the initials. The carving of a dog blowing a horn is virtually the mirror image of one that appears in a *Corpus of Canon Law* from Christ Church (ill. 69). Both are represented in profile, on hind legs, one paw raised to support the horn, the other draped over it as if to finger the notes. Both have long ears, bent hind legs and simple lines to articulate the bodies. Such dogs constantly recur in Canterbury manuscripts. Other carvings, such as the harping grotesque on the north side of the same capital are also related to Canterbury initials (ills. 66, 68). The seminal role of initials in the development of Canterbury sculpture is evident in the smallest of details which may even often reappear on the tail of one of the carved creatures.[35]

51

57. Block capital in the crypt, with angle masks and curling foliage.

58. Initial Q decorated with curling foliage almost identical to the crypt capital, ill.57. Cambridge, Trinity College, MS 0.2.51, f.34.

59. Capital from the cloister of King Henry I's foundation (1121) at Reading Abbey with angle masks and foliage.

Many other sculpted images were similarly inspired by the initials of local manuscripts. The male head and foliage carved on each side of one capital, for example, seems to have been based on isolated male heads used to decorate local manuscripts (ills. 60, 61). In another example, the exotic double-headed female rider with her double-headed dragon steed closely resembles the strange composite creatures of manuscripts from Canterbury and Rochester (ills. 62, 64, 65).[36] The painstakingly carved details of this capital the delicately patterned saddle, the stirrup, the scales clearly imitate a graphic tradition.

60. Block capital in the crypt carved with
full-length bearded heads and foliage.

61. Detail of initial I in Baltimore, Walters Art Gallery,
MS 10.18, f.29 showing a bearded head and foliage.

62. Block capital in the crypt showing
a double-headed monster riding an amphisbaena.

63. Block capital in the crypt showing
a winged monster spearing a running dog.

64. Initial F showing an amphisbaena.
London, BL, Harley MS 624, f.128v.

65. Initial Q showing a double-headed monster.
Baltimore, Walters Art Gallery, MS 10.18, f.152.

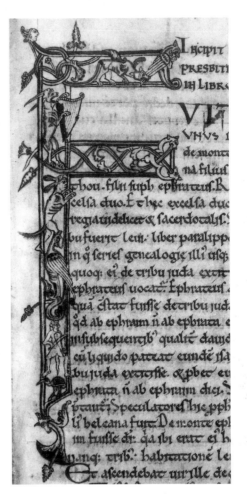

66. *Block capital in St Gabriel's Chapel with animals standing on their hind legs playing musical instruments. There is a close relationship between the motifs used in the manuscripts and sculpture of the Cathedral.*

67. *Initial F showing animals standing on their hind legs playing musical instruments. Cambridge, Trinity College, MS B.2.34, f.117.*

68. *Initial A with grotesques and an animal playing a harp. Cambridge, Trinity College, MS B.2.34, f.79v.*

69. *Detail of animal on hind legs playing a horn. London, BL, Cotton MS Claudius E.V, f.49.*

70. Block capital in St Gabriel's Chapel with grotesques playing musical instruments.

71. Initial N with an animal blowing a horn.
Cambridge, St John's College, MS A.8, f.64.

72. Initial with animals playing musical instruments.
Canterbury Cathedral Library, MS E.42, f.36v

73-74. *Man in cloak playing a fiddle; man playing a horn. Details of capitals on the south side of the choir. Whereas the crypt capitals were produced in the late 11th century, these on the external choir arcade were probably not carved until around 1120.*

75. *Initial T with two men playing harps and a fiddle. London, BL, Arundel MS 91, f.218v.*

76. *Initial B with musicians and a knife thrower. Cambridge, Trinity College, MS B.5.26, f.1.*

I. St Gabriel's Chapel in the crypt of Canterbury Cathedral

II. Capital in St Gabriel's Chapel with grotesques playing musical instruments

III. Capital in St Gabriel's Chapel with animals playing musical instruments

IV. Crypt capital with figure straddling two addorsed grotesques

V. Crypt capital with winged monster spearing a dog

VI. Capital in St Gabriel's Chapel with two addorsed winged grotesques

The capital bearing a pair of addorsed griffins brings us back to the question of the transmission of motifs (ill. 77). A version of the same image is used on the bronze doors of the cathedrals at Trani and Ravello in Southern Italy (ill. 80). The motif may ultimately derive from oriental textiles, such as the Byzantine silks preserved in the church treasuries (ill. 79), and it is presumably from such a source that the motif passed into the vocabulary of Romanesque design hence its use at these two widely separated and unrelated centres.[37] In the case of Christ Church, manuscripts appear to be the most likely intermediary once again (ill. 78): the cat-mask, through which passes the griffins' beaded tails, is a standard feature in contemporary local initials.[38]. An enlarged version of exactly the same motif occurs on a contemporary block-shaped capital which evidently came from one of the monastic buildings at Christ Church.[39]

The subjects of the capitals in the crypt again point to manuscripts as the primary source. Since the figural capitals display a marked predilection for the fanciful and the exotic, meanings are difficult and often impossible to pin down though we have come a long way from the opinion of one eighteenth-century author who attributed them to the 'eccentricity of Egyptian superstition'.[40] The knowledge that this sculpture borrows and reinterprets themes from local manuscripts goes some way to help clarify their meaning.

Many of the subjects represented in the initials of this period derive from the imagery of classical texts of which the library at Christ Church had an outstanding collection.[41] Although we cannot be certain of the contents of the library in the late eleventh century, we have some idea of the holdings while Thomas Becket was archbishop (1162-1170) from a catalogue compiled at the time. The catalogue is incomplete, since it lacks the sections on Law, Theology and Medicine. All that survives is the first three leaves, which document the secular manuscripts, but these are of enormous importance. They convey the astonishing range and diversity of books at Christ Church in the twelfth century, which include not only the Latin classics but books on Astronomy, Arithmetic, Geometry, Music, Rhetoric, Grammar and Dialectic. The rich collection of secular manuscripts alone probably reached approximately two hundred volumes.[42]

This leads us to one of the most interesting characteristics of the arts of the Romanesque period: the way in which classical subjects penetrated the decorative vocabulary of the time and were transformed into random ornament. This process can be followed with some degree of clarity at Canterbury. For example, the *Martyrology* from St Augustine's Abbey (London, B.L., MS Cotton Vit. C.XII) has a zodiacal symbol and the appropriate Labour of the Month throughout; but in the process of copying, the artist misunderstood the meaning of one symbol. Thus, the bull of Taurus (May) is given a halo, presumably by confusion with the symbol of St Luke (ill. 85).[43] This manuscript can also be used to show the transformation of identifiable symbols from their proper context into the general decorative

78. Initial O containing a pair of addorsed winged griffins. London, BL, MS Royal 6 B.VI, f.23.

77. Block-shaped capital in St Gabriel's Chapel with two addorsed winged grotesques with beaded tails passing through a cat mask.

79 (below). Detail of Byzantine silk with addorsed winged griffins.

80 (right). Addorsed winged griffins on the bronze doors of Trani Cathedral, 1180-1190.

81-82. *Opposite sides of a block-shaped capital in the crypt, each with a lion raising his paw.*

83. *Marginal detail of a lion with raised paw. London, BL, Arundel MS 60, f.5.*

84. *Initial topped by a lion with raised paw. London, BL, Cotton MS Vit. CXII, f.134.*

85. *The zodiacal symbol for May. London, BL, Cotton MS Vit. CXII, f.127.*

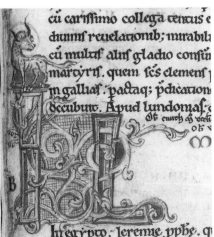

vocabulary of Romanesque. Leo (August) has one foreleg raised and its head twisted towards its tail (ill. 84). A similarly posed lion which has lost all association with the zodiacal symbol Leo, appears as mere decoration in another St Augustine's manuscript (London, B.L., MS Arundel 60, see ill. 83). The two lions carved on one of the capitals in the crypt surely have the same pedigree (ills. 81, 82).

The mutations of astronomical symbols into the Romanesque decorative vocabulary can be followed in other crypt capitals too (ill. 86). The creature with a coiled tail, forepaws and pointed ears that inhabits the shield of a cushion capital also appears frequently in local initials. The physical characteristics of this creature are related to those of one of the constellations, Cetus. This sea-monster can be found in its proper astronomical context in the *Phaenomena* by Aratus, the fundamental text for the calculation of the liturgical year. A Carolingian copy of the manuscript with a picture cycle was in Canterbury by the mid tenth century (ill. 87).[44] Its presence in the library may explain the popularity of this type of grotesque in Canterbury manuscripts and sculpture (ill. 88).

86. Cushion capital with a winged dragon with a twisted tail in the Holy Innocents' Chapel.

87. Image of the constellation Cetus in a Carolingian copy of the classical text *Phaenomena* by Aratus. London, BL, Harley MS 647, f.10. This manuscript was in Canterbury by the mid 10th century.

Astronomical manuscripts were only one of several sources for the images of the crypt capitals. Bestiaries and books of fables were also drawn upon. This can be seen in the humorous capital in St Gabriel's chapel where a donkey stands on its hind legs like a human and plays a lyre (ill. 66). The donkey playing the lyre was a popular image in the Romanesque period. It derives from a fable of Phaedrus in which a donkey finds the instrument in a meadow and tries to play it, saying: 'I do not know music, but if someone else had found this lyre, he would charm the ear with divine harmonies'. The meaning was perpetuated by Boethius in *De Consolatione Philosophiae*, when Philosophy asks her listener, 'Do you hear my words, or are you like the donkey with the lyre?' The same theme was often extended to other animals playing musical instruments, as on the same capital in St Gabriel's chapel (ills. 66, 70).[45]

88. Initial in London, BL, Cotton MS Claud. E.V, f.22v, with a monster similar to ill.87. The standing dog is similar to that blowing a horn in ill.69.

Another capital in the nave of the crypt shows a furry animal with its head bent over its forepaw (ill. 90). According to Bestiary illustrations, this image shows the wolf approaching the sheepfold. It licks its paw to make no sound. If it treads on a stick, it punishes its foot with a bite. A similar representation of an animal with tufts of hair, performing the same action illustrates a Bestiary now in the University Library, Cambridge (ill. 91). The object represented underfoot on the Canterbury capital then must be a twig.[46] The Bestiary was presumably also the source of the pair of addorsed birds tipped inward and pecking their own breasts, represented on the loose capital from the cathedral, now in the City Art Gallery (ill. 277). Single birds in the same pose were used in the *Bestiary* to represent the pelican which supposedly fed its young with its own blood from a self-inflicted wound, symbolizing Christ's Love for the Church (ill. 89).

The images of the crypt capitals derive from other sources too. For example, two sides of one capital depict a man on horseback. The figure on the east side of the capital wears a hooded mantle and points his elongated finger heavenward (ill. 93). Beneath him is a prostrate form. Comparisons with illustrated versions of Prudentius' *Psychomachia* of which at least one copy was produced at Canterbury, suggest that he may be a Virtue treading down a Vice.[47]

But how should the capital (ills. 94, 95) with acrobats on one face and a monstrous centaur on another be understood? The centaur seems to have been concocted from several images, for it resembles the grotesque with a bearded head emerging from its chest in one manuscript (ill. 99), while the fringed skirt is akin to that in another. And what of the strange attributes of this creature? It holds a fish in a horizontal position in one hand, and a brimming bowl in the other. Is there an intentional relationship between these and the vertically held fish and empty bowl of the acrobats on the reverse side of the capital? Fish are certainly one of the most popular motifs in Canterbury illumination. Indeed, it can be argued that their popularity was also due to the symbol of Pisces which often appears in

89. Pelican from the Bestiary MS Ii.4.26, Cambridge, University Library.

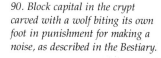

90. Block capital in the crypt carved with a wolf biting its own foot in punishment for making a noise, as described in the Bestiary.

91. A design such as this may have served as a model for ill.90.

92-93. Block capitals in the crypt. Above: a man wrestling with a lion.
The human figure may represent Hercules or Samson, despite the fact that he is here represented with a tail.
Below: a hooded rider, perhaps representing a Virtue trampling a Vice.

94-95. *Block capitals in the crypt. Above: an enigmatic pair of acrobats. Note the empty bowl and headlong fish.*
Below: a two-headed monster. Note the full bowl and the horizontal position of the fish.

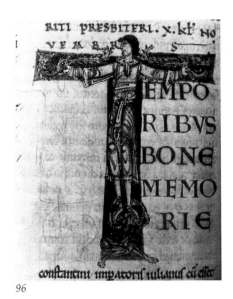

96

97

astrological manuscripts.[48] But the depiction of the monster on the capital beside full and empty bowls suggests other associations. A similar image occurs in the Canon Tables of the Winchcombe Psalter, where lion-headed, human-bodied creatures are seated holding cornucopia in one hand and fish in the other.[49] In classical art the attributes are sometimes held by allegories of the months. For instance, the plenty of June is sometimes represented in this manner. The fish and flask are also frequently depicted in the hands of river gods, as in a number of Carolingian manuscripts and ivories (ill. 98). Although the meaning of these particular images on the Canterbury capital remains ambiguous, there can be little doubt that here again the inspiration came from local manuscripts.

By the time these images were used on the crypt capitals they had been wholly integrated and assimilated into the imagery of the period and in most cases their original meaning had long since been forgotten. Indeed, there is every reason to suppose that had St Bernard of Clairvaux seen the crypt capitals, he would have questioned their meaning and objected to the themes and expense of carving with the same vehemence as he did to those in the offending cloisters of France.[50]

98

99

100. Cushion capital in the crypt at Canterbury with a scallop pattern carved in low relief. Compare the treatment with the Corinthian based capital ill.48.

Strangely enough, the carved mouldings and ornamental details of the imposts and shafts have associations wholly independent from the figural and foliage forms of the capitals. For instance, the variation of egg-and-tongue, and egg-and-dart which appear on four imposts are completely absent from local illuminations. The egg-and-tongue motif on an impost above a cushion capital and a variant on the same motif above a volute capital came from classical art (ills. 101, 102).[51] So does the design of three other abaci, with motifs closer to the classical leaf-and-tongue. Some of the columns of the crypt also reinterpret antique designs. Two with meandering scroll pattern, and seven with a fluted decoration are variants of Roman designs (66, 118, 119). Some of the similarities with Roman remains are especially noteworthy, as for instance the fluted columns with round-ended lappets filling the tops (ill. 33).

The reliance on antique models is nowhere more evident than in the elegant feather motif on a shaft in the Innocents chapel (ill. 104). This

decoration is relatively common on antique columns, altars and funerary monuments.[52] A less elaborate variant is the scale pattern found on several imposts and capitals in the crypt (ills. 36, 37). The association of this particular motif with classical works is confirmed by the twelfth-century sarcophagus at Fordwich, a few miles from Canterbury, where the gabled lid has scale ornament (ill. 103). The similarity of this tomb to Roman sarcophagi strongly suggests that the sculptors were consciously drawing on antique models in the vicinity. The likelihood that local classical remains were the source for the motifs is given additional weight by the fact that the ornamental patterns alluded to above do not appear in Canterbury manuscripts which, as we have seen, were such an important source for the figural sculpture. In Italy, Provence, or even parts of Germany there would be nothing remarkable about direct borrowings from classical remains, but in England such obvious cases are unusual.[53]

101-102. Details of carving on two imposts in the crypt.

103. Sarcophagus with scallop motif on the lid, early 12th century, Fordwich, near Canterbury. The form and the scallop motif on the lid show that the design was based on antique models.

104. Shaft with scallop decoration in the Holy Innocents' Chapel.

We can only guess at the path by which motifs used in precious manuscripts and in ornamental designs from Roman remains may have reached the crypt capitals. It was presumably with the help of a pattern book. A very small number of such sketch books survive, but among them are a few important examples.[54] One collection of sketches from the late tenth or early eleventh century was compiled by a monk from Saint-Martial, Limoges. There is of course no possibility of this exact book having been used at Canterbury, but its contents have important implications here. Among the texts it illustrates are the *Psychomachia* of Prudentius, the *Astronomicon* and *Fables* of Hyginus, all of which provided some of the subjects that inspired the Canterbury sculptors. A second model book of the early tenth century, probably from the Loire Valley, has a series of pen and ink sketches which are based on a variety of sources, from Roman friezes to Carolingian and Insular manuscripts.[55] The fact that the crypt sculpture at Canterbury was also inspired by a mixture of motifs to be found in local manuscripts and surviving classical sculpture suggests that similar notebooks or collections of sketches were relied upon by the artists at Canterbury Cathedral.

The pattern book is certainly believed to be the usual means for the transmission of images from the scriptorium to the masons' lodge. But in this instance several factors suggest that another possibility should also be considered. At first the distribution of sculpture in the crypt seems largely arbitrary, yet on closer inspection certain elements can be seen to

68

follow a logical sequence. The carved cushion capitals are confined to the eastern crypt. Both of the free-standing carved capitals in the Innocents chapel are cushion-shaped, and so too is the easternmost capital in St Gabriel's chapel. The eastern capital, that in the entrance to the apse, is also of cushion form. The eastern apsidal chapel was dismantled by William of Sens, but it must have been the first part of the church to be rebuilt. As such, it too probably contained carved cushion capitals. The western, free-standing capital in the middle of St Gabriel's chapel, however, abandons this type; here, suddenly, the block shaped capital is introduced. All of the other figural capitals further west in the nave of the crypt are of block form.[56]

What was the reason for the sudden abandonment of the cushion form? As building progressed westward, speed and economy appear to have become pressing concerns. This may explain the unfinished pieces (ills. 34-38). An attempt to increase the rate of work may also shed light on the rejection of the cushion form and the introduction of the block capital instead. The confined fields provided by the cushion capital are more complex and intricate than the open, truncated rectangles of the block capital.

The carving on the cushion capitals strictly adheres to the structure of the capital. Each face acts as an independent unit, and the borders between them are awkward and abrupt. This is most obvious in one of the first block capitals to be carved, the capital in the nave of St Gabriel's chapel (ill. 219 and Colour Pl. IV). The plain frame following the upper horizontal edge and extending partially down the sides is reminiscent of the cushion capitals. It is hard to resist reconstructing the cushion form in one's mind's eye. But the frame is abruptly terminated, thus creating a clumsy convergence of the motifs at the angles of the capital. The artist's discomfort with this design is evident in his introduction of a feather at one angle (ill. 219), an attempt to mask the junction of the capital faces. In most of the other block-shaped capitals this difficulty is resolved by reducing the designs, and leaving raised ridges along each angle to form a division (ills. 90-92, 94-95).

Although the cushion capitals may be more successful from the point of view of design, their shape acted as a constraint on the subject matter. The motifs within the shields of the cushion capitals are limited to foliage, or single images, for instance, dragons and lions. On the block capitals by contrast, more complex and dynamic compositions are introduced: groups of animals playing musical instruments, monsters in combat, horses and riders, griffons and birds holding snakes.

The source of these motifs may help explain the sudden abandonment of the carved cushion form and the introduction of the block-shaped capital in its stead. Perhaps the semicircular shape of the shield was found too restrictive for any but simple decorative carving since its width is greatest at the top and it diminishes rapidly towards the bottom. Block capitals on the other hand, presented more convenient fields: truncated rectangles, like the pages of a manuscript.

69

105. Cushion capital in
St Gabriel's Chapel with a lion.

106. Double cushion capital with lions in the shields
in the royal nunnery at Romsey Abbey.

In view of the fact that nearly all of the images can be traced to the
scriptorium and that the sculptures were originally polychromed, there is
a strong possibility that it was actually manuscript illuminators themselves
who were responsible for the carving of these fine capitals. This hypothesis
would certainly account for the absence of all but the most rudimentary
sculpture at Christ Church before the crypt capitals. It would also account
for the artists' approach to the capital, whereby each side is treated as an
independent field for decoration.

Three sides of one of the block capitals are unfinished and it provides
important evidence about the way the artist was trained (ills. 34-35). We
learn from it that the motifs were first engraved on the stone and only
then carved. They were conceived as purely two-dimensional forms with
little interest in modelling or contour. Each is worked almost as if it were
a flat surface: they are carvings in a graphic tradition.[57] The ease with
which some artists were able to switch from the pen to the chisel is illustrated by the case of Master Hugo of Bury St Edmunds Abbey who, according to the *Gesta Sacristanum*, was competent in several techniques: he
carved a huge Rood, he cast the abbey's bronze doors and bells, he seems
to have made the abbey seal, and perhaps he even painted the lavish Bury
Bible.[58]

Whatever their original training, the sculptors who carved the crypt
capitals were clearly men of outstanding artistic ability, for when compared
with most contemporary English sculpture, the crypt capitals stand out as
something quite exceptional. The late eleventh-century capitals from Ely
Cathedral, for example, have simple decorative motifs which are tentatively chiselled. The hesitant carving is a far cry from the bravura and
assurance of form at Canterbury. The capitals from Hereford Cathedral
(*c*.1100), although carved with narrative scenes and in a forceful style, are
technically crude in comparison with Canterbury. In other instances, as
for example Durham Castle chapel (*c*.1072), or the crypt at Gloucester

70

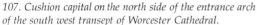

107. Cushion capital on the north side of the entrance arch
of the south west transept of Worcester Cathedral.

108. Cushion capital presumed to
come from Evesham Abbey.

Cathedral (*c.*1089), straightforward transpositions of Norman capitals were produced, such as simple volute capitals with central masks and chip carving. From what we know, given the small amount of surviving sculpture, few English monuments can have rivalled the avant-garde sculpture of Christ Church, although the narrative capitals from Westminster Hall and the recently discovered panel from Winchester give some impression of the high standards that could be achieved.[59]

Considering the outstanding quality of the capitals, it would be reasonable to expect that they provided an impetus to the development of sculpture elsewhere in England and, indeed, some possible instances of Canterbury's influence can be traced. In the south transept at Worcester Cathedral, for instance, there is a series of cushion capitals carved with 'Winchester acanthus' foliage and decorative devices such as a dragon and the half-figure of an angel (ill. 107).[60] In concept the Worcester capitals are close to Canterbury, but the examples at Worcester seem more assured. The plain horizontal borders at the top of each of the crypt capitals do not appear at Worcester, so the carved designs can extend the full height of the capital. The stalks are thinner and more densely enmeshed and the foliage is not steadfastly symmetrical as it is in the crypt at Canterbury. A cushion capital that has by chance survived from Evesham Abbey (ill. 108) offers further evidence of an interest in developments at Canterbury, because its curved foliage branches are very similar to those on the capital in the Innocents chapel at Canterbury.

The carved cushion capitals at Christ Church find parallels elsewhere in England in the first third of the twelfth century. The choir of the aristocratic nunnery at Romsey Abbey contains a series of single and double cushion capitals bearing shields filled with grotesques, and acanthus foliage below (ill. 106).[61] The capitals of the nave and chapter house doorways at Durham Cathedral were probably also inspired by Canterbury, though the Durham examples express greater freedom, with dragons swinging like acrobats from the shields (ill. 138).

71

109. Cushion capital with 'Winchester acanthus' in the Holy Innocents' Chapel.

110. Capital with 'Winchester acanthus' on the external arcade of the north-east transept.

111. Fragment from Westminster Abbey with 'Winchester acanthus' foliage.

The block capitals at Christ Church provided inspiration for other centres as well. A capital from Westminster Abbey has a symmetrical design of 'Winchester acanthus' foliage which could have been inspired by the designs of capitals in the Innocents chapel, if it is not directly based on a manuscript source (ills. 109, 111). Experiments related to the block capitals in the crypt were still being made half a century on, as in a splendid example from Winchester, each face of which is carved with a centaur, a griffin or a grotesque in bold relief.[62]

The crypt capitals therefore played an important role in the development of sculpture at major Benedictine houses across England. The survivals give clear testimony of this; only the means of transmission of their influence remain difficult to pin down. It is true that Canterbury books played some part in the expansion of the library at Worcester, so it is just conceivable that the impact of the decorated initials from Canterbury accounts for the similarities in sculpture. In the same way, the links between the sculpture at Durham and Canterbury may owe something to the influence of Canterbury manuscripts at Durham.[63] But the use of the cushion form must also be accounted for, and neither manuscripts nor model books can be invoked for that.

The similarities between the carvings of Canterbury Cathedral, Rochester Cathedral and St Augustine's Abbey are easier to explain. The close relations between the monastic communities of Christ Church and of Rochester naturally resulted in artistic links, with Canterbury playing the dominant role in both manuscript illumination and sculpture. It must be remembered that Ernulf, the builder of the Canterbury crypt, became bishop of Rochester in 1114, when he is credited with erecting new monastic buildings.[64] Not surprisingly, what little sculpture survives in those buildings (there was a fire in 1137) presents similarities with Canterbury — for example, in the bearded male heads, 'Winchester acanthus', and crouching dragons of the chapter house and monks' dormitory (ills. 112, 113). The use of classical subjects at Rochester also brings Canterbury to mind. The *Serpentarius* repeated twice on the bottom voussoirs of the chapter house doorway derived ultimately from astronomical manuscripts in the same way as some of the motifs on the Canterbury crypt capitals.[65]

The remaining fragments from St Augustine's Abbey are of course linked with the sculptural developments in the crypt at Christ Church. Here too, details from manuscripts were a stimulus for stone sculpture. (For example, one capital from St Augustine's has symmetrical branches

112-113. Confronted dragons and foliage. Above: initial P of Baltimore, Walters Art Gallery, MS 18, f.216v; below: impost of the chapter house doorway at Rochester Cathedral.

114. Voussoir with a bearded head flanked by dragons tugging its beard, from St. Augustine's Abbey. The voussoir, inscribed 'Robertus me fecit' is one of the rare pieces of Romanesque sculpture in England which is signed.

115. Head flanked by dragons at the top of an initial T. London, BL, Harley MS 624, f.132.

116. Capital with foliage from St Augustine's Abbey.

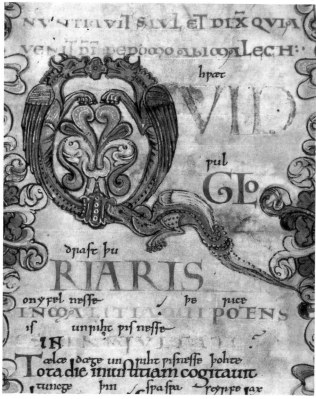

117. Initial with interior foliage. London, BL, Cotton MS Tib. C.VI, f.72.

of foliage with a central clasp, ill. 116, a motif also found in an earlier Winchester Psalter, ill. 117).[66] In another case, a voussoir, probably from the apex of an arch at St Augustine's, is carved with a male head flanked by two inverted dragons tugging at his divided beard, while he in turn clutches their tails (ill. 114). The design is related to a detail in the initial T in a *Passionale* also from St Augustine's, and it confirms the link between manuscripts and sculpture (ill. 115).

None of the surviving sculpture at St Augustine's is *in situ*, so its original location is unknown and the dating must rely on style alone. The similarity to the sculpture at Christ Church suggests that they are approximately contemporary, perhaps even by the same sculptors. As the style of the initials in the two Canterbury monasteries is practically indistinguishable, so the sculpture based on them is related. The question arises whether it was perhaps at St Augustine's that the Canterbury style was initiated, but this is unlikely. The artists who worked in the crypt were clearly experimenting with the problems of applying their motifs as carvings. This is obvious in the shift of capital type and the approach to three-dimensional form. Moreover, the carvers of the crypt capitals were constantly trying out new forms and techniques. The evolution of sculpture discernible in these works make it fairly certain that this style originated in the crypt itself and spread from there to other centres as far afield as Durham and Worcester and as close at hand as Rochester and St Augustine's.

But while the artists of the crypt sculpture blazed a fresh trail by initiating a new fashion for carving at major Benedictine houses, there was virtually no following in parish churches in Kent. One church, at Birchington in north-east Kent, reveals a weak attempt to imitate the volute capitals of the crypt. Otherwise only the simplest geometric patterns were copied, as in the parish churches at Brook, Smeeth and Walmer.[67] But aside from these mechanical patterns which required no special skill to imitate, Anselm's choir did not greatly affect sculpture in the surrounding area probably because of the considerable expense, but above all from lack of experienced sculptors and perhaps the inaccesibility of manuscripts or model books.

The capitals are not the only sculpted element of importance in the crypt. Many of the shafts are also carved. The distribution of the shafts in the centre of the nave adheres to a rational pattern (ill. 32). Pairs of plain capitals supported by patterned shafts are set in alternation with pairs of carved capitals and plain shafts. Although the system is not followed with absolute fidelity, the original intention of the designer seems to have been to use this plan consistently.

When we reach the area of the altar of the Virgin, a noteworthy change occurs. Two pairs of columns with deeply cut spirals flank the sanctuary (ill. 121).[68] These draw attention to the most important area of the crypt, but they may be of wider significance as well. Spiral columns assumed a special meaning in the Middle Ages because of their association with the

118 (overleaf left). Fluted shaft and cushion capital carved in low relief in the crypt.

119 (overleaf right). Shaft carved in low relief and trefoil capital in the crypt.

120 (above). Detail of one of the spiral columns from the shrine of St Peter's in Rome.

121 (below). One of a pair of columns with deeply cut spirals that flank the sanctuary.

shrine of St Peter in Rome. The Constantinian church on that site had six spiral columns, of classical origin, around the shrine, four of which supported the *baldachino* (ill. 120). During the pontificate of Gregory the Great, these were rearranged to form a screen standing before the shrine. This configuration was subsequently enhanced with the addition of six more columns in the time of Pope Gregory III.[69]

Every Christian in the Middle Ages who made the journey to Rome saw the Shrine of St Peter and also the magnificent spiral columns. The columns had an additional meaning during the medieval period for they were universally believed to have been brought to Rome from the Temple of Solomon.[70] This association conferred even greater prestige, and may explain the special use of spiral columns in certain buildings in Northern Europe. The spiral shafts used in the Anglo-Saxon crypt at Repton for instance may refer back to St Peter's.[71] It is presumably then no accident that spiral shafts mark the sanctuary in the choirs at Durham and Norwich or in the crypts of Utrecht, Rolduc, Deventer, Tongres and Lund. The arrangement at Canterbury is yet a further instance of this architectural iconography.

In the case of Canterbury, a specific and conscious reference to the Shrine of St Peter's seems to be confirmed by the documentary evidence. During the course of his description of the Anglo-Saxon church, Eadmer alludes to 'the church of the Blessed Prince of the Apostles, Peter in which the most sacred relics of that man are honoured by the veneration of the whole world'. Later he comments that the church at Canterbury was arranged, 'in the likeness of the crypt of St Peter'. Eadmer was writing about a century after the construction of the Anglo-Saxon church, and his statement could hardly reflect the original intentions of the builders.[72] The comparison he makes may refer to ideas that were uppermost in his mind after his journey with Anselm to Rome in 1099, when he must have seen St Peter's basilica, since the Council in which Anselm participated was held around the saint's tomb.[73] It could be speculated that Eadmer was describing the Anglo-Saxon crypt in terms of the appearance of and intention behind the recently completed Romanesque crypt.

The studied references to the Shrine of St Peter's takes on a special meaning given the political climate at Canterbury during Anselm's episcopate and his concern for the question of obedience. Unlike Lanfranc whose main allegiance had been to the Crown, Anselm insisted that his first loyalty was to the pope, and his high-minded stand on this issue forced him into exile in 1097. But Anselm faced an equally serious problem in the struggle with York for the primacy. This matter came to the fore on the very day of Anselm's investiture, when Archbishop Thomas of York, on being required to consecrate Anselm as primate of all England, retired to the vestry and refused to budge until the offending words relating to the primacy of Canterbury were deleted from the ceremony.[74]

In this atmosphere there was good reason for the authorities at Christ Church to wish to underline Canterbury's special relation with Rome. Anselm's strong belief that the pope and no monarch was the successor to St Peter could only have strengthened the desire to preserve Canterbury's special relationship with the Church in Rome. When understood in this context, the hypothesis that the twisted columns in the crypt at Canterbury were intended as visual propaganda appears an attractive possibility. The architectural allusion made to St Peter's appears to have been a thinly veiled reference to the special relation between Rome and Christ Church.

The Choir

Gervase recorded that after the fire of 1174, the new architect, William of Sens, was instructed by the monks to preserve as much of Anselm's choir as possible. It is clear that William went some way to meet the request. With the exception of the nave arcade, much of Anselm's building is buried within the walls of the Gothic choir.[75]

122. The Choir, Canterbury Cathedral.

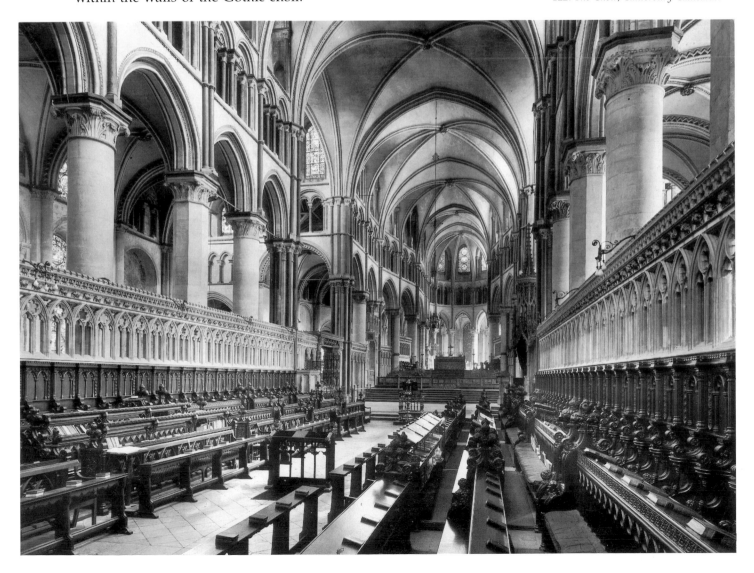

123. Tau-cross capital from the choir of St Anselm, re-used in the crypt after the fire of 1174.

124 (right). Tau-cross capital from the 9th century in the nave of San Vincenzo in Prato, Milan.

The most dramatic example of the architect's adherence to the wishes of the monks is the reuse in the crypt of three of the large columns (albeit shortened) from the choir ambulatory of the upper church with their original capitals and bases (ill. 123). One of these capitals has been recarved, but two others retain their original form, each with a broad T-shaped projection on the central face and broad, flat angle volutes.

This capital type seems to have originated in the ninth century in Italy, the first notable examples being those at San Vincenzo in Prato, Milan (ill. 124).[76] This form may already have reached English shores late in the reign of Edward the Confessor with the Norman masons who built Westminster Abbey (ill. 125). The architectural filiations between the royal abbey and the abbey church at Jumièges (1040-67) are well known, and it is probably no accident that modified versions, with the central projection, but minus the T-shaped cross bar, occur in the nave of Jumièges (ill. 127). The appearance of the tau-cross capital in the dorter at Westminster may indicate that originally their use was widespread in the abbey church there. Tau-cross capitals were also used in St John's chapel in the Tower of London: by the 1070s or 1080s they were a standard feature in buildings of the London basin (ill. 126).[77] Their use in the choir arcade at Canterbury some twenty years later was, therefore, a rather conservative choice. In chronological terms they might fit more comfortably in Lanfranc's church, but several factors rule this out completely. First, the curved impost of one of these capitals shows that it comes from an ambulatory, and Lanfranc's church did not have an ambulatory.[78] Secondly, certain geometric patterns used on the choir capitals also feature on sculpture in Anselm's crypt. The scroll on the necking of one the tau-cross capitals occurs on two shafts in the crypt and the x-in-square motif on a base is also used, albeit inconspicuously, on one of the crypt capitals.

125. Tau-cross capital of the 9th-century dormitory at Westminster Abbey.

126. Tau-cross capital from the 11th-century ambulatory of St John's Chapel, White Tower, London

127. Capital with chamfered angles and a central projection, from the 11th-century nave of Jumièges Abbey.

The simplicity of the geometric motifs is characteristic of the decoration of Anselm's choir. The most common pattern on window heads and arches consists of two bands of slightly raised disc ornament flanking a band of indented lozenge (ill. 128). The same indented lozenge pattern also occurs with a continuous strip of large and small billet (pipeline billet) on the heads of the blind arcade of intersecting arches which is supported by shafts, capitals and bases on the external wall of Anselm's choir beneath the tall windows (ill. 129).

Apart from these capitals and traces of geometric ornament, little other interior choir sculpture remains. It is a tiny body of material from which to try to draw any conclusions. The picture presented on the basis of this evidence is of austere and conservative sculpture — which seems a far cry from the magnificence proclaimed by William of Malmesbury.[79] But when we turn to the exterior arcade we are confronted with capitals and shafts of the same high calibre as those in the crypt, and it becomes clear that William of Malmesbury was not exaggerating the splendour and sophistication of the choir decoration.

The external arcade of the choir corresponds to a similar blind arcade on the interior of the choir. The capitals of the interior arcade are uniformly plain: there is no carving except for some of the arch heads where geometric motifs are used. Much of the external arcade is also plain, but there are some carved capitals and shafts of outstanding quality. The north wall of the north-east transept and the south and west walls of the south-east transept have abundant foliage and figural carvings of the highest calibre. Further east on the south side of the choir, there is a string of simple foliage capitals.[80]

The corrosion of the stone has hindered study, but recent cleaning and conservation of the transepts has allowed the sculpture to be assessed afresh.[81] Among other things, this has shed new light on carving technique. Markings remain on the back of one of the shafts which show that the pattern was incised before carving began. It is impossible that these lines were made once the shaft was in place. The carving was without question prepared before installation.

The motifs on the capitals of the transept arcades fall into several types, ranging from dynamic scenes of hunt and chase, with wolves devouring tumbling men and armed figures stalking birds and wild boar to arched, whirling grotesques with spindly necks and tails, and robust full-length masks spewing small monsters (ills. 130-134, 144-150). There are balanced foliage capitals, with long graceful stalks and swelling leaves, organized in symmetrical designs, and figures playing on musical instruments. Other capitals seem completely anecdotal, such as that with a row of figures, each holding the leg of its predecessor. This rich variety is repeated in the diversity of the patterned shafts.

The subjects of the capitals and the use of patterned shafts are like those of the crypt. So too is the treatment of the upper zone of some capitals, carved with jewel-like bands or thin parallel grooves. But there are also

128-129. Details of a window head with disc and lozenge ornament in the apse of St Anselm's Chapel, and an exterior window between the south-east transept and St Anselm's Chapel.

82

130. (right) Capitals and arcading on the exterior of the north-east transept.

131. Capital on the external arcade of the north-east transept depicting a boldly carved nude figure devoured by grotesques in the place of angle volutes.

distinctive differences. The two-dimensional approach to carving in the crypt is entirely superceded by a more sculptural technique. The scenes on the arcade capitals spread freely across all three sides. There are no awkward joins at the angles as with the crypt capitals. The arcade capitals are smaller, and the carvings are even more delicate and refined than those of the crypt, though at the same time the modelling of the arcade capitals is more vigorous and three-dimensional. This is particularly obvious in the capital on the north transept showing a pair of projecting angle masks devouring a very realistically depicted nude figure (ill. 131).

The differences between the capitals in the crypt and those of the arcade are forcefully conveyed by the divergent approaches to 'Winchester acanthus' foliage. In the Holy Innocents chapel the leaves are lush, broad and stretched into wide, flat shapes (ill. 109). The motifs stand proud: the background has been chiselled away. On the arcade they have become more spindly and brittle and the forms are deeply undercut (ill. 110). The arcade capital is altogether more three-dimensional. The foliage design even meets at the capital angles so that the faces of the capital are integrated, not treated as separate units, as in the crypt.

84

132. *Detail of a hunting scene on the external arcade of the south-east transept. This side of the capital shows a hunter blowing his horn while leading his hound. The other faces of the capital show the hunt in progress. The narrative encompasses the entire capital and is not confined to one scene on each side as on most of the crypt capitals.*

133. *Detail of a capital on the external arcade of the south-east transept showing a fanciful nude holding an axe over one shoulder riding a monster with a beaded foliage tail.*

134. *Winged grotesques with whirling tail on the external arcade of the north-east transept.*

135. *Winged grotesques with whirling tails on a capital from the cloister of the royal abbey at Reading.*

136. *Detail of a cushion capital with foliage from the entrance-arch of the south transept of Worcester Cathedral.*

The arcade sculpture is similar to that in the crypt, but there are telling differences of style. While the arcade is clearly contemporary with the fabric of Anselm's crypt, the stylistic transformation suggests that its date should be pushed as late as the archaeological evidence allows, to around 1120. This date seems to be confirmed by the close relationship of the Canterbury arcade capitals to sculpture elsewhere in England. These carvings seem to have influenced the capitals at Romsey Abbey (ills. 140, 141), Durham Cathedral (ills. 138, 139), and more particularly the capitals from the cloister at Reading Abbey.

The royal abbey of Reading was founded in 1121 by King Henry I as his mausoleum, and as a result no expense was spared. Canterbury Cathedral was a natural model to turn to at the start of Henry's enterprise. Little sculpture survives at Reading aside from that of the cloister, but these vigorous carvings bring to mind the Canterbury capitals, especially those of the external arcade. There are links between many individual pieces, and details are also alike. For instance, the Canterbury capital with grotesque masks at the upper angles is copied in no less than three examples at Reading (ills. 57, 59). The energetic interlocking dragons of another Reading capital perpetuate the dynamic force and clarity of form

137. *Foliage capital on the external arcade of the south-east transept.*

86

and relief of Canterbury (ills. 134, 135. Even the carving of the heads, the wings, the foliate tails and the beaded spines correspond. Other Canterbury details are also reflected at Reading: the upright leaves and the egg-and-tongue motif on the abacus of a Reading capital are drier, more schematic versions of the precedents in the Canterbury crypt (ills. 47, 48, 135). Moreover, the basic approach to sculpture is similar. The carved forms have a three-dimensional quality, and neither at Canterbury nor at Reading do the angles of the capitals act as barriers. The figures and motifs cross them with complete freedom. There is a strong case for suggesting that one of the Reading cloister sculptors trained in the workshop at Canterbury Cathedral. There would be nothing suprising in this, for the royal foundation had the prestige and the money to attract the best talent available.

The sources of the late eleventh-century capitals in the crypt and, some twenty years later, the capitals on the exterior of the choir at Christ Church have been traced to local manuscript illumination, particularly to the type of grotesque and acrobatic initials that flourished in post-Conquest books. These innovations in the decoration of books emerged, albeit tentatively at first, in the scriptorium established by Archbishop Lanfranc. The few initials in the books produced in Lanfranc's scriptorium in the 1070s and 1080s with a double-headed peacock, lions and small dotted dogs, are the earliest anticipations of the magnificent initial style that was soon to flourish at Christ Church under Anselm.

The inspirational power of manuscript initials cannot be overestimated. They were the primary force behind the new sculptural innovations at Christ Church and they repeatedly emerge as a powerful influence in the later sculpture at Canterbury. Their fundamental appeal initiated a local style in sculpture which, as we shall see, persisted in modified forms until the end of the twelfth century.

138 (left). Cushion capital with foliage on the south doorway at the west end of the nave of Durham Cathedral.

139 (right). Detail of foliage on the external arcade of the north-east transept at Canterbury.

*140. External arcade capital
on the south side of the choir.*

*141. Choir capital from
Romsey Abbey.*

The capitals of the Canterbury crypt were carved at a crucial period in the history of medieval art. For the first time since the Roman Empire a truly international style had emerged, and monumental stone sculpture was revived with a vigour that had not been seen since antiquity. From Apulia in the south, to Santiago de Compostela in the west and in numerous centres in France, notably Languedoc and Burgundy, great masterpieces of sculpture were being created. The reliefs of Wiligelmo at Modena roughly coincide with those of Gilduinus at Toulouse, with the Cluny ambulatory capitals, the cloister capitals at Moissac, the cloister capitals at Silos, and so on across Europe. Every ecclesiastic travelling from England to Rome would have certainly travelled along the Via Emilia, and thus he would have seen Modena Cathedral as it was being built. Toulouse was on the main pilgrimage road to Santiago, and English pilgrims doubtless stopped to pray at the shrine of Saint-Sernin. Apulia was visited by crowds of pilgrims for it had two famous centres, Monte Gargano, the centre of the cult of St Michael, and Bari, the centre of the cult of St Nicholas.[82]

Yet despite this traffic across Europe, the Canterbury crypt capitals show little sign of being specifically indebted to Continental sculpture.[83] Perhaps it was only the general knowledge of the new popularity of architectural sculpture that contributed to the wish of the monks to create similar works at their own church. As they made daily use of books in the cloister and choir, they were very familiar with the painted initials in those books, so they knew exactly where to turn for models. There was no need to look across the Channel for inspiration.[84] Thus the idea of carving the capitals may have been stimulated by developments abroad, but the actual choice of motifs and methods for transferring them to stone was a matter largely settled within the precincts of Christ Church.

88

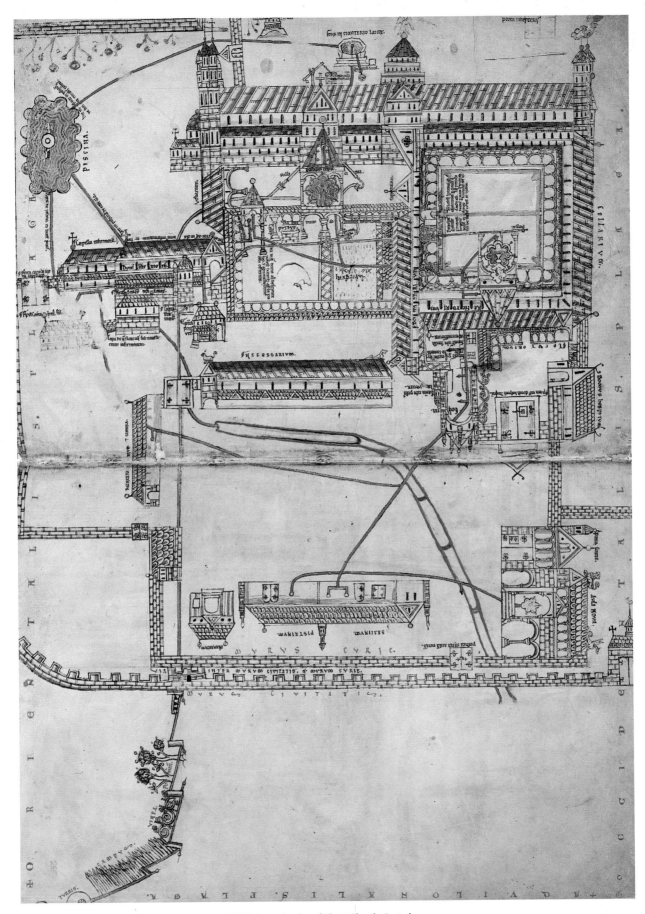

VII. Waterworks plan of Christ Church, Canterbury.
Cambridge, Trinity College MS R.17.1, ff.284v-285

VIII. Capital in St Gabriel's Chapel with a lion

IX. Capital in St Gabriel's Chapel with double-bodied lion

X. Crypt capital with angle mask and foliage

XI. Capital on the external arcade
of the south-east transept

XII. The south-east transept of Canterbury Cathedral

142-143. *Details of two of the carved shafts on the external arcade of the south-east transept.*

144. Falling figure on a capital on the external arcade of the south-east transept.

145-146. *Capitals on the external arcade of the south-east transept will full-length grotesque masks.*
One issues monsters from its open mouth, the other stretches its mouth open, displaying teeth.

147 (above). *Capital on the external arcade of the north-east transept with a nude figure devoured by angle masks.*

148 (below). *Capital of the external arcade of the south-east transept with a figure holding a shield on horseback on the left, and a tumbling figure clutching the jaws of a grotesque that attacks his genitals on the right.*

149-150. *Two faces of a capital on the external arcade of the north-east transept with a hunter stabbing a wild boar (above), as his foot it bitten by a winged bird (below). The imagery is not confined to the three separate faces of the capital but spreads freely across all the sides creating a harmonious work.*

151. External view of the main water tower c.1155. Aside from minor 14th-century alterations, particularly to the upper level, the building retains the same form as shown on the drawing (ill.154).

III. Sculpture under Archbishop Theobald

T HERE WAS A LULL in building activity at Christ Church from the dedication of 1130 until around the middle of the century. Then soon after the installation of Theobald as archbishop in 1139 there was a great expansion and an extraordinary campaign to rebuild at the cathedral, especially in the monastic precinct. Theobald was a cosmopolitan figure: his activities created a climate in which there was a new receptiveness to a range of artistic currents, both local and foreign. Many of these are reflected in the various styles of sculpture that flourished at the time.

The period during which Theobald was archbishop was marked by a great awakening of intellectual life, and by international exchange of every description. A letter drafted by Theobald's secretary and assistant, John of Salisbury, reports that Henry II, king during the later years of Theobald's archiepiscopate, had created anew the golden age.[1] This is certainly no exaggeration, for Henry II's dominions included not only England, but Continental territories from Normandy as far south as the Pyrenees (see Map, p. 206).[2] The monarch consolidated and maintained this, the so-called Angevin Empire, by constant travel, which made him appear ubiquitous to his contemporaries. 'Now in Ireland, now in England, now in Normandy, he must fly rather than travel by horse or ship', the King of France was led to exclaim.[3] Henry's subjects travelled no less readily within these extensive territories.

Theobald is an excellent example of the mobility characteristic of this period. Born of Norman stock, he became a monk at Bec between 1093 and 1124. He was made prior there in 1127, and elected abbot in 1137. Upon his appointment as archbishop of Canterbury, he travelled to Rome to receive the pallium. In 1144 he revisited the papal city and returned through Paris where he was the only prelate from outside France to participate in the consecration of Saint-Denis on 11 June.[4] Three years later he was again in Paris, and the following year (after attending the Council at Reims) he returned to Canterbury for only a brief period before re-crossing the Channel to escape the wrath of King Stephen. It was then that he resided in several houses in Northern France and the Low Countries, among them Arras and Saint-Bertin. On his return, Theobald remained in England until 1152, when he again evaded the king by spending a few months' exile in Flanders.

At Christ Church, particularly in the later, more stable phase of his archiepiscopate, Theobald created one of the most pre-eminent households of twelfth-century Europe, collecting round himself students of philosophy and jurisprudence. With hindsight it is possible to judge just how important Theobald's *curia* was, for it produced no less than six future bishops and four archbishops, some of whom also played a part in England's secular government. The best known figure to emerge from the service of Theobald was Thomas Becket. In addition, some of the great intellectuals of the age also congregated at Theobald's side among them Master Vacarius, an Italian jurist and author on canon and civil law as well as theology, the historian Gervase and the poet Nigel Wireker, best known for his satire on the students of Paris. Perhaps most important of all was John of Salisbury. The author of many letters and remarkable books, notably the *Policraticus* and the *Metalogicon*, he was at the very forefront of the movement which led to a revival of scholarship in the classical humanities.[5] His career also epitomizes the international character of the era. Born in Old Sarum he died bishop of Chartres in 1180, having spent his intervening years in Canterbury, Paris and Rome.

A man of Theobald's experience and breadth of vision could not have failed to encourage the monks in their efforts to modernize and enlarge the monastery. This emerges, perhaps surprisingly but most clearly, in an elaborate hydraulic system designed to carry water to all parts of the precinct (see ill. 154, Colour Pl. VII). The survival at Canterbury of this monastic hydraulic system, the pipes, the drains, the conduit and even a water tower offers remarkable insight into the many facets of the period not least its artistic development. There is ample evidence of Theobald's interest in the internal welfare of the priory and his approval of the new hydraulic system in particular, as evinced by the fact that he himself granted the spring at Horfalde which fed the water supply to the monks.[6]

However, responsibility for the fabric of the cathedral and monastic buildings lay not with the archbishop but with the prior, who in this period at Christ Church was Prior Wibert. Wibert's priorate began under Theobald but spanned the first five years of Becket's archiepiscopacy as well. We know from Wibert's *obits* that he played a major role in the installation of the new hydraulic system at Christ Church: 'among the many other good works which he did for the church [he] caused to be made the watercourse with its ponds, conduits and fishpools; which water he marvellously brought over 1000 paces from the town into the precinct and so through all the offices of the precinct'.[7] Wibert began his career at the cathedral as a monk, but by 1148 was promoted to the rank of subprior, becoming prior four or five years later, in 1152 or 1153. His priorate began towards the end of a stormy period in Canterbury's history. In 1150 the monks of Christ Church found themselves in severe financial difficulties. The chronicler Gervase suggests that while the depletion of funds was partly due to the disruptions caused by the Civil War during the reign of King Stephen, responsibility for their mismanagement lay specifically with Wibert's predecessor, Prior Walter Parvus who, 'although a learned man, lacked practical skills'.[8] The monks applied to Archbishop Theobald for assistance and he responded by taking charge of the conventual property in 1150. Certain of the reforms which he introduced, notably a restricted diet, incensed the monks. A heated dispute ensued and by 1152 the archbishop had to relinquish control of the monastic finances, although he

96

152. (right) The ground storey of the water tower. The large central pillar concealed the water pipes which rose within its core. Note the refined mouldings, double billet on the ribs, chevron filled with leaves and triangles and a delicate band of dog's tooth on the outer arches.

deposed and imprisoned Prior Walter Parvus for his participation in the monks' revolt.[9]

The request in 1150 that the archbishop should undertake the administration of the conventual estates coincides so exactly with the start of the building campaign that it is difficult to believe that the dire financial straits recorded by Gervase alone prompted the prior to invoke the archbishop's help, and the stringencies which Theobald imposed upon the monks may have been intended to help conserve funds for the building programme. Despite his capitulation to the monks, it was thanks to Theobald that Walter Parvus was deposed and the able Wibert was installed as prior in his stead.

It is curious that the campaign to update and improve the cathedral and monastery at Christ Church is not fully described by Gervase, who was himself a monk there at the time. Stranger still are Wibert's *obits*, for although they credit him with the installation of the hydraulic system they make no mention of any other building activity. His purchases of property, however, leave little room to doubt his involvement. Even during the period of unrest it is clear that Wibert was planning a building campaign in the monastic precinct. In 1152 he repossessed allotments of monastic property which had been rented out, and this reacquired land made possible the advancement of the north boundary wall of the monastery. He also repossessed land in the north-west of the precinct, where the main gate and *aula nova* (probably the monastic guest house or pilgrims' hall) were later built. Wibert's intentions in making these purchases emerge from two records stating that land was bought behind the brewhouse and between the cathedral and city walls 'ad opus ecclesiae nostrae', and that Wibert, subprior, bought land 'ad opus ecclesiae suae'.[10]

The monastery's hydraulic system was central to Wibert's building programme. Most monasteries in the Middle Ages were sited with easy access to natural water sources or else relied on wells, but textual sources indicate that the piped supply at Canterbury was in no way unique in twelfth-century England.[11] Excavations have revealed that at about the same time as Christ Church was modernizing its hydraulic system, the monks of St Augustine's Abbey also built a conduit.[12] Waverley Abbey is recorded as having a piped system by 1179. One of the *Miracles of Thomas Becket* tells of plans to pipe water from a spring to Churchdown in Gloucestershire, which were interrupted when excavations caved in. At Bury St Edmunds, when Walter de Banham became sacrist around 1200 he is said to have 'enclosed in lead the water supply from its head and spring for a distance of two miles and brought it to the cloister through ways hidden in the ground'. Further evidence exists in the remains of five other independent twelfth-century structures for water supplies in English monasteries at Battle, Lewes, Much Wenlock, St Nicholas at Exeter and Durham.[13]

It may be more than coincidence that a water system was being built at about this time at Lichfield Cathedral, for its bishop Walter Durdent was a former prior of Christ Church. In fact it was during Durdent's

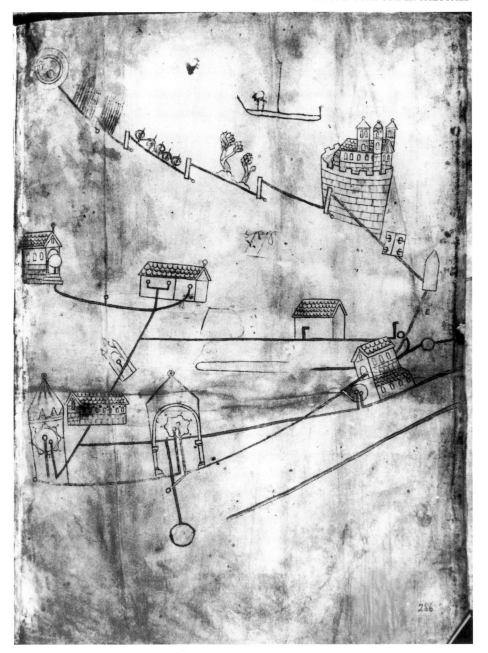

153. Diagrammatic view from the south showing the essential buildings in the precinct at Christ Church Cathedral, Canterbury, in relation to the hydraulic system. Cambridge, Trinity College, MS R.17.1, f.286, c.1165.

priorate at Canterbury (1143-1149) that Wibert became subprior. Perhaps these two men, both later involved in the construction of new water systems at their respective monasteries, had together begun plans for the Canterbury waterworks before Durdent was called to Lichfield.[14]

Our knowledge of Canterbury Cathedral during the third quarter of the twelfth century is enhanced by the happy preservation of two contemporary drawings giving a general layout of the hydraulic system (ills. 153, 154, Colour Pl. VII). As initiator and overseer of the construction of the hydraulic system it is likely that Prior Wibert himself commissioned

99

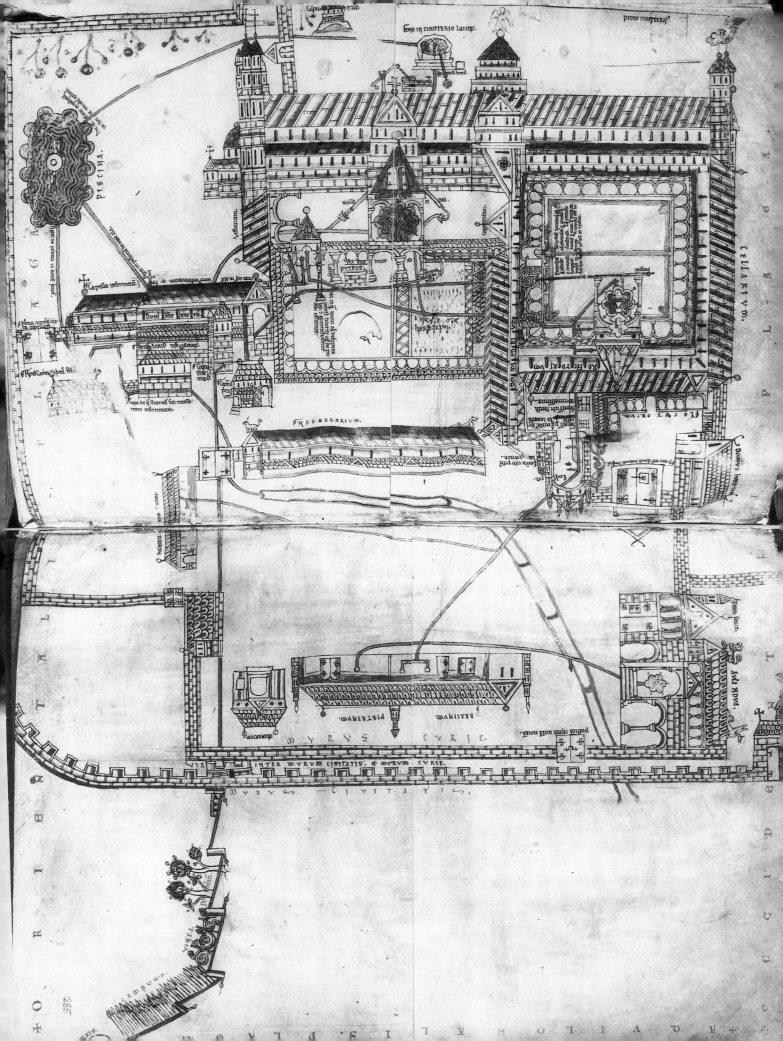

them.[15] The smaller of the two drawings is diagrammatic (ill. 153). It gives a view from the south, showing the plumbing isolated from all but essential buildings. We learn from it that the main supply pipe led from the water source at Horfalde, today on the outskirts of the city, to the conduit house and thence to five settling tanks situated in a cornfield, a vineyard and an orchard. The pipe entered the monastery, passing under the infirmary to the first main outlet, the water tower or laver which still stands near the infirmary cloister, and thence to a second water tower, now destroyed, which was in the principal cloister. These two main outlets are represented by towers with rosette-shaped symbols and conical roofs. From there the diagram (as it will be referred to henceforth) charts the course of subsidiary pipes to other important outlets in the precinct.

The large drawing (or plan, as it will be referred to henceforth) gives a bird's eye view from the north and is far more detailed (ill. 154, Colour Pl. VII). The main outlines are in pen and ink, but the buildings are further highlighted with blue, brown, red, green and yellow pigments. Some thirty different structures and installations are depicted, with detailed captions naming the monastic buildings and explaining the functions of the pipes. The main supply pipe, drawn in green, is shown passing through the same fields and leading to the same two primary cloister lavers as on the diagram. These two main outlets are again shown with conical roofs. The rosette-shaped symbol in the main water tower is represented in the upper storey, with what were evidently spouts where the monks could wash before entering the choir. The fountain in the second tower came to a head on ground level, so that the monks could wash before passing from the cloister into the refectory. The courses of subsidiary pipes are shown in red. In addition, the monastic drainage system, lavatory (*neccesarium*), fishponds, and wells are represented.[16]

The function of the plan is uncertain. On the basis of its fine execution one might conclude that it was meant to impress the distinguished visitors to the monastery, but this could not have been its sole purpose. Its technical nature is clear from the inclusion of small details such as the filter represented on the pipe of the conduit house, the purge pipes shown on the settling tanks and the little bridge that carried the pipe across the ditch into the precinct. The plan thus appears to have been much more strictly utilitarian, as a record of the position of the underground pipes and their functions. The representation of the buildings seems to have been less important than their relationship to the waterworks.

The only remotely comparable work is the plan of St Gall in Switzerland of *c*.820; but this gives an idealized layout of a monastery, while the Canterbury drawings depict relatively realistic representations of the buildings and plumbing. In an age where copying and reproduction were controlling influences, the Canterbury drawings represent a radical departure from the norm.[17]

It is safe to assume that the Canterbury drawings were made before 1174, because in that year the choir built during the archiepiscopate of

101

154 (opposite). This drawing is unique in that it provides a remarkably accurate depiction of the buildings and hydraulic system at Christ Church, Canterbury. It presents a bird's eye view from the north. The buildings and pipes are labelled to explain their functions. Cambridge, Trinity College, MS R.17.1, ff.284v-285.

Anselm which is shown on the plan was destroyed. But their date can be fixed even more precisely. Since it was Wibert who almost certainly commissioned the drawings, they must have been made before his death in 1167. The date of *c*.1165 has been suggested and seems plausible, allowing for the fact that some of the buildings were still incomplete when the drawings were made.[18]

Wibert's activities imply that a building campaign was being planned shortly before 1150. The dire financial straits of the convent make it likely that actual work on new buildings was begun only after 1152, when Walter Parvus was ousted as prior and Wibert took his place. In view of the scale of the enterprise, it may have continued at a pace of varying intensity until it was disrupted by the fire of 1174. Several distinctive sculptural styles can be identified for the period of the campaign, yet bearing in mind its duration and the variety of functions for which the buildings were constructed, we may nevertheless discern an underlying homogeneity by examining individual buildings in detail.

The main water tower remarkably still stands within the precinct (ills. 151, 152).[19] As depicted on the drawing it is the first structure within the monastic precincts to be fed by the primary supply pipe. The pressure rallied by the height of the conduit house carried the water up to the first floor of the tower. Since the water source at Horfalde was over thirty-two feet above the ground level of the precinct, the pressure would have ensured a constant flow to the washing tower and so throughout the monastery.[20] This was clearly the first structure related to the hydraulic system to be constructed in the precinct, so we may assume that the surviving water tower dates to the beginning of Wibert's campaign, around 1155. From there the pipe brought water to the second water tower, now destroyed, which was situated in the large cloister. These were the sole outlets for the main supply pipe, the rest of the convent being served by subsidiary pipes.

Much of the original water tower is intact, although it was substantially altered in the later Middle Ages. The ground plan has an outer ring of eight piers which encircle a large column articulated by pairs of attached shafts (ill. 152).[21] Two pairs of shafts remain, one with carved trumpet leaves and an impost with palmette joined by beaded frames, the other a linenfold scallop capital, with the same palmette pattern on the impost (ill. 156). The column concealed supply and drainage pipes rising within its core. The rib-vaults encircling the central column have profiles with central rolls flanked by rectangular mouldings and rows of billet and three carved keystones. The mouldings of the outer ring of arches are more complex, with two bands of headlong chevron filled with simple triangles or trefoil leaves flanking a roll moulding. The hood moulding bears delicately veined or beaded dogtooth ornament. Scallop and volute capitals are used with slight variations of pattern, some with fringed or trefoil leaves (ill. 160).

In the upper storey, the only surviving Romanesque features are three shafted windows, two in the east wall and one in the west (ills. 157-159). The heads of these windows have roll mouldings with geometric ornament: deeply cut beaded chevron and sawtooth chevron with a band of fret motif superimposed upon it. The geometric ornament of the arches and vaults is surprisingly subtle and ingenious. The combination of fret superimposed on chevron is unusual, and so at this relatively early date is the appearance of dogtooth motif.[22]

The basin from this upper storey has perished, but there are a number of examples at other sites in England which give some idea of its likely appearance. A fluted basin of Purbeck was recently recovered in front of the Palace of Westminster, and in the Cluniac abbey at Wenlock in Shropshire there is a lobed bowl encircled with foliage and enriched with New Testament scenes. The partly twelfth-century laver at Durham Cathedral was described c.1600: 'Within the Cloyster garth, over against the Frater house dour, was a fair Laver or Counditt for the Monncks to washe ther hands and faces at, being maid in forme round, covered with lead, and all of marble....having many little cunditts or spouts of brass'. The four lavers represented on the Canterbury plan also have a fluted shape. In view of

155 (left). Decorated arch in the nave gallery at Rochester Cathedral.

156 (right). Trumpet leaves and palmette ornament on the central pier of the water tower at Canterbury Cathedral.

157-159. *Upper chamber of the water tower showing the geometric ornament used on the window heads.*

the evidence at Durham, Westminster and Much Wenlock it seems that the multi-foil shapes represented on the plan were intended to reproduce the form of the basins at Canterbury.[23]

The Durham, Westminster and Wenlock basins are made of stones that can take a high polish. Two other surviving English lavers were made of similar materials: the example from the Cluniac Priory at Lewes was of blue lias while that at St Nicholas Priory at Exeter was again made of Purbeck. The Canterbury lavers were presumably made from a stone with similar qualities, so it is of special interest to find that the upper storey window seats were inset with Purbeck.[24]

Apart from the water tower, the only building still standing in the precinct which can be directly related to the plumbing system is the *aula nova* (ills. 162, 163). It was restored in the nineteenth century, and the first floor and west wall are entirely modern. But the enormous projecting twelfth-century staircase is almost all original (ills. 161, 163). According to the plan, the staircase supported a multi-foil laver.[25] The decoration of the staircase is closely related to that of the water tower in many respects. The bases have similar profiles and bands of zigzag on their scotia; the arches have the similar headlong sawtooth chevron and chevron filled with trefoil leaves. The springer-shaped stones with three-petalled flowers are also like the motif as it appears in the water tower. Many of the capitals are of similar scallop type, with delicate trefoil leaves (ills. 160, 161). Purbeck is used in this building also, for several shafts of the staircase. The *aula nova*, therefore, cannot be far removed in date from the water tower.[26]

160. *Scallop capital from the ground level of the water tower, virtually identical to capitals of the aula nova staircase (see below).*

161. *Aula nova staircase, south side. The speckled columns are Purbeck stone.*

162. Detail of the aula nova (guest house) and porta curie (main gate) from the waterworks drawing. There are finials on the roof of this building as on the roof of Westminster Abbey (see ill.16).

163. External view of the aula nova with the grand projecting 12th-century staircase. The edge of the main gateway into the precinct is just visible on the left.

Not all the buildings shown on the plan were part of the hydraulic system. The structure captioned the *vestiarium* had an entirely different function. It was built in such a way that the upper storey could be entered only from St Andrew's chapel (ills. 177), and thus it served as a repository for valuables.[27] This grand, spacious upper chamber was crowned by a parachute-like octopartite rib-vault with a single keystone carved with four lion heads (ill. 171, 186). Of the supporting respond capitals, one is carved with faces and one with birds (ills. 174, 175).

The plan shows the ground level of the building as it now stands, with a pair of capacious arches (ill. 164). Their decoration is most elaborate on the west side, and it is depicted from that vantage point on the drawing. The range of geometric ornament and schematic foliage is as intricate and varied here as in the water tower and the *aula nova*. Aside from sawtooth chevron and beaded fret, there are beaded interlaces. The interior of the ground level has rib-vaults of the same construction as the water tower and again with carved keystones (ills. 170, 173). The capitals also have close parallels in the water tower, though some are even more elaborate. The date of the *vestiarium* cannot be far removed from that of the water tower: *c*.1155-1160.[28]

164. *External view of the west side of the treasury or vestiarium. The upper storey could be entered only through St Andrew's chapel. It thus functioned as a sort of strong box and was a suitable repository for valuable objects and documents. The great open arches on the ground level look almost like a triumphal arch. They allowed passage through the precinct. The enormous columns which support them are of onyx — a rare material in 12th-century England.*

165

166

167

165-167. *Stylized scallop capitals with pleated shields, similar to those on the ground level of the vestiarium. Top left comes from St Albans Abbey. (Since this photograph was taken the capital has been lost). Top right provides a North of England example from Bridlington Abbey in Yorkshire.*

The capitals above come from a doorway built by Bishop Pudsey (1154-1195) at Durham Castle. The earliest experiments with scallop capitals which led to this type were made in the cathedral crypt. This, like so many features, shows the consistent sculptural tradition at Canterbury Cathedral.

168. *Capital on the west wall of the vestiarium.*

169. *(right) Central pillar of the vestiarium at ground level.*

170. Boss from the ground storey of the vestiarium.

171. Boss from the upper chamber of the vestiarium with four lion's heads.

172. Vault boss from the ground storey of the water tower.

173. Vault boss carved with a flower from the ground storey of the water tower.

174. *Mask capital in the vestiarium.*
175. *Bird capital in the vestiarium.*

The shafts throughout the *vestiarium* are strongly emphasized. Some, of Caen stone, have carved designs such as scale motif or hour-glass stalks and palmette (ill. 168). Those on the west face of the *vestiarium* are made from onyx, a most unusual material and one difficult to come by in twelfth-century England.[29] The use of this stone again suggests a preference in twelfth-century Canterbury for stones that take a high polish. The capitals are mainly decorated with geometric or foliage designs. In some cases simple scallop capitals are enlivened with nested-Vs, exactly as in the water tower (ills. 190, 191). In others, scallop capitals are carved as if they were overlaid with crisply folded lengths of fabric again as in the water tower (ill. 169).[30] Where human and animal forms appear they are reduced to schematic patterns, the shapes are awkward and the technique is coarse (ills. 174, 175). The masons responsible evidently were not hired for their ability as sculptors. But their accomplishments as builders may have played a role in their employment at Canterbury.

The chapels of St Anselm (ill. 176) and St Andrew (ill. 177) bring both the shortcomings and the skills of the masons sharply into focus. The chapels were originally built as part of the late eleventh-century cathedral choir, but were later altered by the insertion of two arches in each chapel, one spanning the opening to the apse and another the opening into the choir.

111

176. Capitals on the south side of St Anselm's Chapel.

These insertions do not obscure all traces of the original wider openings, for in St Anselm's chapel the cushion capital of the original arch of the early twelfth century can be seen embedded in the masonry (ill. 176).

Some of the capitals newly inserted in St Anselm's chapel are carved (ills. 194, 196). Beaded, strap-like stalks predominate in the decoration; on two of the capitals such stalks are interwoven in a crisp basket design, while on the other capitals they form flowing curves. These stalks, with parallel rims and sunken central channels filled with beading, are of the same type as those used in the decoration of the *vestiarium* capitals, as for instance on the angle of the bird capital (ill. 175). The north respond capital in the *vestiarium* chamber has five crudely carved heads with bulging eyes, gaping mouths and facial marks which are similar to the two beak-head masks in St Anselm's chapel. Even minor details such as the vertical setting of the eyes is alike (ills. 174, 196). Clearly these two groups of capitals must be roughly contemporary and the work of the same masons who, in this instance, were engaged in a complex patch-up job.

The purpose of the arches which they inserted in the two chapels was clearly not aesthetic. They serve to diminish the span of the original arches, and thus strengthen both structures. Further signs of reinforcement exist directly below these chapels at crypt level, in the chapels of the Holy Innocents and St Gabriel. The apse windows in both chapels have been

112

blocked, and strengthening arches have been inserted in the entrances to both apses.[31] In both chapels modest decoration accompanied the changes, namely the alternating large and small billet on the stringcourses and imposts. The same motif is carved on some of the imposts of the strengthening arch capitals in St Anselm's chapel above. These alterations in the crypt appear to have been made by Prior Wibert at the same time as arches were inserted in the chapels above, and for the same reason.[32]

177. St Andrew's Chapel.

113

178. *The south-east transept tower at Canterbury Cathedral.*

179. *Engraving of the church tower of St Mary's Dover as it stood in 1814. Its abundant geometric ornament appears to have copied the towers at Canterbury Cathedral.*

So much effort to reinforce the walls of the two choir chapels would not have been made without good reason. Examination of the waterworks plan and the second conventual seal (ills. 154, 225) suggest the motive for this activity. The plan shows two tall towers flanked by narrow stair turrets above the chapels. The late eleventh-century design included low chapels with a chamber above each, and a stair turret by which these upper rooms were reached. It was not until Wibert's time that the 'lofty' towers mentioned by Gervase were constructed above the chapels. Gervase describes how the architect of Canterbury's new choir, William of Sens, dismantled the upper storeys of the towers after the fire of 1174, 'being unable to move them entirely'.[33] Since the position of the chapels of St Anselm and St Andrew was a controlling factor in the line of the outer aisle walls, he was forced to reduce the width of the choir and its aisle walls to the east. The preservation of the chapels may have been due to the monks who, as Gervase explains, wished to retain as much of the original church as possible and who may have tried to economize by not replacing them. The towers have a *terminus ante quem* of 1158, the date of the charter on which the second seal of the convent first appears.[34]

Although the reinforcements were made to both chapels at the same time, the capitals of the arches inserted in St Andrew's chapel were left plain while those of St Anselm's chapel were carved (ills. 176, 177). This suggests that St Anselm's chapel was of special importance. The chapel was originally dedicated to St Peter and St Paul, but this was changed following the translation of St Anselm's body from the main church to the chapel. The translation may well have provoked the remodelling of the chapel, including the carving of the capitals and, as recently suggested, the painting of St Paul and the Viper (ill. 278).[35]

The towers above the two choir chapels were dismantled soon after completion but those above the eastern transepts remain, and they help to provide us with a general impression of the appearance of the destroyed towers (ill. 178, Colour Pl. XII). Like other work of this period, the exterior of the transept towers is covered with rich geometric ornament. The arch heads have chevron, billet and a T-shaped moulding. The wall surface is covered with X-in-square and vertical rows of lobing. The upper wall has sunken roundels. Although this was heavily restored in the late nineteenth century, the evidence of an engraving published by John Britton in 1836 shows that the restoration was faithful to the original work (ill. 182).[36]

Since the towers are not represented on the waterworks plan, it is unlikely that they were executed or even conceived until after the drawing was completed. The red burn marks on the interiors of the stairwells demonstrate conclusively that the towers were in existence during the fire of 1174, so they can also be dated within a fairly short span of time.[37]

An important alteration to the late eleventh-century crypt can be dated from several salient features to this same campaign. The doorway leading from the north transept to the crypt is usually considered to be contemporary with the crypt (ill. 183); indeed, at first sight the capitals of the

180. Detail of the north entrance to the crypt.

181. Volute capital and carved impost from Hackington, St Stephen's. These are roughly contemporary with the crypt doorway at Canterbury.

crypt doorway (ill. 180) appear very close to the late eleventh-century volute capitals of the crypt. But what is common to these capitals is the type, not the execution. In the crypt, the volutes are cut with a crispness entirely lacking on the two capitals of the doorway. Moreover, no chevron ornament survives anywhere in the late eleventh-century crypt or choir, although it is common enough in the buildings at Christ Church of the third quarter of the twelfth century.[38] Its use on the arch of the crypt door-way speaks strongly against a late eleventh-century date for the doorway.

Evidence that the north doorway to the crypt was inserted during Wibert's priorate emerges in a comparison with the parish church of St Stephen, Hackington. Here the west doorway was renovated during the nineteenth century, but one of the Romanesque volute capitals and imposts with a debased egg-and-dart motif remains, as do a few voussoirs enriched with chevron (ill. 181). These features are identical with those used on the crypt doorway at Christ Church, and must be works of the same or closely related masons. A nineteenth-century engraving[39] shows the west doorway of St Stephen's in a more complete state (ill. 184), including a scallop capital with a moustachioed angle head, like one of those in Caen. The final proof that the crypt doorway was inserted during Wibert's priorate is provided by the right-hand shaft of that doorway. Like the columns of the *vestiarium*, this too is of onyx.[40]

182. Engraving of 1822 of the south-east transept tower of Canterbury Cathedral.

115

183. North entrance to the crypt at Canterbury Cathedral. The left hand shaft has been removed.
The remaining right hand shaft is of onyx, like the shafts of the west face of the vestiarium.

The south wall of the passage leading to the doorway has carved lattice (ill. 183). This lattice pattern does not run smoothly from one ashlar block to another, a proof that the blocks were carved before they were installed. The doorway too was probably prepared in the workshop, and when inserted the sides of the arches had to be trimmed to fit exactly. The wall with the lattice pattern was obviously added after the doorway, for it overlaps the arch of the doorway.

The north wall of the south passage to the crypt is faced with lozenge-shaped *opus reticulatum* stones.[41] A twelfth-century doorway may have been added on this side too, but if so it was replaced by a later Gothic insertion. The two western bays of the north and south sides of the central aisle arcade of the crypt are filled with masonry, and this work seems likely to be contemporary with the inserted doorway. All of the reinforcements occur beneath or slightly east of the central tower. Perhaps Lanfranc's tower needed strengthening. As we have seen, its stability was a matter for concern even in the late eleventh century. But could this work not be evidence of a plan to raise the central tower? Among the lower courses of the present fifteenth-century tower are some reused stones decorated with pinwheel motif, similar to that found in the *vestiarium*, the *aula nova* and the cemetery gate. Perhaps they were reused from a twelfth-century remodelling of the tower.[42]

The sculptural decoration and reinforcements made in the crypt and choir may provide evidence of a move to enhance the cathedral exterior. The two western towers, together with the pair of transept towers and those over the axial chapels, as well as the heightened central tower, would have created a powerful silhouette of seven towers, deeply impressive when approaching Canterbury from the capital of London and from Kent's coastal roads.

The twelfth-century cathedral at Christ Church would not have been the first multi-towered church in England. Exeter Cathedral had seven towers, and transept towers may have been intended at Winchester Cathedral in addition to its low west and central towers. But it was in the Low Countries and in Germany that multiple towers featured most frequently, and these could surely have provided the inspiration for the seven massed towers at Christ Church.[43] As will be seen shortly, there were abundant links with Flanders and adjoining regions at this time.

The decorative features that characterize Prior Wibert's buildings may be summarized as follows. Archivolts and string courses are mainly enriched with geometric motifs. Fret and beaded interlace are frequent devices, and chevron is also abundant, sometimes taking the form of simple sawtooth, or else with the V-shapes filled by carved trefoil leaves. A broad range of scallop capitals is used, the shields are often beaded or filled with small leaves. But there is a total absence of narrative carving. Even figural sculpture is rare, appearing only in St Anselm's chapel and in the *vestiarium*. Where original vaulting remains, the bosses are usually carved too. The

184. Engraving of 1822 of the south-side capitals of the west doorway of Hackington, St Stephen's.

117

185. The vault of the upper chamber in the church of Montivilliers.

few survivals of foliage sculpture make no concessions to natural forms: the stalks are reduced to veined or beaded bands with small awkward leaves. The sculptural evidence points to a group of masons operating at Christ Church between 1150 and 1160, but there is no earlier work in the region that explains the emergence of this style. It can be understood only by looking across the Channel to developments in the duchy of Normandy.

The type of octopartite rib vault found in the *vestiarium* is unusual in England (ill. 186). Such domed ribbed vaults have been shown to have originated in Lombardy. From there they were adopted in Normandy and then in England. The specific relationship between the profiles of the vault of the *vestiarium* and that of the first floor of the crossing tower of the Norman abbey of Montivilliers was noted by Bilson over seventy years ago (ill. 185).[44] The architectural links between Christ Church and Normandy have been reinforced by the observation that the vaults of La Trinité at Caen and those of the *vestiarium* also belong to the same family. What

118

186. The octopartite rib vault that crowns the spacious upper chamber of the vestiarium.

187-188. *Two scallop capitals on the west side of the vestiarium. The finger-like leaves that fill the shields are similar in form the those filling the shields of capitals supporting the vaulting at La Trinité, Caen (see ill.192).*

189. *A tower capital from St Clement's, Sandwich, with finger-like leaves in the shields as in ills.187, 188, 192.*

has so far escaped notice, however, is the close relationship between the sculpture of Wibert's buildings and La Trinité.[45]

The eleventh-century naves of the two Caen abbeys, Saint-Etienne and La Trinité were remodelled in the course of the following century.[46] At Saint-Etienne, which was renovated first, plain fret decoration was used around the clerestory windows; and following its introduction there, it appeared at the neighbouring abbey of La Trinité, and became popular throughout Normandy, also passing into England. This is not to suggest that fret ornament had been previously unknown in England. The ornament occurs on some of the fragmentary carvings from Old Sarum, c.1130, and this was clearly influential in the choice of the motif for the decoration of the three doorways of Lincoln Cathedral of around 1150-1155. But the relationship between the sculpture of La Trinité and Christ Church consists of more than merely a shared range of geometric motifs.[47]

The sculpture at La Trinité has been heavily restored. Many of the nave capitals there were re-tooled during the reconstruction of the vaults by the nineteenth-century architect, Ruprich-Robert. However, he seems to have remained faithful, at least in general terms, to the original compositions of the capitals (ills. 197, 198).[48] Many of these are related to sculpture in Wibert's group of buildings the water tower, *vestiarium* and St Anselm's chapel.

One should not lose sight of the areas of architectural overlap and the general similarity of the character of geometric ornament, but in order to prove this relationship, some small, seemingly insignificant sculptural details should be noted. For instance, the thin parallel grooves used on a capital in the *vestiarium* are similar to the striations in the place of volutes on several of the vault support capitals at La Trinité (ills. 190-193). The beaded shields of the capitals are alike and so too are the nested-V patterns of the shields. The shields of some of the capitals in the water tower, *vestiarium* and *aula nova* staircase are filled with leaves, fleur-de-lis and small geometric motifs; again, similar enrichments are used at La Trinité.

120

190. (left) Scallop capital in the upper chamber of the vestiarium. The nested Vs at the angles are similar to those used in the water tower capitals. Also of interest are the multiple striations on the left-hand side of the capital. These should be compared to the similar markings in the place of the volute on capitals from La Trinité, Caen (see ill.193). Also similar are the beaded shields of all capitals on this page.

191. (right) Scallop capital from the water tower.

192-193. Vault support capitals in the nave at La Trinité, Caen.

194. *Capitals in St Anselm's Chapel, carved with strap-like veined or beaded stalks and simple indented leaves with bowed heads.*

195. *Vault support capital from La Trinité, Caen carved with foliage similar to that in ill. 194.*

196. *Capital with angle masks and beaded intertwined stalks in St Anselm's Chapel.*

197. *Vault support capital from La Trinité, Caen, similar in design and style to that of St Anselm's Chapel.*

The finger-like leaves used in the shields of various capitals are nearly identical (ills. 187, 188). The few foliage capitals are related; they are characterized by veined and beaded stalks and small fan-like leaves (ills. 194, 195). The forms of many of the trefoil capitals, with thick bands of drilled beading are also alike (ills. 190, 193). So too are the interlaces on a capital from La Trinité and that used so freely at Christ Church. Taken on their own, such individual links would be irrelevant, but (as the comparative photographs demonstrate) the cumulative evidence is striking.

The similarity between the mask capital of St Anselm's chapel and one at La Trinité is also clear (ills. 196, 197). Although the Caen capital has two beaded shields on its front face, the capitals are otherwise very close. In both examples there are angle masks emitting beaded stalks which twist around the faces of the capitals. These grotesque heads have bulging eyes and incised caps of hair. The Christ Church heads differ from those at La Trinité in that the masks are like beak-heads, but in this they closely resemble another Caen capital carved with a beak-head at the angle (ill. 197). The horizontal head which the Caen beak-head clasps is in itself like those on the *vestiarium* capital. There are only two other examples of beak-head in Kent, both corbel heads: one is at Rochester, the other at Barfreston although there are numerous examples in adjoining counties. Thus the isolated beak-head at Canterbury was most likely derived directly from Normandy.

Further comparisons with Christ Church may be seen in rural Norman churches influenced in their turn by the sculpture associated with the revaulting of La Trinité. At Creuilly, a few miles from Caen, the range of capitals with angle masks, strap-like foliage and scallop capitals is comparable to that in St Anselm's chapel. The disc and foliage capital at Vieux-Saint-Sauveur in Caen has a similar, though simplified version of the design used in St Anselm's chapel.[49] The moustachioed head at the angle of one of the scallop capitals at Vieux-Saint-Sauveur (ill. 199), derived presumably from those at La Trinité, recalls the capital known to have existed at Hackington (ill. 184).

198. Capital supporting the vaults of La Trinité, Caen.

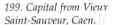

199. Capital from Vieux Saint-Sauveur, Caen.

Norman influences, so pervasive during the period immediately following the Conquest, are generally assumed to have died out in the twelfth century, and Normandy itself is believed to have become in its turn receptive to artistic influences from England. The artistic links described here suggest that the situation was not so straightforward.[50]

Here again it is essential to be aware of the historical context in which this building campaign took place. It is significant that most of the stone used for building in the mid twelfth century at Canterbury was still quarried in the region around Caen. Carriage by water was cheaper than by land so it was worth importing stone from Normandy to Canterbury, especially since it could be transported by water almost from site to site. It was brought from quarries around Caen, down the Orne, across the Channel and up the Stour to Fordwich, from where it was carted to

200

201

202

200-202. Two scallop capitals with masks from the nave of St Margaret-at-Cliffe, and (below) a similar vault support capital from La Trinité, Caen.

Canterbury. The sculptural filiations suggest that masons associated with the Caen quarries travelled from Normandy with the shipments of stone brought to Canterbury at this time.[51] It must be assumed that some of these craftsmen had a hand in building proceedings at Canterbury. These were highly skilled technicians. As they had recently revaulted the nave at La Trinité they were an appropriate choice to cope with such problems as inserting arches, heightening towers, and tackling complex vaulting and perhaps the intricacies of installing a new plumbing system. They were surely hired for their skill as builders and structural engineers, not as sculptors.

The geometric style of sculpture introduced at Christ Church in the water tower, *vestiarium* and St Anselm's chapel generated a large following in the region around Canterbury. The same range of motifs can be traced to other important local centres, notably St Augustine's Abbey and Leeds Priory, but its effect was the most marked in parish churches in the region.[52] In the twelfth century the western part of Kent was still covered by the dense forest of the Weald, and the influence of the style was mainly confined to East Kent.[53] It does not appear to have spread across the Thames estuary into neighbouring Essex, in the diocese of London.

Numerous doorways and chancel arches in East Kent have the same geometric motifs as observed at the metropolitan church. The beaded interlace ornament was frequently imitated in various forms as may be seen in the fragments at Minster-in-Thanet, St Augustine's Abbey, Chislet, St-Margaret-at-Cliffe and Sandwich (ills. 206, 207). These geometric interlaces may even have had an influence on the sculpture of Westminster Abbey, for some of the remains from the twelfth-century abbey have similar patterns.[54]

124

203. The west face of the entrance arch to the vestiarium.

204 (below left). West doorway of St Michael's and All Angels, Throwley. The design of the doorway and the beaded interlace around the head are similar to those of the vestiarium.

205 (below). Doorway leading from the cloister to the dormitory in the precinct of Canterbury Cathedral. Note the fret decoration around the head of the doorway which came into fashion at Canterbury as a result of its prominent use in Normandy.

206. Small tympanum from St Clement's, Sandwich. It is decorated with beaded interlace and beaded wicket ornament; in the upper right is a stag.

207. Font in St Martin, Canterbury, decorated with beaded interlace. It has been suggested that this font is composed of re-used stones from the well-head (puteus) seen on the waterworks plan (ill.154).

Some parish churches made almost exact copies of features that appear at Canterbury. At Throwley, for example, the arches of the *vestiarium* were virtually reproduced (ills. 203, 204). According to the pre-restoration engraving of 1814, the tower of St Mary's in Dover was a reduced version of those above the cathedral transepts (ills. 178, 179). But the impact of the style is perhaps best revealed at St-Margaret-at-Cliffe and at Sandwich.[55] These are both large buildings as befits their role in serving prominent coastal towns which flourished as ports during the twelfth century. The sculpture of both parish churches is related to that at Christ Church. However, more interestingly, some of the sculpture is similar to carving at La Trinité at Caen. Several of the nave capitals at St-Margaret-at-Cliffe are of scallop type, with small human heads taking the place of angle volutes (ills. 200-201). At St Margaret one of these heads is bearded, and the striations of the beard are continued onto the cone of the scallop capital. An identically applied bearded head decorates a capital at La Trinité (ill. 202). Other heads at the two churches have similar quizzical expressions. To take another example, the hybrid volute trefoil capitals at La Trinité also occur at Sandwich and St Margaret-in-Cliffe, although they are not used at Christ Church. These may appear trivial details at first sight, yet such features must be the result of intimate knowledge of the original model. The popularity of the Norman-inspired style which was introduced to Canterbury soon after 1150 and then adopted throughout the region in the third quarter of the twelfth century was, at least in part, due to the ease with which such geometric carving could be produced relatively cheaply and quickly.

208. Detail of a shaft of the dormitory doorway (ill.205) decorated with beaded interlace. Note the fragmentary shafts, carved with beaded interlace similar to that around the heads of the doorways in ills.203 and 204.

209. Small tympanum from the turret doorway at St Mary's, Chislet.

210. Upper part of the main gateway (porta curie) leading to the monastery at the north-west corner of the precinct. This western view of the gateway would have been seen when approaching the precinct from outside.

211. Fragment of shaft from Saint-Bertin, now in the Musée de l'Hôtel Sandelin in Saint-Omer. The ornament is similar to that on the gateway above.

The sculpture inspired by Normandy which makes such frequent use of geometric ornament was not the only style practised at Canterbury in Wibert's time. This is most clearly illustrated by the decoration of the grand main gateway, captioned the *porta curie* on the waterworks plan, and leading to the monastery at the north-west corner of the precinct (ills. 162, 210).[56] The carved decoration of its western face, seen when approaching from outside the monastery, is abundant and elaborate. The two wide arches are carved with 'Winchester acanthus' foliage, with sturdy stalks and broad leaves in alternating round and lozenge trellis frames (ills. 212-213).[57] They are interspersed with roundels containing delightfully fanciful motifs: a mermaid, a pair of lovers, acrobats, animals and musicians. These are all carved in relatively low relief, and the forms are two-dimensional. The capitals, on the other hand, have the deeply cut forms of headlong dragons, coiled snakes, a large grotesque head with flaming hair and an acrobatic group of animals (ills. 216, 218, 221, 222).

The figural and foliage carving of the main gate is both sophisticated and naturalistic,[58] and the workshop responsible for it belonged to a very different sculptural tradition from those whose style has been associated

128

212-213. Details of the main gate with foliage, and a musician and an acrobat.

214. Carved head from the refectory at Dover Priory with similar facial features to musician (ill. 212) above.

215. London, BL, Arundel MS 60, f.85v with foliage border similar to Cathedral gateway.

216 (above). Capital on the main gateway of Canterbury Cathedral, with grotesque issuing foliage.

217 (above right). Capital with grotesque mask issuing foliage, on the east end of Sens Cathedral.

with La Trinité at Caen. Various distinctive features imply that the sculptors of the main gate were well familiar with the carving of South-east England. The figure style of the main gate archivolts, for instance, closely resembles the row of carved heads in the refectory at Dover Priory (ill. 214). The faces are flattened and smooth, with high cheek-bones and blank, undrilled eyes. A similar facial type is also found on the font at St Nicholas, Brighton, and some of the foliage fragments recorded at Lewes are related to the acanthus of the gate.[59]

But the sculptural sources of the gate should be sought even closer to home, indeed at home. The archivolts in their two-dimensional approach recall the capitals of the crypt. Moreover, the jugglers, acrobats, musicians, hunters, grotesques and acanthus foliage of the main gate recall the same subjects as were used in the cathedral crypt and on the choir arcade. Sometimes the similarities are quite specific: for instance, the 'Winchester acanthus' foliage of the main gate, with tapering beaded leaves and folded tips, is similar to the foliage of the Innocents chapel. The mask capitals of the gate repeat those of the external choir arcade. But the most telling example of all is the image of a human straddling two addorsed grotesques, which was first used on a capital in the crypt, and is virtually reproduced on a capital of the main gate (ills. 218-219).[60]

The recurrence of motifs used in the crypt has several implications. While this 'revival' could testify to the enduring importance of the crypt capitals, it is doubtful that the later sculptures were direct copies of their predecessors in the crypt.

The repetition of motifs used in Anselm's choir at Christ Church also occurs in buildings of the third quarter of the twelfth century with Norman filiations. For instance, the heavy double scallop capitals of the *vestiarium*

130

and infirmary cloister indicate a knowledge of capitals in the late eleventh-century crypt. The patterns of the shafts of the crypt capitals and choir arcade are also repeated in the *vestiarium*: there are several shafts with scallop motif, others with palmette, and others with similar geometric motifs. It is interesting that both these motifs could have been inspired by the decoration of the shafts of Archbishop Anselm's crypt and choir. The continued use in the third quarter of the twelfth century of motifs and images initiated in the previous quarter century is an important characteristic of this period. These repetitions of form and motif suggest that a model book with images derived in the first instance from local manuscripts, and used for the crypt capitals, may have been preserved and augmented, and still used in the second half of the twelfth century.

What these comparisons make abundantly clear is that local artistic traditions were not forgotten in the mid twelfth century, despite the introduction of the new taste for sculpture in the geometric style from Normandy. Artists who knew local manuscripts and sculptures were obviously also at work. But the perpetuation of these motifs reveals an important general characteristic of Canterbury sculpture. Like the artistic productions of so many established institutions, sculpture at Canterbury Cathedral is fundamentally conservative. Its artistic productions remained firmly rooted in its own traditions, even though it was receptive to fashionable developments made in other centres and to innovative foreign workmanship. These trends are evident during Wibert's campaign of the third quarter of the twelfth century, and they emerge again with great force in the last quarter of the twelfth century.

218-219. Capital from the Cathedral gateway with a central figure straddling two addorsed grotesques. The image is so similar to that of the late 11th-century crypt capital (ill.219) as to suggest the use of the same model book for both works.

218

219

The sculpture of the *porta curie* may have been embedded in local traditions, but it also came under the sway of Continental artistic currents. Although the links are more tenuous than with the Norman style they nevertheless merit close examination. The relationship between South-east England and that stretch of coast east of Normandy which includes Picardy and Flanders was predetermined geographically, for it is here that the Channel reaches its narrowest point of under thirty miles. Nor did the Channel act as a barrier: in this period where roads were difficult, passage by water facilitated contacts and trade between England and Flanders, as the wool trade proves (see Map p. 206).[61]

For the art historian, no region could be more problematic than North-east France and Flanders. The flat, open territories have been victim of successive European wars, and medieval buildings are reduced to a pitifully small number. Most monuments of primary importance have been lost: the cathedrals of Arras and Cambrai,[62] of Thérouanne, of Notre-Dame-la-Grande at Valenciennes, and the abbeys of Anchin, Saint-Amand and Saint-Vaast at Arras. However, among the scanty remains at Saint-Bertin Abbey in Saint-Omer two fragments of engaged columns with beaded lozenge frames filled with foliage have survived, and they are similar to the archivolts of the main gateway at Christ Church ((ills. 211-213).[63] The relationship may merely be the result of common manuscript sources, but evidence of artistic links between Christ Church and Saint-Bertin would come as no surprise at this period.

In the twelfth century the contour of the Flemish coast presented a very different picture from today, and the sea extended inland almost as far as Saint-Omer, which became for Canterbury a direct gateway to the Continent. The close relationship which had existed between Christ Church and Saint-Bertin since Carolingian times had increased in importance by the mid twelfth century. When Archbishop Theobald returned to Canterbury in 1148 from the Council of Reims which he had attended in defiance of the wishes of King Stephen he was expelled from England and found refuge at Saint-Bertin until he was permitted to return to Canterbury. It was perhaps for this reason that St Bertin was included in the mid twelfth-century martyrology of Canterbury.[64] Later it was in Saint-Bertin that the monks of Christ Church found a temporary home when they were compelled to abandon their monastery shortly before the Interdict of 1208.[65]

There were other important political links with Flanders. After Archbishop Theobald the second most powerful landholder in Kent was the Flemish nobleman and military leader, William of Ypres. He was at the head of the large number of Flemish mercenaries who supported King Stephen in his fight against the Empress Matilda. During the Civil War years, partly as a result of its geographical position and partly because of support in the county for Stephen, Kent was more closely allied in many ways with Flanders than with the rest of England.[66]

That artists travelled as freely as military men between the County of Flanders and England is demonstrated by architectural links and by the evidence of enamel objects and manuscripts. The gospel book made for Liessies Abbey (Hainault) in 1146 is a prime example. It was written by a Continental scribe and illuminated by an English painter whose master-piece, the Lambeth Bible, was probably produced in mid twelfth-century Canterbury. Indeed the Flemish contribution to the arts of Canterbury can be seen more clearly in manuscripts than in any other medium.[67] The broad flat blossoms with cross-hatched interiors on the gate at Christ Church are stylistically related to Flemish productions such as the Floreffe Bible and the later productions of Anchin Abbey (ills. 220-221). The lavish initials produced during the most active period of Saint-Amand, that is during the abbacy of Hugh II (1150-1168), may also have been influential. Large splendid letters, often with elongated dragons creeping through the foli-age, are the hallmarks of the Saint-Amand scriptorium.[68] The gateway capital at Christ Church with a long-bodied dragon set in springy coils of foliage is closely related to these.

Other forms of ornament at Christ Church derived from the adjoining regions of the Soissonais and Picardy. The extensive use of dogstooth ornament, for example, in the water tower at Canterbury is extremely rare in England at this time and must have originated from those regions, where it featured frequently (ill. 152).[69]

Canterbury Cathedral's ecclesiastical links were not confined to the coastal regions of Flanders. Indeed, they extended far inland. When Becket escaped England in 1164, he fled from the port of Sandwich to the Flemish coast and thence, via Soissons, to Sens. From there he proceeded deeper into the diocese of Sens, to Pontigny, some thirty miles from the cathedral city, where he remained for the next two years. There is evidence of this historical connection in contemporary carving. In another case, one of the capitals of the main gate at Christ Church has a fierce angle head emitting

220. Initial P from London, BL, MS Add. 17738, f.13v.

221. Capital from the Cathedral gateway with a dragon in foliage.

222. Two capitals with headlong dragons on the main gateway.

223. Capital with a headlong dragon formerly in the Schnütgen Collection in Cologne.

coils of foliage that spiral on the two faces of the capital. A similar work is to be found among the Early Gothic capitals at Sens (see ills. 216, 217).

Further testimony to the relationship with the region around Sens is found in the façade at Rochester Cathedral. One of the capitals there has confronted birds in foliage which closely resemble another capital in Sens Cathedral. Other capitals at Rochester have tightly wrapped coils of foliage that recall the spring-like spirals of the richly decorated initials of the manuscripts of the diocese of Sens. Other important foliage capitals at Rochester also reflect types generally confined to Northern France and Flanders. One has a motif with circular stalks that split into feather-shaped leaves which closely resemble examples at Villiers-Saint-Paul and several in Cambrai. The design of the Rochester Cathedral doorway itself with its *Majestas* tympanum and its column figures probably derived from examples in Northern France, which in turn reflect developments in the Ile-de-France.

The geographical situation of Flanders, open to the North Sea and cut by easily navigable rivers, encouraged links with many regions of Europe. By the mid twelfth century it had become the foremost predominately 'industrial area' in Northern Europe. At that time much Flemish trade was with England, but there were also important ties with other parts of Europe. Flemings appear to have frequented the markets of Cologne, the Upper Rhine and Saxony, as far as the Elbe.[70] This perhaps explains certain notable similarities with sculpture from the Rhineland and Lower Saxony. Two of the gateway capitals at Christ Church have headlong birds with bodies that dwindle into foliage coils (ill. 222). Birds in this position are common enough in English metalwork, where they frequently decorate the feet of candlesticks and reliquary boxes, but they are relatively rare in English sculpture. On the other hand, they do occur with some regularity in capitals found in Germany and the Low Countries.[71] A Rhenish capital (formerly in the Schnütgen Collection in Cologne) with a headlong bird at the angle and the coils of its tail transforming into foliage on each face, provides the closest comparison with the capitals on the *porta curie* at Canterbury (ill. 223).[72] The multiple towers at Canterbury may be recalled here as further evidence of a link with the Rhineland and the Low Countries, where multiple church towers were a typical feature in the twelfth century.

The scale of rebuilding at Christ Church during this period was enormous. In addition to what has been examined above are many other remains of buildings with sculpture in the same styles: the cemetery gateway, the dorter doorway (ill. 205), the archdeacon's kitchen, the infirmary chapel and cloister (ills. 270, 274). Fragmentary remains suggest that the main cloister was also remodelled at this time. Most important are the three Purbeck arches, with foliage like that of the *aula nova* staircase and the water tower (ill.224). The small span of these arches suggests that they may have come from a cloister. There were clearly other new buildings erected at the same time which have vanished without trace, such as the

224. Fragment of arch from the Infirmary cloister.

water tower in the main cloister and that in the infirmary cloister. The depiction on the large drawing of both the *camera vetus prioris* (old lodgings of the prior) and the *nova camera prioris* (new lodgings of the prior), implies that the latter was also a new building.

The colossal scale of this construction and remodelling must have involved a very substantial workforce, and the sculptural decoration goes some way to help us reconstruct it. Several concurrent styles have been distinguished. The geometric style of sculpture associated with Normandy was perhaps less remarkable than the structures themselves. But despite this, the masons who worked on these buildings were prolific carvers and their work in turn strongly influenced regional sculpture. Other carvings are steeped in Canterbury's own artistic traditions. These roots, together with a fresh inspiration from Northern France and Flanders, created a sophisticated sculptural style with an air of naturalism that grew even more pronounced in the last phase of twelfth-century sculpture at Canterbury.

The three sculptural styles distinguished here give some identity to the sculptors in a period when artists' signatures were a great rarity. But the situation is complicated by the fact that the styles are not fully segregated and often occur in the same buildings. For example, the largely geometric decoration of the first building examined in this chapter, the water tower, is ostensibly the work of masons with Norman filiations. But the occurrence of dogstooth ornament in this structure suggests Northern French influence. The trumpet leaves on the central pillar of the water tower occur also in the nave of nearby Rochester Cathedral, so local sculptors too had a hand in this work. This shows that in some buildings these distinctive sculptors or groups of sculptors actually worked side by side.

136

The continuity of local artistic traditions is nothing extraordinary in the Middle Ages. Nor for that matter is the extension of artistic influence in neighbouring territories. It is no surprise to find Norman artistic elements east of Normandy in the region around Beauvais or, for instance, to find the influence of Cluny III not only in Burgundy but in adjoining regions. But English developments are usually seen as separate from those of the Continent. Our views are prejudiced by its geographic isolation and its present political identity. The period considered in this chapter is one of the many instances where it is grossly misleading to talk of medieval art in terms of today's national frontiers and conditions. With the political unification of England and Continental lands as far south as the Pyrenees under Henry II, England became more tightly linked with the international network of politics and economic and artistic life (see Map p. 206). It was only natural that the influence of territories such as Normandy, Northern France and Flanders should have emerged with such vigour on the neighbouring shores of England.

225. View of Canterbury from the south on a 12th-century seal.

226. *Canterbury Cathedral, male head, presumably from the choir screen c.1180.*

IV. Sculpture after the Death of Becket

FROM THE INSTALLATION of Lanfranc until the death of Theobald, all the archbishops of Canterbury (with the exception of William de Corbeil) were Benedictines who perpetuated the essentially monastic character of the cathedral priory. The chain was broken when Henry II appointed his chancellor, Thomas Becket in 1162.[1] Although Becket was a familiar figure at Christ Church, having served as archdeacon under Theobald, he was not a member of any religious order, and he became a priest only one day before his installation as archbishop. The distance the monks felt from Becket is attested by the fact that upon the death of Prior Wibert in 1167, they applied to the king, not the archbishop, for permission to elect Prior Odo as his successor. Nor was Becket particularly involved in the life of the community: out of the six hundred letters remaining from Becket's exile, only three were addressed to the monks.[2] Thus, Becket's role in the monastery was mainly formal and peripheral. As a result it comes as no surprise that Becket did not become greatly interested in the building programme initiated by Archbishop Theobald.[3]

In any event, Becket's long absences and other activities made involvement in building impossible. The year following his consecration he was mostly at the King's side. In the second year, Becket experienced a private conversion and a profound change in his character, which led him to transfer his loyalties whole-heartedly from King to God. This brought about the well-known rupture in relations with Henry II in 1164 that forced Becket into exile for the next six years. It was during this period, spent in monasteries in the North of France and Burgundy, that Becket entrusted Herbert of Bosham with the task of editing Peter Lombard's glosses on the Psalter and the Epistles of St Paul, then fashionable in learned circles in Northern France. These volumes eventually passed into the library at Christ Church, together with other books also produced in Northern France and decorated with the same type of sumptuous initial, displaying tightly coiled foliage, neatly painted leaves and blossoms and small white dogs, usually set against gold backgrounds and within coloured panels. These books provide a further link in the artistic relationship between Christ Church and Northern France.[4]

It is ironic that it was only after his murder, on the evening of 29 December 1170, that Becket became a truly significant figure with regard to the art and architecture at Christ Church, for his martyrdom brought the cathedral priory to the centre of European attention. Becket's cult spread swiftly throughout Europe, and he was canonized only three years after his death. In July 1173, King Henry II did penance at the martyr's tomb in the crypt.[5]

139

Becket's tomb in the cathedral crypt quickly became the focus of popular pilgrimage and the scene of visions and miracles. It attracted the pious of every social class, from the humblest to the most aristocratic: even King Louis of France journeyed to England to pray at the saint's tomb.[6] The potential importance and revenues of the nascent cult must soon have become apparent to the monks, but the siting of the tomb in the crypt gave it neither adequate prominence nor access.[7] The only suitable location was in Anselm's choir, and evidently even this appeared too cramped for the purpose. The rebuilding of the choir must have been discussed as the only possible solution.

In the years immediately following the martyrdom, the monks of Canterbury became engaged in a bitter struggle with the King over the election of the next archbishop. It was not until 1173 that they formally selected their own prior, Odo, as Becket's successor. Not surprisingly, the monks' candidate encouraged the new Becket cult. Because of this Odo was unacceptable to Henry II, who forced the election of Richard, Prior of Dover. Despite the fact that the monks eventually accepted Richard, his election was a significant defeat for the community and a victory for the king, who was thereby saved from an archbishop likely to perpetuate Becket's policies or promote his cult. Richard proceeded to Rome, where he was duly confirmed by the Pope. On his return he met and conferred with Henry II in Normandy before reaching England on 3 September.[8] He travelled from Southampton to London, and the news of his return and confirmation must have reached the monks on 4 or 5 September. During the night of 5 September a fire gutted the cathedral choir.

Gervase writes that the fire began just outside the precinct. This, it seems, distracted the citizens so that they failed to recognize that the church itself was burning:

'During an extraordinarily violent south wind, a fire broke out before the gate of the church, and outside the walls of the monastery', whence, 'sparks, carried aloft by the high wind were deposited upon the church, and being driven by the fury of the wind between the joints of the lead, remained there among the half rotten planks and shortly glowing with increasing heat, set fire to the rotten rafters; from these the fire communicated to the larger beams and their braces, no one yet perceiving or helping'.[9]

It is hard not to see these circumstances as suspicious.[10] The news of Richard's confirmation as their new archbishop and his friendly meeting with the king probably reached the monks as Richard was travelling to London. There must have been anxiety in the community about the possibility that Henry II might have enlisted Archbishop Richard's support to curtail the Becket cult which was an embarrassment to the King. The fire of 5 September presented the opportunity for a major rebuilding of the choir such as would suitably accommodate the shrine of the murdered saint as well as the anticipated flocks of pilgrims. The 'disaster', was so fortuitous for the community as to suggest that the conflagration may have been started deliberately. The fact that no one noticed it or helped may also be viewed as suspicious especially in conjunction with the fact that the flames were quenched before significant harm was done to the monastic buildings: according to Gervase, only 'the infirmary with the chapel of St Mary' was damaged.[11]

Had the fire been deliberate, it would indeed help account for a variety of factors. Why was Gervase so insistent that the timbers in the choir were rotten when they were only sixty or seventy years old? And why did he take such great pains to justify the rebuilding of the choir? Why in fact did Gervase compose this unusual text at all?

The account by Gervase is remarkable, indeed unique. It chronicles not only the destruction, but the rebuilding of the cathedral, year by year, from 1174-1184. As a result, it is possible to date the architectural sculpture that remains *in situ* in the cathedral with unusual precision. According to the text, the monks summoned both English and French architects in the wake of the fire. These masters had differing opinions on how much of the burnt out shell of the choir it would be possible to incorporate into a new design. Some believed that the church could safely be rebuilt using the existing structure, others that it would have to be dismantled and built anew. In the end the monks chose the French architect William of Sens, 'On account of his lively genius and good reputation'.[12] The choice of an architect who no doubt promised a building in the same style as those going up in France, is entirely in keeping with the cosmopolitan tastes previously exhibited by the community at Christ Church. The building he erected was both exotic and avant-garde for England, as it was pronouncedly Gothic in style (ill. 122).[13]

Any notion that William of Sens might have had of basing the ground plan of the new choir on those current in France was soon abandoned. The convent was adamant that as much of Anselm's old choir as possible should be retained.[14] This was probably partly a measure designed to keep down the cost of the new choir. But economy alone cannot account for the preservation of the old walls. The very fabric of Anselm's choir seems to have taken on holy associations as the location of Becket's murder. It was, so to speak, sanctified by the martyrdom, and as a result the structure of the old choir itself became a kind of relic worthy of veneration.

William of Sens started work just to the east of the west transept, where he set two half columns into the masonry of the older principal piers. By 1177, the third year of building, five pairs of columns had been placed. These had the same diameter as those in Anselm's choir and their alternating round and octagonal pattern may even have reflected the arrangement in Anselm's church; but they were a full twelve feet higher.[15] The main arcade arches which they supported were not round but pointed, and they were topped by a triforium based on French designs, bearing above it a clerestory with a wall passage.

141

The four piers at the crossing of the east transept were put up in 1177 and 1178. Here colonnettes in marble were introduced around the columns according to the fashion set by Notre-Dame at Valenciennes.[16] All this was crowned by sexpartite vaulting. During the fourth year of building, two more bays went up and the scaffolding was prepared for the great vault over the crossing. Then, in 1179, William of Sens was hurt in a fall from the scaffold and forced to give up work and return to France. The remaining task of rebuilding was passed to William the Englishman, who vaulted the transept and started work on the roof over the high altar. He extended the eastern crypt as a foundation for the eastern chapels, including the Trinity chapel and the Corona. Lack of funds prevented this work from being finished until 1184, though the choir itself was used from the year 1180, when it was dedicated.[17]

In certain respects, William the Englishman showed greater familiarity with French architectural developments than his predecessor, despite his curiously nationalistic name. The Trinity chapel, for example, has a true triforium wall passage, and it seems that the twin columns may have been copied from designs at Sens Cathedral.[18]

The grand foliage capitals of the choir arcade, both those put up by William of Sens and those placed by William the Englishman, manifest a clear knowledge of French designs.[19] It has recently been revealed that the models for the choir capitals were concentrated in the north-eastern region of France (including Flanders) and in the area around Paris. The first two capitals, which abut the piers of the earlier structure, have simple overlapping water leaves. Similar capitals existed at Sens, but some interest in the type was already shown at Canterbury, in foliage capitals of the infirmary cloister. The next four pairs of capitals directly reflect French models. The chief influence on this homogeneous group came from the region that stretches in an arc around Paris, from Saint-Leu-d'Esserent to Reims. The capitals of the eastern transept piers are closer to designs at Laon. There are hints that capitals at Arras, Cambrai and Valenciennes inspired the designs at Canterbury, but the destruction of these major churches leaves little evidence except for the strong links between Arras and the capitals of the double columns in the Canterbury choir.[20]

The carved bosses naturally reflect the same sources. Like the capitals, they are mainly carved with plain foliage (ills. 228-230), and occasional figures and animals were introduced too.[21] The bird grotesques carved on two of the bosses are close to the grotesques on the capitals at Sens.

227 (opposite page). Canterbury Cathedral, detail of choir aisle. The arch mouldings here are similar to those used roughly twenty years earlier in the water tower (ill.152). Note especially the rows of billet ornament on the ribs, the chevron and the dogs-tooth ornament. This suggests a greater continuity between work carried out in the third quarter of the 12th century and the Gothic choir than is often assumed.

228-230. Three bosses from the choir aisles at Canterbury Cathedral. The foliage is stylistically similar to the choir screen fragments (e.g. ill.258).

The documentary evidence confirms the precision with which certain elements of the choir were based on French designs. According to Gervase, the preparations for building by William of Sens included the delivery of templates from France for the shaping of stones.[22] This presumably ensured that some of the mouldings employed at Canterbury would be consistent with those in use across the Channel. It is unusual to find a foreign architectural and sculptural style so readily accepted, but the long-standing artistic connections with France had apparently paved the way for its adoption.

However, it would be a mistake to think that sculpture at Christ Church was entirely taken over by these new developments. The Romanesque style did not terminate neatly with the construction of the choir. Many of the traditional features used by previous generations continued, even in the Gothic choir itself. For example, the idea of arranging dark, polished shafts around a monolithic limestone core may have derived from Flanders, but the taste for unusual polished stones was hardly new at Canterbury. During Theobald's archiepiscopate, not only was Purbeck used but onyx too. Nor is it surprising that two of the choir capitals were made from Bethersden 'marble'. Already around 1145-1150 the royal abbey of Faversham, near Canterbury, had capitals made from Purbeck.[23] Other developments of the third quarter of the twelfth century also persisted in this next phase of building. Masons with Norman filiations had made innovative new experiments with vaulting, as in the *vestiarium*. These men were also clearly familiar with the sexpartite vaults of La Trinité at Caen. When it came to the choir, these factors may have increased local receptiveness to the developments of the sexpartite vault made in fashionable French buildings, particularly at Sens, at Laon and at Notre-Dame in Paris. The power of past local architectural tradition is further manifested by the fact that many mouldings from the previous building campaign were repeated in the new 'Gothic' choir (ill. 227). For example, the profiles of the choir aisle ribs virtually reproduce those of the outer ring of arches of the water tower (ill. 152). Both have the same downward pointing chevron and dogtooth in the hollow of the roll, and this despite the fact that William of Sens is said to have imported templates from France.

The decorative mouldings of the choir are consistent with those of Theobald's building campaign, and this suggests the continued presence at Christ Church of some craftsmen active before the fire. These men were already in close touch with artistic developments across the Channel, and the new ideas and fashions introduced by William of Sens and William the Englishman obviously struck a responsive chord in the local workshop. But the persistence of the local artistic vocabulary also represents a fundamental characteristic of the art of Canterbury. The importance of old traditions at Christ Church ran deep. There was a stubborn conservative strain in the artistic productions of the convent. This is in direct contrast to the radically new styles accepted in Canterbury, not least the wholesale introduction of Gothic architecture at this phase.

We are sadly ignorant about the furnishings of the choir. There was, of course, Becket's magnificent shrine of 1220 at the top of the ascending series of floor levels in the choir. But this suffered the same fate as most of the metalwork at Canterbury and it was melted down at the time of the Dissolution of the monasteries in the sixteenth century.[24] There are, however, important remains of one of the furnishings from the choir in the form of a beautiful group of sculptures, many of which have only recently been discovered. Together with the sculptures from St Mary's Abbey, York and the doorways to the Lady Chapel at Glastonbury, they form one of the largest groups of figure sculpture from the late twelfth century to survive in England. As will be seen, there is good reason to think that they came from the choir screen, the barrier between the lay nave and the monastic choir. The appearance of the sculptures differs considerably from previous work, and they represent a turning-point in the style of sculpture at Christ Church, indeed in England as a whole. They are discussed here as a group for the first time, and so they will be treated in some detail.[25]

The first piece came to light in the eighteenth century (ill. 232). It was found reused as building material in the wall of the *aula nova*, and was moved to the Faussett Pavilion, which housed the collection of the Kentish antiquarian, Reverend Bryan Faussett.[26] It is carved with a sunken quatrefoil containing the three-quarter length figure of a bearded, crowned man. The right hand of the figure peeks out above the collar of his mantle, the left points upward. A second related panel, again with a half-figure of a crowned, bearded man in a sunken quatrefoil, was preserved in the chapter library until soon after the Second World War (ill. 233). The right hand of this figure is pressed close to the torso, the left hand points upward. Fortunately it is less damaged than the Faussett sculpture. It retains the moulded frame of the quatrefoil and also has a roll mould at its upper

231. Canterbury Cathedral. Female figure in quatrefoil frame presumably from the choir screen c.1180.

232. Canterbury Cathedral, three-quarter length King pointing upward, in a quatrefoil frame, presumably from the choir screen. The piece was found re-used in the aula nova and was saved by the antiquarian Brian Faussett.

edge. A third relief carved with a woman in a sunken quatrefoil, was found in the precincts shortly after the war (ill. 231). The face and left hand have been cut away, but her loose head-covering and right hand (gesturing upward, palm towards the spectator) are intact, and so are the surrounding mouldings.

Between 1968 and 1972, a series of spectacular additional finds were made at Canterbury. More pieces, obviously related to these three reliefs, were recovered from buttresses and above the arcade during restoration work in the north-west corner of the cathedral cloister. Among these were four more panels with quatrefoil frames containing figures,[27] nine roundels containing heads, and one roundel with a three-quarter length figure as well as a large group of architectural fragments, including string-courses, annulets, and small animal-headed label-stops. Despite their varied poses and physical types, it is clear from the similar decorative devices that enclose the figures that they formed part of the same group. All of the frames have similar facetted mouldings, and the backgrounds are deeply cut, so that the figures project forward in bold relief. Stylistically too, the figures form a homogeneous group, although there are slight nuances within this common style. The half figures in quatrefoils are swathed in heavy folds of cloth cascading down the torsos. Similar rich crescent folds sweep across a female head in a roundel (ill. 246). All of the forms are

146

233. Canterbury Cathedral, three-quarter length King pointing upward in a quatrefoil frame. The moulding along the upper edge suggests that this piece was one of several from the top of the choir screen.

articulated in a way that conveys an extraordinary sense of roundness, weight and bulk.

These fragments pose a thorny problem: they have no architectural context. And since they are badly damaged and appear to represent only a small percentage of the original number, it is difficult to reconstruct the decorative scheme to which they belonged. Moreover, no archaeological records were kept when the stones were found. Some pieces, including twisted colonettes, were left embedded in the vaulting of the cloister and not recorded. Thus, the only evidence which helps in the task of reconstruction is the physical condition of the sculptures, their iconography and comparative material from elsewhere.

The crisp lines and the undisturbed detailing of the surfaces suggest a completely protected setting, presumably indoors. This of course leaves open a range of possibilities. Could the pieces have come from a tomb for instance? Since roundels and grotesques were an important part of the decorative scheme of twelfth-century tombs, the number of grotesques in the Canterbury group does not itself militate against the possibility.[28] By the early thirteenth century, quatrefoils also featured in tomb sculpture. The Purbeck tombs of Archbishop Hubert Walter (d.1205) in the cathedral choir (ill. 234) and of Bishop Gilbert de Glanville (d.1214) at Rochester Cathedral have quatrefoils filled with projecting heads on their gabled lids.

147

The representation of the shrine of St Edward in the thirteenth-century manuscript, the *Life of Edward the Confessor* is shown decorated with quatrefoils containing three-quarter figures. But the iconography of the Canterbury figures in quatrefoils is not compatible with their use on a tomb. To put it quite simply, the gestures of the figures across architectural frames show that they are interacting in a manner which does not occur in tomb sculpture before the end of the thirteenth century.[29]

The fact that the majority of the fragments were discovered in the cloister has suggested to some that this was the origin of the pieces.[30] Elaborate cloisters with sculpture that extended onto shafts and archivolts did indeed feature in the second half of the twelfth century, especially in France. The superb figures from Châlons-sur-Marne are the most eloquent witness of this.[31] In France, there are even a few cloisters where roundels carved with grotesques are used in the arcade spandrels.[32] But such an arrangement is unlikely at Christ Church because the roundels are carved on rectangular blocks, which are not compatible with the spandrel shape. The two trapezoid shaped stones, on the other hand, have moulded tops which suggests that they formed a sort of parapet. This cannot be paralleled in any remaining cloister. Moreover, both of the figures set in quatrefoils on the spandrel-shaped stones point upwards (ills. 232-233, 238). This would have been a meaningless gesture had they been set below the cloister roof.[33]

234. Tomb of Bishop Hubert Walter (†1205) in Canterbury.

The third, and by far the most likely possibility is that the pieces came from the cathedral choir screen or *pulpitum*. By a fortunate chance, there is a documentary reference to the screen in the new Gothic choir, which records that after the fire of 1174 and for a period of five years, the sorrowing monks were separated from the people by a low wall in the nave (*muro parvulo*) an arrangement which was evidently deemed improper.[34] Then, early in the spring of 1180, Gervase tells how the monks were 'seized with a violent longing to prepare the choir so that they might enter it at the coming Easter. And the Master (William the Englishman), perceiving their desires, set himself manfully to work, to satisfy the wishes of the convent. He constructed, with all diligence, the wall (*murus*) which encloses the choir and presbytery'.[35]

The idea that the screen was conceived at the beginning of the year and erected before Easter is, of course, out of the question. Preparations must have begun sometime in advance, a year or two before the accident of William of Sens in 1179. In 1178, in fact, William of Sens had already built the low screen with arcading on the ambulatory side in the presbytery, so it is reasonable to assume that plans for the main screen were already in the hands of sculptors by around 1177 or 1178 at the latest. As will be seen, the style of the fragments is entirely consistent with this date, so there is a good chance that the pieces under discussion came from the very screen mentioned in Gervase's account, a possibility which will be explored in detail shortly.

First let us consider the screen that Gervase describes in the earlier choir of Anselm's church. It was sited to the east of the crossing with marble slabs ('tabulis marmoreis compositus') along its sides, which separated the choir from the aisles.[36] This probably returned across the west end with entrances in it.

The Rood above it must have been very splendid, for Gervase says: 'At the eastern horns of the altar were two wooden columns, gracefully ornamented with gold and silver, and sustaining a great beam, the extremities of which rested upon the capitals of two of the pillars. This beam carried across the church above the altar, and decorated with gold, sustained the representation of the Lord, the images of St Dunstan and of St Elphege, together with seven chests covered with gold and silver and filled with the relics of divers saints. Between the columns there stood a gilded cross, of which the cross itself was surrounded by a row of sixty transparent crystals'.[37]

The structure of the 1180 screen probably did not differ much from this, although the ornamental details were obviously not the same. There must have been a large Rood, as in all churches, and there was a barrier wall between the choir and aisles.

During Prior Chillenden's years of office (1390-1411), the west face of the 1180 choir screen was dismantled and replaced by the screen that remains today. Chillenden was responsible for much rebuilding at Canterbury, and among his achievements was the reconstruction of the cloister,[38] where many of the sculptures from the 1180 screen were found reused. Perhaps one of the sources for the stone of Chillenden's cloister was the 1180 screen which he had just demolished. The new supply was not exclusively reserved for the cloister though. It was evidently used for some of Chillenden's other extensive repairs in the precincts. This would explain why one of the fragments emerged from a buttress in the *aula nova*.

Gervase makes only a cryptic reference to the 1180 screen, which does not shed light on its appearance. However, later documentation gives some clue to its physical structure. The passage through the lateral doors was evidently kept open, for in 1298 one of Archbishop Robert of Winchelsey's statutes direct the prior to put up doors:

'a fair and strong wooden door with a strong and decent lock at the entry of the choir towards the west with a fitting lock so that it can be shut; and let it be kept and shut at the proper times lest free ingress through the choir be open to anyone passing, and so that greater security by this means may be provided for the upper part of the church, where great peril could often threaten'. The statute also directs that 'two small doors were placed under the great loft, between the body of the church and the choir, through the two sides next to the altar under the great Rood of the church shall remain shut except by reason of divine service, or when the unavoidable egress and ingress of a minister is imminent, or in time of solemn processions'.[39]

The 1180 screen was subsequently renovated by Prior Eastry between 1304 and 1305, following the installation of new stalls. This included the addition of a new facing on the east side of the west wall. The arrangement of the additions by Eastry must reflect the form of the 1180 screen because they abutted one another. The 1180 screen as we have seen was taken down by Chillenden, but Eastry's screen remains, although hidden behind the choir stalls. When it was temporarily uncovered in 1875, three doors were revealed — an arrangement which surely mirrored that of the 1180 screen.[40]

Although the *pulpitum* was an essential part of the furnishing of every

235. Reconstruction of the 12th-century choir screen formerly at Ely Cathedral by James Essex who removed the screen from the cathedral in the 1770's. The row of quatrefoils at the top which presumably contained carved or painted figures, suggests the type of arrangement that may have existed in the screen at Canterbury Cathedral.

monastic church, not a single English Romanesque example survives *in situ*, and there are dismally few fragments.[41] Nevertheless, a brief look at the remaining material sheds light on the use of the Canterbury sculptures.

As for the English survivals, excavations at Old Sarum revealed the plan of the *pulpitum* of the church enlarged by Bishop Roger (1103-1139).[42] This was a full fourteen feet deep. There were stairs within it leading to a rood loft above, and on a platform flanking the choir door were two altars. Two panels from this screen were reused in the thirteenth-century screen at Salisbury Cathedral, but they were cut back and all trace of carving was destroyed. Complete narrative screen panels remain at Chichester Cathedral (*c.*1130) and at Durham Cathedral (*c.*1155), both carved with New Testament scenes showing Christ's redemptive powers. In addition, there is a portion of the mid twelfth-century screen from the nunnery of All Hallows, Barking in Essex. This has a Crucifix flanked by the attendant figures of St John and the Virgin set before a lively backdrop of carved geometric pattern. A fine twelfth-century example stood in Ely Cathedral until its removal in the 1770s by James Essex. Had it survived, it might have helped considerably with the reconstruction of the Canterbury sculptures. Fortunately, a few drawings were made just before the screen's destruction, and they show that it had moulded quatrefoils, trefoil arches and turned shafts, capitals and bases, although there is no record of the sculpture or painting that decorated these moulded frames (ill. 235). A new discovery from Southwick Priory in Hampshire adds to the list of English choir screens.[43] It has a row of large arches, with the representation of a city above. Presumably here too the arches were filled with painted figures.

The surviving material in France is even more limited. There are fine thirteenth-century choir screens, notably at Bourges Cathedral, Chartres Cathedral and the Cathedral of Notre-Dame in Paris, but there are no earlier examples which bear comparison with the screen at Christ Church.[44] A few twelfth-century examples remain *in situ* in Italy, as at Sant'Ambrogio, Milan, Modena and Vezzolano. But for the purpose of comparison with the sculptures at Canterbury, by far the most interesting examples are to be found in Germany. Portions of a fine mid twelfth-century screen with narrative scenes survives from the Mariengraden church in Cologne (ill. 248). Here, figures of great simplicity are set in sunken frames, much as at Canterbury. The magnificent late twelfth-century examples from the Liebfrauenkirche in Halberstadt (ill. 236) and St Michael in Hildesheim (ill. 240) are by far the most complete, with large stucco figures and voluminous drapery under round-headed arches. These are topped by smaller open arches with little figures or decorative friezes.[45]

Even this cursory glance at the most important comparative material indicates that there was no standard design or iconography for the choir screen in the twelfth century. But they do at least provide a general context for the Canterbury pieces. With these other screens in mind we can turn to the question of how the Canterbury fragments might have been used, if they did in fact come from the 1180 screen.

236-237. *Screen and Rood at the Liebfraukirche, Halberstadt. The prophets here hold scrolls and some point upwards to the Rood above. This evokes the way the figures in quatrefoils might have been used in the choir screen at Canterbury Cathedral.*

238-239. *Bearded figures in quatrefoil frame presumably from the choir screen, c.1180, at*
Canterbury Cathedral. One points upwards, perhaps a prophet, the other may be holding a scroll.
The moulding along the upper edge suggests that both were placed at the top of the screen.

The horizontal moulding on the upper edge of each of the quatrefoils suggests that these pieces were set along the top in a straight row (ills. 233, 238-239). The quatrefoil, with a figure carved on trapezoid-shaped stones, presumably filled the spandrels between arches or gables or doorways (ill. 232).[46] The drawings of the Ely *pulpitum* show that this was precisely the arrangement used there; immediately below the moulded parapet was a line of quatrefoils (ill. 235). The surviving late twelfth-century choir enclosure at Halberstadt sheds more light on the Canterbury quatrefoils. On the east face of the screen at Halberstadt, three-quarter length figures are set immediately below the Rood (ills. 236, 237). They have beards and hold scrolls and books, which suggests that they were prophets. As in the case of the Canterbury fragments, the upper edge is also moulded. These figures are framed not by quatrefoils but by trefoil canopies. Nevertheless, they help suggest a setting for the figures in quatrefoil at Christ Church.

The absence of architectural mouldings on the roundels makes their context more difficult to determine. Several of them clearly represent devils, with hair fanned out into flame-like tufts: one grimaces, another

240. *Detail of the late 12th-century choir screen at St Michael, Hildesheim*
showing that grotesques and foliage were deemed appropriate ornaments for the sides of the screen.

241 (above). Canterbury Cathedral, roundel with a grotesque head presumably form the choir screen of c.1180.

242 (below). Canterbury Cathedral, roundel with a three-quarter length figure holding a martyr's palm.

243-245. Canterbury Cathedral, roundels presumably from the choir screen of c.1180. The caps worn by the male heads (ills.243,244) may be intended to indicate that they are Jews.

sticks out his tongue, and one has the unmistakable horns of a devil (ills. 245, 262-263). Two of the roundels have bearded heads, with long moustaches, prominent ears and the type of peaked cap sometimes used to denote Jews (ills. 243, 244). Another has the finely modelled head of a youth, with a band drawing back his tufted hair and a sixth defaced roundel seems to have been similar to this (ill. 226).[47] However incongruous such profane representations may seem in the heart of the church, they did occur in the context of other screens. The *jubé* of around 1230-1240 at Chartres, for example, had quatrefoil reliefs with animals, insects and hunting scenes decorating the rear side of the parapet. At Hildesheim, a string-course with grotesque birds, harpies and humans forms a horizontal division between the row of prophets and pierced arches (ill. 240). The grotesques from Christ Church could have been used in a similar way.

But not all the images contained in roundels depict incarnations of evil or grotesques. Some are clearly linked to other themes. One of the roundels stands apart from the rest: it depicts not a head, but a three-quarter length figure. It holds a palm frond and gives a sign of blessing, so presumably it represents a martyr (ill. 242). The drapery used here may seem rather more archaic than most other examples, but the type of three-dimensional fold characteristic of the other figures is evident in the swag of cloth on the right side of the figure. The size of the roundel matches that of the others, so it certainly belongs to this group.

156

244

245

246. Canterbury Cathedral,
roundel with a female head
presumably from the choir screen
of c.1180. The veil pulled across
the forehead may indicate that
this is Luna or Synagoga.

The eighth roundel, carved with a female face half covered by a veil,
pulled asymmetrically across her head is the most enigmatic (ill. 246). Her
downward gaze and the cloth which covers her eyes, suggests that she
could have represented the allegorical figure of *Synagoga*.[48] The personifi-
cation of *Synagoga* is associated with the Crucifixion. She featured in
French sculpture, as in the examples on the font from Sélincourt (in the
museum at Amiens) or the doorway of Berteaucourt in Picardy. She also
appears with a veil on the large ivory cross now in the Cloisters Museum,
New York, and on the font from Stanton Fitzwarren (Gloucestershire) (ill.
247). Alternatively, this female head, half covered by a veil, could represent
Luna. Amongst the possible parallels for *Luna* is that on the choir screen
formerly in the Mariengraden church in Cologne (ill. 248).[49] Here a female
figure with a veil across her forehead appears in a roundel on one side of
the Enthroned Christ.

Each of the quatrefoils is filled with a three-quarter figure. Of these, two
are uncrowned males, two are crowned males, one is a female figure and
the sixth is too damaged for identification. A further clue of the original
arrangement of the quatrefoils may be provided by the gestures of the
figures they contain. Three of the male figures point upward, the crowned
ones with the left hand, the uncrowned ones with the right hand (ills.
232-233, 238). Their pointing fingers invite spectators to focus their gaze
upward. The pose of the fourth figure is ambiguous, but the left hand

158

appears to cross in front of the body and hold the top edge of a scroll (ill. 239). The female figure raises her right hand, as if in salutation or blessing (ill. 231). We know from a late medieval description that the twelfth-century screen at Durham Cathedral depicted the story of the Passion of Christ, and it had two tiers of figures of English kings (benefactors of Durham) and figures of the bishops of Lindisfarne and of Durham.[50] Since the monks at Canterbury had no reason at that time to be particularly pro-royal, the crowned figures are more likely to be biblical kings. And since it was customary to have a crucifix (or rood) above the centre of the *pulpitum*, the pronounced upward pointing gestures of the figures may have been directed towards this central part of the composition. The kings might then have represented the royal ancestors of Christ: David, Jesse and Solomon. If the fourth male held a scroll, then he was probably a prophet. The identity of the female figure is uncertain. The gesture she makes with the palm of her hand towards the viewer is that often made by the Virgin at the Crucifixion, so again, the position of this figure at the top of a screen and below the rood would be consistent. The roundel representing *Luna* or *Synagoga* would also fit with the iconography of the screen, though it could have been used in several ways.[51]

247. Detail from the font at Stanton Fitzwarren (Gloucestershire) showing figure of Synagoga with a blindfold.

248. Enthroned Christ with Luna in roundel on the right, from the 12th-century choir screen formerly in Mariengraden church, Cologne, now in Bonn, Landesmuseum.

*249. Jesse page.
Paris, BN, MS lat. 8846, f.4.*

Manuscripts provide additional insights. Some light may be shed on the arrangement of the Canterbury fragments by a folio in the Paris Psalter, which is the last of three extant copies of the Carolingian Utrecht Psalter to be made at Canterbury around 1180-1190. One page (ill. 249) has ranks of medallions containing half figures and at the top, in the centre, is Christ flanked by Peter and Paul. Below them are the remaining Apostles and John the Baptist. The Virgin is represented under Christ, and lower still are her royal ancestors, with Jesse at the bottom. Some of the figures point upwards towards Christ, and it is tempting to imagine the reliefs in a similar composition, but with the half figures in a horizontal row at the

160

250-53. Figures with fingers emerging from within the cloak: Detail of f.66, Paris, BN, MS lat. 8846; an antique statue in the Vatican Museum, Rome; king from the choir screen at Canterbury; figures from the south doorway at Barfreston Church.

250

251

top, with the female figure, the Virgin Mary, in the centre, directly below Christ. The drapery in this manuscript is stiffer and the poses are more mannered than the sculpture fragments, but there are compositional and stylistic similarities.[52] The folds of the king's drapery on the Faussett Pavilion relief, for instance, are like those of the king third from the bottom, centre, on the Jesse folio of the Paris Psalter. The pose assumed by the king in the Faussett relief (with one arm hidden beneath his toga-like cloak and only his fingers showing, holding the collar) is very rare in medieval art, and significantly enough it is also found in the Psalter (ill. 250). The odd position of the hand probably derives from Roman portraiture (ill. 251). When used in Roman art it shows the practice of older orators who kept one hand inside their mantle instead of indulging in gesticulation.[53] Of course in these representations at Canterbury the origin and meaning of the gesture had been forgotten. But this unusual pose gives irrefutable evidence of a link between the Psalter and carvings under discussion.

252

Various architectural fragments also survive. There are four segments of a string-course, three of which have a similar pattern of framed palmette flanked by trefoil leaves and beaded diagonal strips. The fourth piece has an octopus leaf with spindly tips (ill. 116). These presumably represent only a portion of the original lengths of string-course that would have been necessary as divisions and supports.

Of the three small label-stops, the calf's head with a protruding tongue, remains attached to part of an arch (ill. 254). The head emerges from the bottom of the moulding, which is decorated with beaded palmette and billet. The heads on the two other label-stops were evidently broken off similar arches. One has a long bent nose and a windswept mane, the other has little leaf-like ears and grips a tiny human head between its jaws (ills. 255-256). The use of arcades with small label-stops in the form of human or animal heads, became increasingly popular in the second half of the twelfth century, and may be seen, for example, in Malmesbury Abbey and St Andrews at Steyning in Sussex.

The other group of architectural fragments from Christ Church is the annulets. These are of two types: one pair is cigar-shaped, decorated with

253

broken or pipeline billet, the others are cylinder-shaped and decorated with foliage motifs (ill. 258). Annulets were devised in Roman architecture to facilitate the placing of one segment of column upon another, and from there they passed into use in Early Christian and Byzantine buildings.[54]

In the region around Canterbury the best known Romanesque annulets are those of the portal at Rochester. But the closest comparison for the Canterbury annulets is provided by the chancel arch at Barfreston (ills. 257, 259).[55] Here, spiral-decorated and plain shafts are jointed with annulets, the foliage of which extends to form part of the string-course. Not only is their form related to the Canterbury annulets, but the rippling leaves used are also similar. Perhaps the spiral shafts of the Barfreston chancel arch were also modelled on the screen at Canterbury. Spiral shafts were after all found with the other fragments at Canterbury, and they could have been joined by these annulets for use in the doorways of the screen. There are other clues that the builders of Barfreston had the Canterbury choir in mind as the model for their little church. The 'swallow tail spur' base at Barfreston, for instance, must be in imitation of those in the cathedral choir, because the type was unknown in England before it was introduced by William of Sens. The screen is reflected elsewhere in this parish church — as in one of the roundels of the south doorway (ill. 253), which is carved with a figure whose hand is in the unusual and distinctive position emerging from under the collar of his cloak, noted above in the Paris Psalter and quatrefoil figure.

254. Canterbury Cathedral label stop with a calf's head, presumably from the choir screen of c.1180.

255. *Canterbury Cathedral, label stop in the form of a grotesque head presumably from the choir screen c.1180.*

256. *Canterbury Cathedral, label stop grotesque holding a human head in its jaws, presumably from the choir screen of c.1180.*

257. Barfreston Church, chancel arch. The church at Barfreston was built at the very same time as the Gothic choir at Canterbury Cathedral was being erected. Many features of the small parish church imitate those of the cathedral choir. The chancel arch of the parish church with its twisted columns and bulbous foliage annulets may reflect those of the cathedral choir screen.

None of the sculptures from the choir screen reflect the designs of the grand capitals in the choir. However, there are stylistic links between the choir screen and other less prominent carvings in the aisles of the choir. Several of the bosses of the choir aisle vaults have round-tipped leaves with indented centres (ills. 228-229). These are sometimes sharply furrowed, and the surface of the leaves has a ruffled effect. The circular compositions of the vault bosses gives the foliage a more windswept appearance than the choir screen foliage, but the general characteristics and leaf forms are similar in both groups (ill. 258).

The only human figure in all of the architectural sculpture of the choir, is carved on a vault boss in the south aisle (ill. 230). This depicts a male head, his two hands raised and wrenching his mouth open. The compact hands with strong fingers, the proportions of the wide, flattened face, the twisted coils of hair, almond eyes and delicate ears are similar to the kings and particularly close to the 'prophet' of the choir screen (ill. 239). This aisle vault boss, and those with foliage referred to above, were prepared in the workshop of William of Sens between 1174 and 1179.[56] It seems very likely that craftsmen were preparing the choir screen at just the same time. It is interesting that no reference to the innovative large choir capitals is evident in the screen sculpture. The style of the aisle bosses, on the other hand, is comparable in several respects. The similarities of sculptural style suggest that the sculptors of these two concurrent projects were on good terms and lent each other a hand from time to time.

164

258. Canterbury Cathedral, annulet presumably from the choir screen of c.1180.

259. Annulet from the chancel arch at Barfreston Church.

Like the sculptors of the large choir arcade capitals, the sculptors of the choir screen were well-informed about Continental artistic fashion. They were, however, in touch with a different facet of international style. The choir screen sculptures show a departure from the Romanesque style in the sense that they no longer exhibit a steadfast concern with purely abstract forms or with surface pattern.[57] The style of the choir screen figures is more relaxed. The drapery is carved in high relief and arranged in soft, flowing folds that emphasize the unity of the figure rather than fragmenting it into separate areas of independent pattern. The proportions of the figures, despite their narrow shoulders and heavy torsos, are relatively naturalistic. Each face has an individual physical structure: the devils are truly ferocious and the kings radiate dignity, while other heads convey a sense of serenity and pathos.

It is generally recognized that the art of the last quarter of the twelfth century in Northern Europe drew inspiration from the Meuse Valley, renowned for goldsmiths work, with superb enamelling and manuscript painting.[58] From the bronze font at Liège at the beginning of the century to the shrines and *pulpitum* of Nicholas of Verdun towards the close, Mosan artists were developing a style in which classical elements were blended with a Romanesque love of pattern and line. The fame of Mosan art was such that when Abbot Suger wanted the best craftsmen for the works at Saint-Denis, he brought them from that region, and such a discriminating patron as Bishop Henry of Blois also commissioned enamel works from Mosan artists.[59] French sculpture of the 1170s onwards for more than thirty years fell under the spell of the classicizing style of Mosan art, and a similar effect can be observed in England in many media.

That metalwork undoubtedly stimulated the choir screen is clear from a number of technical as well as stylistic features. The sharpness of line evident in the fragments alone reveals the influence of metalwork conventions, but there are specifically technical similarities as well. Cross-hatching is used on the background of one of the damaged roundels (ill.

260. Detail of the St Heribert shrine in Deutz showing a roundel with a cross-hatched background. This technique was common in metalwork. It had the important effect of making metal objects shimmer in candle light.

166

261). This device is common on metal objects, as shown in the roundels of the well-known shrine of St Heribert of Deutz, or in numerous other examples (ill. 260).[60] Another technical feature which the fragments share with metalwork is the striking use of the delicate decorative incisions of the rocking chisel (ills. 244, 263). This tooling device is also frequent in metalwork.

The common influence of metalwork probably accounts for the similarities between the screen sculptures and certain carvings in France, especially a series of capitals in the chapter house at Saint-Rémi, Reims.[61] These share with the Canterbury fragments not only their diminutive size and the delicacy of their execution, but also striking similarities of tooling, particularly the faintly incised zigzag line, so-called rocking chisel.

Given the close interrelationship between stone sculpture and art in other media during the eleventh and twelfth centuries at Canterbury Cathedral, it is not surprising to find that some of the contemporary stained-glass in the choir at Christ Church is stylistically linked to the screen fragments.[62] The carved octopus leaf on what was probably a string-course from the screen is closely related to painted examples like those of the Jesse window with low, fleshy buds from which feathery leaves emerge.[63] To take another example, a stained-glass roundel from the choir shows King Herod draped in a mantle exactly as on the carved panel from

261. Fragment presumably from the Cathedral choir screen with cross-hatching similar to ill.260, showing the important influence of metalwork.

262-263. Canterbury Cathedral, two grotesque heads presumably from the choir screen of 1180.
The delicate zig-zag line around the rim of the circular frame (also see ill.244) is a technique
known as 'rocking chisel' which is common on metalwork of the 12th century.

264. Rochester Cathedral, grotesque head in a roundel.

265. St Bartholomew's, Bobbing. Small octagonal shaft with St Martial and an unidentified figure probably came from St Augustine's Abbey, Canterbury.

the Faussett Pavilion. The long sweeping folds of the cloak are gathered over the left elbow of each figure, and the broad collars and borders are all similar as are the proportions of the figures, with narrow shoulders, bulky hips and spindly arms.

As was the case with the sculpture of the other major building campaigns at the cathedral, the carving of this period seems to have sparked imitation at other major houses in the region. At Rochester Cathedral, a roundel with a grotesque head has the same grimacing expression and three-dimensional modelling as the roundels from the screen at Canterbury (ill. 264); and a diminutive shaft fragment with two figures, formerly from St Augustine's Abbey, is also related (ill. 265).[64] The inscription *S. Marcialis pius patronus*, identifies one of the figures with a mitre, pallium, staff and halo as St Martial of Limoges. St Martial was not especially popular in England: the only evidence of his veneration in the entire country is at St Augustine's Abbey.[66] Like those of the screen, these figures have real weight and bulk. The attendant tonsured figure holds his garment bunched up in a loop a common convention in metalwork and sculpture of *c.*1180-1200, and also occurring on one of the screen pieces. But the faces on the fragment from St Augustine's are coarser and the drapery more schematic than on the choir screen fragments.

The style of the screen fragments persisted at Canterbury and in the surrounding region until the end of the century. It can be seen in its most refined form on the second seal of St Augustine's Abbey, which can be precisely dated to between 3 September 1198 and 6 April 1199 (ill. 266). It bears the figure of St Augustine, flanked by two heads in quatrefoils.[67] On the reverse are the seated figures of St Peter and St Paul, holding a roundel with the heads of various other saints. The drapery on both sides of the seal is remarkably soft, flowing and logically arranged. The bodies beneath are anatomically convincing, their poses and gestures natural and relaxed. The classicism of this style is undeniable, and a characteristic reference to Roman times occurs in the inclusion of a crouching figure labelled *Nero*, the emperor under whom the two apostles suffered martyrdom.[68]

169

266. Second seal of St Augustine's Abbey, Canterbury.
Note the similarity of the heads in quatrefoils with ill.267.

But as is clear from the tombs of Hubert Walter who died in 1205 (ill. 234), and Bishop Gilbert de Glanville of Rochester who died in 1214, the style did not last at Canterbury much beyond the year 1200. By the time the tomb of Archbishop Hubert Walter, who died in 1205, was carved, sculpture had taken a very different turn.[69] A new awareness of the possibilities of line and the interplay of shapes appears, as for instance where the slanting gable of the tomb passes behind the edges of the quatrefoil frames. The architectural elements also make a new departure. The bell-shaped capitals and elaborately moulded stepped bases on the side of the tomb are wholly in keeping with those of the Early English style.

Naturally some familiar earlier features were carried over. Like the screen fragments and the seal of St Augustine's Abbey, the tomb has quatrefoils from which human heads emerge (ill. 267). These are carved

170

in deep relief, finely chiselled and modelled with great sensitivity. And yet the graceful, flowing style of the screen busts is lacking here. The cascading locks of hair and beard are replaced by tight stylized curls. The forms are carved with sharp lines, knife-edged eyebrows in elegant arcs continuing from the bridge of the nose, and crisply defined lips. The tomb is carved from Purbeck stone, but the material alone cannot be responsible for the stiffening of line and general hardening of style. The emergence of a new style is evident in the frozen heads of the tomb.

267. Canterbury Cathedral, detail of a male head in a quatrefoil from the tomb of Bishop Hubert Walter.

Epilogue

ROMANESQUE TRADITIONS lingered in some regional churches beyond the end of the twelfth century, but hardly beyond the year 1200 at Canterbury. It is not difficult to understand why. Aside from anything else, the upheavals of the reign of King John, felt throughout the country, were especially severe at Canterbury. Once again, the trouble centred around the problem of archiepiscopal elections. When Archbishop Hubert Walter died, King John tried to install his own candidate, John de Gray, then Bishop of Norwich. For their part, the monks proposed their own sub-prior, Reginald. It was only as a result of the intervention of Pope Innocent III that a third candidate, Stephen Langton, was elected archbishop. This satisfied the monks and pleased the Pope, but the King was enraged. He responded with an Interdict on 23 March 1208, confiscated the possessions of the house, and had its buildings occupied by his agents. Most of the monks fled to Saint-Bertin. The duration of the monks' exile is unclear, but as Prior Geoffrey died in Rome in 1213, it can be assumed that the majority remained in exile until that year, when the Interdict was lifted. Normal life was resumed only in 1215, after the signing of Magna Carta. By then the Romanesque style at Canterbury had run its course.

Appendix I

The Infirmary Complex

The sculpture of the infirmary complex is so damaged that it is impossible to date with certainty, and so it would not be useful to discuss it within the main text. Nevertheless, the buildings are of interest in themselves as well as for the light they shed on the refurbishing of the monastery as a whole.

The Infirmary Hall

The only remains of the infirmary hall are six columns of the south aisle arcade with round, scallop capitals (ill. 269). On the waterworks plan, the infirmary hall is represented as a basilican structure with a nave and flanking aisles, a clerestory and a steep pitched roof (ill. 268). This spacious building was designed to accommodate monks who were too sick to participate in the normal life of the community. To the east of it lay the infirmary chapel, of which only four piers of the south aisle remain (ill. 270) The plan shows that its construction was similar to that of the hall, and that originally it terminated with a semicircular apse. Traces of this apse remain, but it was replaced soon after its construction with a square east end a part of which is still evident today.

The infirmary buildings were so badly damaged in the fire of 1174 that Gervase singles them out for comment, saying that in addition to the choir 'the infirmary, with the chapel of St Mary' was consumed.[1] What survived the fire was destroyed in the period after the Dissolution of the Monasteries, except for the south walls, which were spared because they were incorporated into new buildings.[2] Willis compared the round columns and scallop capitals of the infirmary hall to those at the bottom of the *aula*

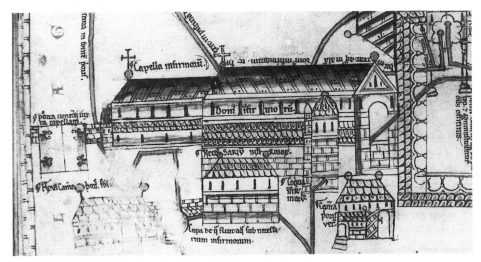

268. Detail of the waterworks plan, Cambridge, Trinity College., R.17.1, f.284v, showing the range of infirmary buildings in the precinct of Christ Church Canterbury.

269. *Remains of the Infirmary Hall.*

nova staircase (ill. 163), but such features were common throughout the twelfth century, so this is no criterion for dating.[3] All that can be said for certain from the masonry joins is that the infirmary hall pre-dates the *vestiarium*. The position of Lanfranc's infirmary is unknown, but it is unlikely to have occupied the current site, which is far to the east of the first Anglo-Norman cathedral. Perhaps the construction of the new infirmary followed Anselm's enlargement of the cathedral.

174

270. *Remains of the Infirmary Chapel.*

The Infirmary Chapel

There is at least a *terminus post quem* for the infirmary chapel. In 1114, the boundary of the monastic precinct was extended to the east. It has been suggested that this land was purchased with a view to extending the choir, but this had already been largely built by 1114.[4] The land was more likely bought with a view to enlarge the monks' cemetery and to construct the infirmary.

175

271. *Capitals from the Infirmary Chapel with grotesque.*

272. *Capital from the Infirmary Chapel decorated with confronted grotesques.*

273. *Capital from the Infirmary Chapel decorated with a flower.*

The capitals of the piers are in very poor condition.[5] The carving of the south side has deteriorated beyond recognition, although that of the other three faces is marginally better preserved. From what is still visible it appears that the foliage and geometric motifs are related to other buildings in the precinct dating from Wibert's priorate, especially the main gate. The shields of one capital are filled with daisy-like flowers similar in type to those on the east face of the main gate (ill. 273). To take another example, the 'indented finger leaves' of the infirmary chapel are akin to those of the scallop capital of the main gate and of the *vestiarium*. Two of the capitals which top the flat pilasters of the infirmary chapel piers survive on the north side, and these have foliage medallions which are closely matched by those of the outer archivolt of the west face of the main gate with their sun-burst centres and their folded leaves. Even the beaded geometric interlaces of the chapel are similar to those voussoirs on the east face of the main gate.

The grotesques in the infirmary chapel are also related to sculpture of the third quarter of the twelfth century. One is carved with a dragon related to the snake-like creature of a capital in the *porta curie*. Another has a pair of addorsed animals with a decorative band of striated leaves above. Similar leaves are used in the decoration of St Anselm's chapel (ills. 176, 194, 272).[6] One of the capitals is carved with two dragons with intertwined necks. Despite their weathered condition, there is at close range a clear similarity between these and the same image which occurs on an oak box probably made in Canterbury around 1150-1160.[7]

The first design of the chapel was planned with an apse, such as is shown on the large waterworks drawing. Traces of the springing of the barrel vault of this apse are still evident, and one pilaster capital which supported the vault remains *in situ* on the north side of the building.[8] This capital is decorated with cusping and a cable moulding, and it is in the style of the surviving capitals of the south aisle of the chapel. Pilaster capitals were also used on the north and south faces of the infirmary piers, which seems to confirm that the apse is contemporary with the remaining south aisle. The square east end was added to the chapel at a later date, but before 1174. This may have been necessitated by subsidence of the earlier apse of the first campaign. The square east end was lit by two shafted windows on the north and south sides, each carved with flat chevron. A richly carved beaded water-leaf capital remains *in situ* in the north window. There are two additional chevron-headed windows in the east wall.[9]

The Infirmary Cloister

To the west of the infirmary stood the infirmary cloister. The large drawing
shows that it had its own washing tower and well (ill. 268). Six arches of
the east walk remain (ill. 274). There are monolithic onyx shafts with squat
scallop capitals (as in the *vestiarium*), a pair of slender Purbeck shafts
carved with a spiral design, a pair of Purbeck shafts with chevron crowned
by foliage capitals, and a group of four Purbeck shafts with delicate annulets at their mid-point. The dating here is relatively secure. The remains
of the infirmary cloister are clearly contemporary with the enlargements
to the precinct made while Theobald was archbishop. But the capital forms
and spiral shafts suggest a later date, perhaps just around the time of the
1174 fire.

274. (opposite) Infirmary cloister,
Canterbury Cathedral. As the
waterworks plan (ill.268) shows,
this originally enclosed a garden
which produced herbs and plants
grown for medicinal use.

Appendix II

Twelfth-century Carved Images of Becket at Canterbury

The cult of St Thomas rapidly became one of the most important in Western Christendom and with its popularity came the proliferation of Becket images.[1] Among the earliest to survive is probably the panel now at Godmersham (ill. 276). Immediately after Becket's murder, a marble tomb was set in the eastern crypt.[2] This became obsolete when the body was translated to a splendid gold and bejewelled shrine in 1220. A gable-headed panel, presumably one end of the first hastily constructed tomb, was evidently preserved as a relic and moved to Godmersham, where the archbishops of Canterbury held a manor.[3] It is carved with the seated figure of an archbishop in full regalia, holding a crozier and making a blessing. The figure is conceived in very low relief, but the proportions of the body are well understood and the style, although rustic, fits comfortably with the date of Becket's martrydom. The twisted shafts and capitals of the arch that frames the figure are of the type current at Canterbury in the 1170s (e.g. the infirmary cloister and the choir screen). Moreover, the form of the mitre, with its single peak, confirms that the relief was produced after the 1160s when a new, single-peaked form of bishop's mitre was introduced.[4] The fact that the relief is of poor quality, not really worthy of a great archbishop, implies that it was hastily made by whatever sculptor happened to be available at the time.

Other stone figures at Christ Church may also represent the new saint. A segmental arch head over the entrance to the *domus hospitum* has a figure robed in archiepiscopal garb, with a Seated Christ in the arch above (ill. 275).[5] In 1640, the imagery of the doorway was said to include 'the resemblance of the Holy Ghost in the Dove's form descending on Our Saviour and under his feet the statue of an Archbishop...'.[6] The foliage capital supporting the arch clearly imitates those of the Gothic choir and so must post-date 1174. Though weathered, the figure takes on a new significance as one of the earliest images of Thomas Becket.

Another fragmentary figure in episcopal robes was carved on separate blocks, two of which remain. The head is missing, but the vestments and position of the arms (the right hand raised in blessing, the left carved as if holding a crozier) suggest that here too is a representation of the saint. The style of the drapery closely resembles the screen fragments, and it is just conceivable that the figure may actually have come from the screen discussed above.

Images of the saint also appear to have penetrated local parish church iconography. The figure of a blessing bishop surmounts the apex of the south doorway of Barfreston (ill. 7)[7] and the chancel doorway at Patrixbourne, two of the most richly carved parish churches in Kent.

275. Entrance to the 'domus hospitum.'
In the segmental tympanum is the image of an archbishop, probably Becket.
The arch above contains the seated figure of Christ.

276. Gabled end of a sarcophagus now at St Lawrence, Godmersham.
The figure of the archbishop is presumably Becket (see also ill.5). This may be one end of the first hastily constructed tomb
which held the body of Becket before it was translated to a gold shrine in the choir in 1220.

Notes to the Text

Notes to Preface

1. Gervase, I, pp.27-28; Willis (1845), pp.59-60.

Notes to Introduction

1. This is most clear cut in the case of secular architecture. The castle, a type of building unused in Anglo-Saxon times, proliferated in England once the Normans had taken control; see R.A. Brown, 'The Norman Conquest and the genesis of English castles', *Château Gaillard ... European Castle Studies Conference at Battle, Sussex 1966*, ed. A.J. Taylor, London/Chichester, 1969, pp.1-15.

2. See Z.N. Brooke, *The English Church and the Papacy from the Conquest to the Reign of John*, Cambridge, 1931, pp.231-235.

3. J. le Patourel, 'The report of the trial on Penenden Heath', *Studies in Medieval History presented to F. M. Powicke*, ed. R. Hunt *et al.*, Oxford, 1948, pp.15-26.

4. Southern, *St Anselm*, pp.130-142; D. Nicholl, *Thurstan of York 1114-1140*, York, 1964, pp.36-37.

5. From 1163 attempts were made to have Anselm canonized, and this finally happened in 1494; see R.L.P. Milburn, *Saints and Their Emblems in English Churches*, Oxford, 1949, p.20.

6. *English Historical Documents*, ed. D.C. Douglas, Oxford, 1981, pp.766-770; see especially p.768, n.1 for Maitland's assessment of the controversy.

7. Knowles, Ch. XXXVI, 'The cathedral monasteries and the bishop's abbeys', pp.619-631. Some doubt must be cast on the shared life of the monks and the archbishop by the discovery that Lanfranc's archiepiscopal palace is the largest known example to survive in the whole of 11th-century Europe; see T. Tatton-Brown, J. Bowen and J. Rady, 'The archbishop's palace at Canterbury', *JBAA*, forthcoming.
The monks' privilege to elect the archbishop was confirmed in 1158 by the English Pope Hadrian IV; see *Papsturkunden in England*, ed. W. Holtzmann, II, Göttingen, 1935, pp.288-289.

8. R.S. Hoyt, 'A pre-Domesday Kentish assessment list', *A Medieval Miscellany for D.M. Stenton*, eds. P.M. Barnes and C.F. Slade, *Pipe Roll Society*, new series, XXXVI, London, 1962, pp.189-202. The unit of assessment in Kent is not the usual hide but the sulung, which equalled two hides or about two hundred acres; *VCH, Kent*, III, p.184.
In the Domesday Book estimates of Canterbury's holdings vary somewhat; see *VCH, Kent*, III, ed. W. Page, London, 1932, pp.177-269. Southern, *St Anselm*, puts it at £730, below Glastonbury and Ely at £830 and £770 respectively, while Knowles, p.702, calculated it was £687, below the incomes of Glastonbury (£827) and Ely (£768); see also the *Domesday Monachorum*, which records the episcopal and monastic estates of Christ Church in the last years of Lanfranc's archiepiscopate, D.C. Douglas, *The 'Domesday Monachorum' of Christ Church Canterbury*, London, 1944.

9. For the history of the abbey, see *Historia Monasterii S. Augustini Cantuariensis by Thomas of Elmham*, ed. C. Hardwick, *Rolls Series*, VIII, 1858, and *William Thorne's Chronicle of St Augustine's Abbey, Canterbury*, trans. A.H. Davis, Oxford, 1934. For the buildings, see A.W. Clapham, *St Augustine's Abbey*, London, 1955; D. Sherlock and H. Woods, *St Augustine's Abbey. Report on Excavations, 1960-1978*, Kent Archaeological Society, Maidstone, 1988.

10. Estimates of the values given in Domesday Book vary. Knowles, p.702, assesses St Augustine's at £635.

11. Gervase went so far as to describe its bishop as 'proprius et privatus Cantuariensis ecclesiae capellanus' (Gervase, I, p.133). See I.J. Churchill, *Canterbury Administration*, London, 1933, pp.279-287.

12. Kahn, *ERA*, p.182; B.J. Philp, *Excavations at Faversham. First Research Report*, Kent Archaeological Research Group Council, Maidstone, 1968, pp.42-43. For some of the other important monuments which have been destroyed, see C.R. Haines, *Dover Priory*, Cambridge, 1930; P.J. Tester, 'Excavations on the site of Leeds Priory', *AC*, XCIII, 1977, pp.33-45 and XCIV, 1978,

p.75ff.; id., 'Excavations at Boxley Abbey', *AC*, LXXXVIII, 1973, pp.129-158.

13. D.M. Wilson, 'Scandinavian settlement in the north and west of the British Isles', *Transactions of the Royal Historical Society*, fifth series, XXVI, 1976, pp.95-113. For the impact of the Viking armies on English politics and culture see N.P. Brooks, 'England in the ninth century: the crucible of defeat', *Transactions of the Royal Historical Society*, XXIX, fifth series, 1979, pp.1-20.

14. L. Webster and J. Cherry, 'Medieval Britain', *Medieval Archaeology*, XVIII, 1974, p.179.

15. *VCH, Kent*, III, pp.26-27. Many fragments of the monument at Richborough have come to light, including pilasters, inscriptions, capitals and parts of gilt bronze statues. Although it was partly destroyed in the 3rd century, enough remained in the 16th century for Camden to comment on it; see W. Camden, *Britannia*, London, 1586, p.176.
For the Roman theatre see S.S. Frere, 'The Roman theatre at Canterbury', *Britannia*, I, 1970, pp.83-113, and ibid., VIII, 1977, pp.423-425.

16. Some 36 pre-Conquest books from Christ Church alone remain; see James, pp.xxi-xxix. The wealth of the library of St Augustine's Abbey was also considerable. It housed not only such a key book as the Gospels of St Augustine, but also Carolingian manuscripts of immense importance. The lavishly illustrated copy of the astronomical treatise by Aratus cast such a spell in England that it was copied at least five times in the early Middle Ages, while the famous Utrecht Psalter (Utrecht, University Library, MS 32) was copied at least three times: once in the 11th century and twice in the 12th century. For the Gospels of St Augustine, see F. Wormald, 'The miniatures in the Gospels of St Augustine, Cambridge, Corpus Christi College, MS 286', *Francis Wormald. Collected Writings. Studies in Medieval Art from the 6th to the 12th Century*, London, 1984, pp.13-27. For the Utrecht Psalter, see ibid., pp.36-46. For the Aratus Treatise, see F. Saxl, *Lectures*, London, 1957, pp.96-110.

17. Knowles, 515-516; Eadmer records that books, 'sacred and profane' perished in the fire; see Eadmer, *Vita Bregwini, Anglia Sacra*, II, p.187.

18. London, B.L., MS Cotton Claudius, C.VI, f.173; see Dodwell, p.17 for translation. See also James, p.xxx. For manuscripts at Christ Church: N.M. Ker, *English Manuscripts in the Century After the Conquest*, Oxford, 1960, pp.10-11. A list of the earliest manuscripts is also given in Dodwell, p.17. For reliance on Bec, see *S. Anselmi Opera Omnia*, ed. F.S. Schmitt, III, Edinburgh, 1946, nos. 23, 25, 26; G. Nortier, 'Les biblio-thèques médiévales des abbayes bénédictines de Normandie', *Revue Mabillon*, 1957, pp.57-83.

19. The Gloucester candlestick is now in the Victoria and Albert Museum. For the attribution to Canterbury, see A. Harris, 'A Romanesque candlestick in London', *JBAA*, XXVII, 1964, pp.32-52. For a more recent view and full bibliography, see Stratford, *ERA*, p.249, who suggests that the candlestick was made by a professional artist, active in South-east England, but does not assign it a Canterbury provenance.

20. Zarnecki, *Regional Schools*, pp.48-49, first recognized the two pierced whalebone plaques in the Victoria and Albert Museum as Canterbury works. See also Williamson, *ERA*, p.221. For the croziers, see T.A. Heslop and G. Zarnecki, 'An ivory fragment from Battle Abbey', *Antiquaries Journal*, LX, 1980, pp.341-342. There is no reason to attribute the beautiful walrus ivory pectoral cross in the Victoria and Albert Museum to Canterbury as does J. Beckwith, *Ivory Carving in Early Medieval England*, London, 1972, p.128. Beckwith dates the object 1100, but it is demonstrably pre-Conquest. Wood was also used in the production of luxury small-scale objects. There is evidence to suggest that an oak casket for secular use was produced at Canterbury; see G. Zarnecki, 'A Romanesque casket from Canterbury in Florence', *Canterbury Cathedral Chronicle*, 64, 1969, pp.37-43.
For the 12th-century glass, see M.H. Caviness, *The Early Stained Glass of Canterbury Cathedral*, Princeton, 1977, and id., 'Romanesque "belles verrières" in Canterbury', *Romanesque and Gothic*, pp.35-38. For a general look at Canterbury wall-paintings, see O. Demus, *Romanesque Mural Paintings*, London, 1970, p.509.
That the Bayeux Tapestry was a Canterbury work was first proposed by F. Wormald, *The Bayeux Tapestry*, London, 1957, p.34. The monks of Christ Church were well known abroad for their textiles. For example, the Archbishop of Benevento took great pride in the cope made at Canterbury which he received from them in exchange for the arm of St Bartholomew; see Eadmer, *Hist. Nov.*, pp.107-110.

21. Urry, pp.112-123. For Terric the goldsmith, one of the greatest citizens of the town c.1180, see pp.174-176. We know little of how metal workshops were organized at this period, and whether the craftsmen were monks or laymen. Occasionally a document sheds light on the problem: for instance, when fire damaged the shrine of St Edmund at Bury St Edmunds in 1198, the monks called upon a *lay* goldsmith to repair the damage (see *The Chronicle of Jocelin of Brakelond*, ed. Sir E. Clarke, London, 1903, p.165).

Notes to I : Lanfranc

1. Eadmer (c.1060-c.1144), *Vita Bregwini*, Migne, *PL*, CLIX, cols.757-758. This was written after 1123 (see Southern, *St Anselm*, p.285, n.2. The translation was taken from Willis (1845), p.9; see also A. Gransden, *Historical Writing in England c. 550-1307*, Ithaca, 1974.

2. For Stigand, see F. Barlow, *The English Church 1000-1066*, London/New York, 1979, pp.77-81. The best account of Lanfranc's activities is Gibson, *Lanfranc*; also *The Letters of Lanfranc, Archbishop of Canterbury*, eds. H. Clover and M. Gibson, Oxford Medieval Texts, Oxford, 1979. For Lanfranc's *Consuetudines* or *Statua* see Knowles, pp.122-123, and *The Monastic Constitutions of Lanfranc*, ed. D. Knowles, London, 1951; see also F. Barlow, 'A view of Archbishop Lanfranc', *Journal of Ecclesiastical History*, XVI/II, October 1965, pp.163-177.

3. Eadmer, *Hist. Nov.*, p.13. The translation is given in G. Bosanquet, *Eadmer's History of Recent Events in England*, London, 1964, p.13; see also Gibson, *Lanfranc*, pp.162-167.

4. Eadmer, *Hist. Nov.*, p.13, 'Ecclesiam praeterea quam spatio septem annorum a fundamentis ferme totam perfectam reddidit'. For consecration see Gibson, *Lanfranc*, p.115.

5. Henry held the position of prior until 1096, when he became abbot of Battle. See Southern, *St Anselm*, p.269; *The Chronicle of Battle Abbey*, ed. E. Searle, Oxford, 1980, p.100. For the recently excavated remains at Battle see J.N. Hare, 'Battle Abbey. The eastern range and the excavations of 1978-80', *Historic Buildings and Monuments Commission for England, Archaeological Report No. 2*, London, 1985.
Gundulf had a reputation as a highly competent builder. He was referred to as 'in opere cementarii plurimum sciens et efficax'; see *Textus Roffensis*, ed. T. Hearne, Oxford, 1720, p.146. He also worked on the Tower of London, Rochester Castle and possibly on Colchester Castle; see *The History of the King's Works*, I, eds. R.A. Brown, H.M. Colvin and A.J. Taylor, London, 1963, pp.28-31; R.A.L. Smith, 'The place of Gundulf in the Anglo-Norman church', *The English Historical Review*, LVIII, July 1943, pp.259-260.

6. On the mysterious absence of Lanfranc from the dedication ceremony, see M. Baylé, *La Trinité de Caen*, Paris, 1979, 13B, n.26.

7. Willis (1845), pp.64-68, was the first to make a detailed comparison between Saint-Etienne and Canterbury. For an account of the appearance of Lanfranc's church, see R. Gem, 'The significance of the 11th-century rebuilding of Christ Church and St Augustine's, Canterbury, in the development of Romanesque architecture', *BAA CT*, Canterbury, 1982, pp.1-19, and F. Woodman 'Lanfranc's cathedral at Canterbury', *Canterbury Cathedral Chronicle*, LXXI, 1977, pp.11-16.

8. The first excavations of the crypt were made in 1895. See A.W. Clapham, *English Romanesque Architecture After the Conquest*, Oxford, 1934, p.21; C.F. Routledge, W.A. Scott Robertson and J.B. Sheppard, 'On discoveries in the crypt of Canterbury Cathedral', *AC*, XVIII, 1889, p.254. T. Tatton-Brown (see 'Researches and discoveries in Kent', *AC*, XCV, 1979, pp.276-278), excavated the west end of the crypt in 1979. It was discovered that the foundations of the west wall and corner pier base foundations were built at a lower level than, and were cut by, the foundations of Anselm's crypt, so the west wall must belong to Lanfranc's crypt. Tatton-Brown argued that the opening in the west wall was the doorway to the crypt; however, this seems an improbable arrangement, particularly as the opening did not reach floor level and would have required steps. It is more likely that the opening was a niche for a tomb. For the crypt at La Trinité see Baylé, op. cit. note 6, pp.40B, 100A, who believed that the crypt was added (or rather inserted) c.1090. This theory is difficult to accept; see the review by G. Zarnecki in *The Burlington Magazine*, April 1980, p.260.

9. H.J.A. Strik, 'Remains of the Lanfranc building in the great central tower and the northwest choir/transept area', *BAA CT*, Canterbury, 1982, pp.20-26.
The watercolour by Buckler is in the Society of Antiquaries of London, *Red Portfolio*. The southwest tower was reshaped in Gothic times, but the north-west tower survived until 1834. The new tower, by George Austin, was finished in 1840; see W.D. Caröe, 'The three towers of Canterbury', *Architectural Review*, XVII, 1905, pp.3-12.
For the cushion capital on the central crossing pier see C.E. Woodruff and W. Danks, *Memorials of the Cathedral Priory of Christ in Canterbury*, London, 1912, p.29. The capital came to light when holes were cut into the western piers of the crossing tower with the purpose of filling the cores with liquid cement for strengthening the tower.

10. Eadmer, *Miracula S. Dunstani*, ed. W. Stubbs, *Rolls Series*, LXIII, London, 1874, p.232; translation by Willis (1845), pp.14-15.

11. See V. Ruprich-Robert, *L'architecture normande aux XIe et XIIe siècle en Normandie et en*

Angleterre, I, Paris, 1884, p.177; J. Strzygowski, *The Origin of Christian Church Art*, Oxford, 1923, p.146.

12. G. Baldwin Brown, *The Arts in Early England. Anglo-Saxon Architecture*, II, London, 1925, p.255, cites Brixworth as an Anglo-Saxon example, but when examined at close range this cannot be accepted as a cushion capital. H.M. Taylor, *Anglo-Saxon Architecture*, III, Cambridge, 1978, p.1050, claims that the cubic (cushion) capital was developed in Anglo-Saxon England independently of the Continent, but the extant evidence does not support this.
It has recently been suggested that the cushion capital was first introduced to England through the Canterbury workshops around 1070 (see R. Gem, 'Canterbury and the cushion capital: a commentary on passages from Goscelin's De Miraculis Sancti Augustini', *Romanesque and Gothic*, pp.83-97). According to Gem, cushion capitals were roughly shaped at the quarry in Marquise (near Boulogne) and shipped from there to Canterbury. Until further petrological tests can be made, this must remain an attractive, but open issue.

13. For the relationship of sculpture of the duchy with that of England see G. Zarnecki, 'Romanesque sculpture in Normandy and England in the eleventh century', *PBC*, I, 1979, pp.168-189.

14. Eadmer, *Hist. Nov.*, I, p.7; and Gervase, I, p.10.

15. Eadmer, *Hist. Nov.*, p.13; Willis (1845), p.14 and Willis (1869), pp.2-3.

16. Willis (1869), pp.21-29, 47-59.

17. J. Bony in 'Durham et la tradition saxonne', *Etudes d'arts médiéval offerts à Louis Grodecki*, eds. S. McKnight Crosby, A. Chastel and A. Prache, Paris, 1981, pp.79-92, argues that the patterned columns were a continuation of pre-Conquest tradition.

18. For a full description of the stones and their possible use at Canterbury, see D. Kahn, 'Recently discovered eleventh-century reliefs from Canterbury', *Gesta*, XXVIII/1, 1989, pp.53-60.

19. N.P. Brooks and H.E. Walker, 'The authority and interpretation of the Bayeux Tapestry', *PBC*, I, 1979, pp.1-34, especially p.18 for the Canterbury provenance of the Tapestry; D.J. Bernstein, *The Mystery of the Bayeux Tapestry*, Chicago, 1986, especially Ch. III.

20. A. Lawrence, 'Manuscripts in Canterbury 1060-1090',unpublished M.A. thesis, Courtauld Institute, 1977, pp.3-9.

21. It was Lanfranc who suppressed the Feast of the Immaculate Conception and dropped St

Dunstan from the Canterbury Calendar; see F. Barlow, opcit. note 2, p.279, n.7.

Notes to II : Anselm

1. *The Monastic Constitutions of Lanfranc*, ed. D. Knowles, London, 1951.

2. Eadmer, *Hist. Nov.*, p.75. Apparently the finances of the cathedral priory were not seriously affected either by William Rufus or by Henry I, each of whom in turn appropriated the revenues while Anselm was in exile; see *VCH, Kent*, II, ed. W. Page, 1926, p.29.

3. C.F. Routledge, W.A. Scott Robertson and J.B. Sheppard, 'On discoveries in the crypt of Canterbury Cathedral', *AC*, XVIII, 1889, p.254. According to St John Hope's reconstruction, the monks' choir occupied two or three bays of the nave, enclosed on the west by a *pulpitum*; see W. St John Hope, 'Quire screens in English churches, with special reference to the twelfth-century quire screen formerly in the cathedral church of Ely', *Archaeologia*, LXVIII, 1916-1917, p.70.

4. Eadmer, *Epistola ad Glastonienses*, Migne, *PL*, CLIX, col.805; Gervase, II, p.368. For a count of the numbers of monks, see also R.A.L. Smith, *Canterbury Cathedral Priory*, Cambridge, 1943, p.3; and Knowles, p.714.

5. The Life of St Odo is published in *Anglia Sacra*, II, pp.122-142. For writings on St Dunstan (d. 988) see *Memorials of St Dunstan*, ed. W. Stubbs, *Rolls Series*, LXIII, London, 1874. The Life of St Bregwin (d. 762) can be found in *Anglia Sacra*, II, pp.184-190. Eadmer also wrote a Life of St Oswald of Worcester at the request of the monks of Worcester, and a Life of St Wilfrid of York, whose relics reputedly rested at Christ Church. For Eadmer as a hagiographer, see A. Gransden, *Historical Writing in England c.550-c.1307*, London, 1974, p.129.

6. Eadmer, *The Life of St Anselm*, ed. and transl. R.W. Southern, Nelsons Medieval Text, Oxford, 1962, pp.50-53.

7. F. Wormald, *English Kalendars before AD 1100*, and id., *English Benedictine Kalendars after AD 1100*, Henry Bradshaw Society, 1939, lxxii and lxxvii. Both St Dunstan and St Elphege were former archbishops of Canterbury. The latter, an English hero, was killed by the Danes and venerated as a martyr at Canterbury. For changes made by Lanfranc to the Christ Church Calendar, see also F.A. Gasquet and E. Bishop, *The Bosworth Psalter*, London, 1908, pp.27-39. At the dedication of Lanfranc's new cathedral in

1077 there was no ceremonial translation of the church relics as was usual on such occasions, but a procession of the consecrated Eucharist; see Gibson, *Lanfranc*, pp.171-173.

8. Gervase, I, p.13.

9. Eadmer, *Hist. Nov.*, pp.179-181; Gervase, I, p.13; E. Bishop, *Liturgica Historica*, Oxford, 1918, p.116. It was under the influence of Anselm's nephew, Anselm of Bury, that the Feast of the Virgin was restored in England; see R.W. Southern, 'The English origins of the miracles of the Virgin', *Medieval and Renaissance Studies*, IV, 1958, pp.176-216.

10. 'Arnulfus prior Cantuariae factus est abbas Burgi; hic dormitorium, capitulum, refectorium et necessarium fecit construere, ac viginti libras dedit conventui, ad capas et alia ornamenta emenda'. *Chronicon Angliae Petriburgense*, ed. J.A. Giles, *Rolls Series*, London, 1845, p.74. Part of the surviving fabric of the west end of the nave of the cathedral at Peterborough may have been erected by Ernulf. But there is no or-namental sculpture at Peterborough which can be attributed to Ernulf's time as abbot (1107-1114). My thanks are due to L. Reilly for dis-cussing her results before submitting her Ph.D. thesis entitled *The Architectural History of Peter-borough Cathedral*, to the Institute of Fine Arts, New York University. For Ernulf at Rochester, see W. St John Hope, *The Architectural History of the Cathedral Church and Monastery of St Andrew Rochester*, London, 1900, p.142.
For Ernulf's biography, see Southern, *St Anselm*, pp.269-70. It is unclear whether he was a monk of Saint-Simphorien or Saint-Lucien at Beau-vais; see D. Knowles, C.N.L. Brooke and V. Lon-don, *The Heads of Religious Houses in England and Wales 940-1216*, Cambridge, 1972, p.33.

11. *Anglia Sacra*, I, p.342.

12. *Anglia Sacra*, I, p.137.

13. Ralph, a man of noble birth, was trained in Normandy before being driven out by Robert Belleme. He was consecrated bishop of Roches-ter in 1108 and became the administrator of the diocese of Canterbury upon Anselm's death in 1109, while the See was kept vacant by Henry I; see *The Ecclesiastical History of Orderic Vitalis*, ed. M. Chibnall, IV, Oxford, 1973, pp.170-172.

14. This is the dedication date given by all the major chroniclers (see O. Lehmann-Brockhaus, *Lateinische Schriftquellen zur Kunst in England, Wales und Schottland vom Jahre 901 bis zum Jahre 1307*, I, Munich, 1955, p.200), except Matthew Paris, who gives 1114/1115 (obviously in error); see Matthew Paris, *Historia Anglorum*, ed. F. Madden, *Rolls Series*, I, London, 1866, p.219.

Archbishop Ralph's successor, William de Cor-beil, was also of Norman descent. He became a pupil of Anselm of Laon, a clerk of Ranulf Flambard, and subsequently a regular canon and prior of the Augustinian canons of St Osyth in Essex before he was chosen, under pressure from Henry I, as archbishop of Canterbury. He was involved with building at both Rochester Cathedral and Rochester Castle.

15. See the *Anglo-Saxon Chronicle*, I, ed. B. Thorpe, *Rolls Series*, XXIII, London, 1861, for the year 1130. Among those present at the dedication, the King of Scotland stands out as an unusual participant. He was, however, Queen Matilda of England's brother which led to his consider-able political involvement south of the Scottish border; see G.W.S. Barrow, 'David I of Scotland 1124-1153. The balance of new and old', *Stenton Lecture*, Reading, 1984, p.17. King David was in the South in 1130, to preside over the court which tried the charge of treason brought against Henry's powerful agent, Geoffrey Clin-ton; see Chibnall, op. cit. note 13, pp.276-277. Unlike his brother-in-law, David was a deeply pious man, and the special ties with Canterbury established by Queen Margaret of Scotland may have contributed to his decision to attend the ceremony at Canterbury; see G.W.S. Barrow, 'A Scottish collection at Canterbury', *Scottish His-torical Review*, XXXI, 1952, pp.16-28. The same dignitaries attended the dedication at Rochester Cathedral a few days later, so it appears that the event was purely ceremonial and bore no relation to the condition of either church. This occasion is not, therefore, a reliable tool for dat-ing.

16. William of Malmesbury, *Gesta Pontificum Anglo-rum*, ed. N.E.S.A. Hamilton, *Rolls Series*, LII, 1870, p.138. For the translation, see Willis (1845), p.17; cf. also Gervase, I, pp.9-16.

17. Gervase, I, p.28. For the only detailed descrip-tion of the crypt, see W.A. Scott Robertson, 'The crypt of Canterbury Cathedral', *AC*, XIII, 1880, pp.17-80, and pp.500-552.

18. The columns in St Gabriel's chapel are nearly a full foot taller than those of the Innocents cha-pel. This was presumably necessary in order to compensate for the sloping ground level.

19. E. Fernie, 'St. Anselm's crypt', *BAA CT*, Canter-bury, 1982, pp. 30-31.
For links with German crypts, see G. Zarnecki, 'The capitals of the crypt', *Arch Jnl*, CXXVI, 1970, p.246. Hall crypts were also a frequent feature of Italian architecture, but these bear no apparent relationship with Christ Church Canterbury. For a survey of the Italian material, see M. Magni, 'Cryptes du haut moyen âge en

Italie: problèmes de typologie du IXe jusqu'au début du XIe siècle", *Cahiers archéologiques*, XXVIII, 1979, pp.41-85.

For Speyer, see H.W. Kubach and W. Haas, *Der Dom zu Speyer*, Berlin, 1972, pp.255-293. For Cologne, see H. Rahtgens, *Die Kirche St. Maria im Kapitol zu Köln*, Düsseldorf, 1913. Writing about Romanesque crypts, Lasteyrie notes that the largest examples were built in England and the Rhineland. He singles out Speyer, Winchester, Worcester and above all Canterbury as the grandest. But the learned archaeologist was wrong in believing Canterbury was a conglomeration of various structures built at different times. Only the crypt under the Corona was an addition. R. de Lasteyrie, *L'architecture religieuse en France à l'époque romane*, Paris, 1929, p.307.

20. R. Gem, 'The significance of the 11th-century rebuilding of Christ Church and St Augustine's, Canterbury, in the development of Romanesque architecture', *BAA CT*, Canterbury, 1982, pp.9-10. The plan fanned out to several major Benedictine centres in England, notably Worcester Cathedral and Bury St Edmunds Abbey.

For reference to Normandy cf. the crypt at Rouen, which has a central apsidal chamber, enclosed by a continuous wall. This is divided into three aisles by rows of columns, and terminates in an ambulatory and three radiating chapels with free-standing columns supporting the vaults; see G. Lanfry, 'La crypte romane de l'onzième siècle de la cathédrale de Rouen', *BM*, 95, 1936, pp.181-201.

21. The view that the crypt capitals were carved *in situ* has been current for a considerable period; see for instance J.K. Colling, *English Medieval Foliage*, London, 1874, p.21. The crypt was dated to 1096-1100 by Willis (1845), and to 1100 by Robertson, op. cit. note 17, p.27. E.S. Prior and A. Gardner dated the capitals as late as 1150; see *An Account of Medieval Figure-Sculpture in England*, Cambridge, 1912, pp.31, 164. A.W. Clapham, *English Romanesque Architecture After the Conquest*, Oxford, 1934, p.142, did not stray far from this with his date of 1140. In his thesis of 1950, Zarnecki accepted the theory that the capitals were carved *in situ*, dating them c.1130 (see Zarnecki, *Regional Schools*, pp.55-60), but he later abandoned this view. See G. Zarnecki, 'The Romanesque capitals in the south transept of Worcester Cathedral', *BAA CT*, Worcester, 1978, p.39.

22. R. Gem, 'Canterbury and the cushion capital: a commentary on passages from Goscelin's *De Miraculis Sancti Augustini*', *Romanesque and Gothic*, pp.83-97.

23. St Emmeram, Regensburg is a German example; see R. Strobel, 'Katalog der ottonischen und romanischen Säulen in Regensburg und Umgebung', *Jahrbuch für fränkische Landesforschung*, XXII, 1962, pp.367-368, pls.2, 3.

For Como, see O. Zastrow, *Scultura carolingia e romanica nel Comasco. Società Archeologica Comense*, Como, 1978, pl.88. For Milan, see A.K. Porter, *Lombard Architecture*, II, New Haven/London, 1917, p.528, pl.115, fig.1.

24. J. Raspi Serra, 'English decorative sculpture of the early twelfth-century and the Como-Pavian tradition', *Art Bulletin*, LI/4, 1966, pp.357-8. This article seriously distorts the relationship between Lombard and English Romanesque sculpture. A more recent attempt to examine the issue goes someway to redress the balance; see J. Meredith, *The impact of Italy on the Romanesque architectural sculpture of England*, Ph.D. thesis, Yale University, 1980, especially pp.166-167, pls. 108-109. For some new thoughts on the problem, see G. Zarnecki, 'Sculpture in stone in the English Romanesque exhibition', *SAOP*, 1986, pp.9-22. Also see R. Kautzsch, 'Oberitalien und der Mittelrhein in 12 Jahrhundert', *Atti del X Congresso Internazionale di Storia dell' Arte in Roma: L'Italia e l'arte straniera*, Rome, 1922, pp.123-130. For the fundamental work on travelling Lombard sculptors, see G. de Francovich, 'La corrente comasca nella scultura romanica europea, *Revista del R. Istituto d'Archeologia e Storia dell'Arte*, V, 1935-36, pp.267-305. Cf. also, ibid., 'La diffusione', VI, 1937-38, pp.47-129.

25. For Bad Hersfeld see G. Kiesow, *Romanik in Hessen*, Stuttgart, 1984, pp.200-202; Zarnecki, op. cit. note 24, p.9. For Regensburg see Strobel, op.cit. note 23, pp.367-368

26. In France, Emile Mâle, *L'Art religieux du XIIe siècle en France. Etude sur l'origine de l'iconographie du moyen âge*, Paris, 1922, did the most to establish the links between manuscripts and sculpture. In England, George Zarnecki, *Regional Schools*, pioneered the idea.

27. This particular image, a sort of reversed animal protome, was also present in the art of the Near East; see J. Baltrusaitis, *Art Sumerien, Art Roman*, Paris, 1934, p.20. Emile Mâle (op. cit. note 26, pp.344-349) believed that it was transported to the West with the precious textiles so highly prized during the Middle Ages. See also V. Slomann, *Bicorporates. Studies in Revivals and Migrations of Art Motifs*, Copenhagen, 1967. Also of interest on this subject is R. Ettinghausen, 'Muslim decorative arts and painting. Their nature and impact on the medieval west', *Islam and the Medieval West*, ed. S. Ferber, New

York, 1975; id., 'The impact of Muslim decorative arts ... on Europe', *Islamic Art and Architecture. Collected Papers*, Berlin, 1984, p.1079.

28. T.A. Heslop, '"Dunstanus Archiepiscopus" and painting in Kent around 1120', *Burlington Magazine*, CXXVI, April 1984, pp.195-204. Heslop argues that Prior Conrad was himself actually German an attractive if unprovable hypothesis, but one which might help account for some of the similarities. For evidence of artistic links with the Mosan region, see T.A. Heslop, *ERA*, p.307, where the seal of Archbishop Anselm is shown to reflect the classicizing Mosan tradition that produced the Liège font.

29. These are two splendid, large Corinthian capitals and the fragment of a third, probably from Wulfric's church (1047-1059), St Augustine's Abbey, see W. St John Hope, 'Recent discoveries in the abbey church of St Austin at Canterbury', *AC*, XXXII, 1916, p.24. J. Taylor and H.M. Taylor, 'Architectural sculpture in pre-Norman England', *JBAA*, XXIX, 3rd series, 1966, pp.47-49, make an unconvincing comparison with the crypt capitals at Saint-Germain at Auxerre (841-865).
For York, see D. Phillips, *Excavations at York Minster*, II, London, 1985, pls.83, 122-3, for Richmond Castle. For St John's chapel, see G. Zarnecki, 'Romanesque sculpture in Normandy and England in the eleventh century', *PBC*, I, 1979, pp.176-178. For Lincoln, see G. Zarnecki, *Romanesque Lincoln*, Lincoln, 1988, pp.12-14. For Stogursey, see M. Baylé, 'Les chapiteaux de Stogursey (Somerset) ancien prioré de Lonlay l'Abbaye', *BM*, CXXXVII, 1980, pp.405-416.

30. Despite the close similarity of these capitals, Clapham (*English Romanesque Architecture After the Conquest*, Oxford, 1934, pp.135-136) argued that the free-standing example (ill.49) was re-used from Lanfranc's structure of the 1070s, but this was clearly mistaken.

31. See R. Krautheimer, *Early Christian and Byzantine Architecture*, Harmondsworth, 1965, pl.78a; and E. Licht, *Ottonische und frühromanische Kapitelle in Deutschland*, Marburg, 1935, pp.145-146, pl.62.

32. For Bernay, see L. Grodecki, 'Les débuts de la sculpture romane en normandie', *BM*, CVIII, 1950, pp.7-67. For Bibury, see G. Zarnecki, 'The Winchester acanthus in Romanesque sculpture', *Wallraf-Richartz Jahrbuch*, XVII, 1955, pp.1-4, reprinted in Zarnecki, *Studies*. For the block capitals at Milborne Port in Somerset, see G. Zarnecki, '1066 and architectural sculpture', *Proceedings of the British Academy*, LII, 1966, pp.98-99.

33. Zarnecki, *Regional Schools*, pp.4-69. The subsequent discussion of the relationship between Canterbury manuscripts and sculpture makes frequent reference to this pioneering work.

34. 'Winchester acanthus' to decorate capitals was first used in Anglo-Saxon sculpture, as seen in the capitals flanking the chancel arch at Bibury in Gloucestershire. See Zarnecki (op. cit. note 32, pp.1-4).
See F. Wormald, *Decorated initials in English manuscripts from A.D. 900 to 1100*, Appendix I, pp. 69-72 in Volume I of Francis Wormald's Collected Writings for a clear account of the 'Winchester' style. The manuscripts in this style, possibly from Canterbury are: Cambridge, Trinity College, MS B.10.4; London, B.L., Arundel MS 155. The best surviving parallels, however, come from elsewhere (e.g. Cambridge, Pembroke College, MS 301, and Oxford, Wadham College, MS A.10.22) though this is probably the mere result of chance survival. F. Wormald, *English Drawings of the Tenth and Eleventh Centuries*, London, 1952, dates this to *c.*1100.

35. For comparative material in France, see M. Jullian, 'L'image de la musique dans la sculpture romane en France', *Cahiers de civilisation médiévale*, XXX, 1987, pp.33-44.

36. For the amphisbaena, see G.C. Druce, 'The amphisbaena and its connections in ecclesiastical art and architecture', *Arch Jnl*, 67, 1910, p.315.

37. Both sets of bronze doors were made by Barisano da Trani: those at Ravello are dated 1179, those at Trani 1180-90. The design is repeated on twelve panels at Ravello and on three at Trani. See U. Mende, *Die Bronzetüren des Mittelalters*, Munich, 1983, pp.164-169, pls.137, 156.
The motif of addorsed griffins was probably derived from oriental textiles which were used as liturgical vestments, covers and hangings at Canterbury; see Zarnecki, *Regional Schools*, pp.20-21. For Canterbury fabrics, see G. Robinson and H. Urquhart, 'Seal bags in the treasury of the cathedral church of Canterbury', *Archaeologia*, 84, 1934, pp.163-211; A.M. Muthesius, 'The silks from the tomb' in 'Archbishop Hubert Walter's tomb and its furnishings', *BAA CT*, Canterbury, 1982, pp.80-87.

38. The cat-mask clasp was widespread in 'Winchester School' style manuscripts and in Romanesque manuscripts. A particularly close comparison for the capital again exists in the *Pseudo Isidore* from Canterbury: London, B.L., MS Claudius E.V., f.7r.

39. G. Zarnecki, 'A Romanesque capital from Canterbury at Chartham', *AC*, XCV, 1979, pp.1-6. The capital (ill. 277) was recently moved from

a garden in Chartham to the Canterbury Heritage Museum.

40. E. Ledwich, 'Observations on ancient churches', *Archaeologia*, VIII, 1787, p.180. Robertson (op. cit. note 17, pp.29, 41), dismissed them as 'merely wild grotesque devices of the sculptor's unbridled imagination', and related them to Revelation IX: 7-10, 17, 19 passages which cite dreaded monsters, the forms of evil which wage war on men's souls.

41. For the transformation of classical images in medieval art see E. Panofsky, *Renaissance and Renascences in Western Art*, London, 1965; Dodwell, Ch. VI, pp.60-80. The subject is also examined in F. Saxl and R. Wittkower, *British Art and the Mediterranean*, Oxford, 1948; E. Panofsky and F. Saxl, 'Classical mythology in Mediterranean art', *Metropolitan Museum Studies*, IV, 1932-33, pp.228-280. For an important study of the same problem in the ornamental borders of the bronze doors at Gniezno see, Z. Kepínski, 'La symbolique de la porte de Gniezno', *Drzwi Gniézniénskie*, ed. M. Walicki, II, Warsaw, 1959, pp.161-283 (French summary pp.290-297), copiously illustrated, pp.299-381.

42. James, pp.xxxi-xxxv. The leaves of the catalogue are at the end of Cambridge, University Library, MS Ii. 3.12. James calculated that the total number of books in the library was roughly six to seven hundred.

43. For a full description of the decorative use of these symbols, see Dodwell, pp.62-63.

44. London, B.L., MS Harley 647, f.10r. For an important study of this manuscript and its descendants see F. Saxl, 'Illuminated science manuscripts in England', *Lectures*, London, 1957, pp.96-110.

45. Mâle, (op. cit. note 26, pp.339-340); H. Adolf, 'The ass and the harp', *Speculum*, XXV, 1950, pp.49-57; F. McCulloch, *Medieval Latin and French Bestiaries*, North Carolina, 1960.
For the use of fables in French medieval sculpture see J. Adhémar, *Influences antiques dans l'art du moyen-âge français*, London, 1939, pp.223-230. For the fables in the Bayeux Tapestry borders see H. Chefneux, 'Les fables dans la tapisserie de Bayeux', *Romania*, LX, 1934, pp.1-35; A. Goldschmidt, 'An early manuscript of the Aesop Fables of Avianus and related manuscripts', Princeton, 1945.

46. Zarnecki, *Regional Schools*, p.37. M.R. James, *A Bestiary of the Twelfth Century*, Roxburghe Club, Oxford, 1928. G.C. Druce, 'The stall carvings in the church of St Mary of Charity, Faversham', *AC*, L, 1938, pp.24-25.

47. London, B.L., MS Cotton Cleopatra C.VIII of the late 10th century; see *Anglo-Saxon Art*, p.65. There are convincing parallels for the figures in various illustrated versions of Prudentius, notably a Carolingian copy (Brussels, Bibl. Royale, MS 9987-91); cf. A. Katzenellenbogen, *Allegories of Virtue and Vice in Medieval Art*, London, 1939.

48. Dodwell, p.64; see also L. Wehrhahn-Stauch, 'Christliche Fischsymbolik von den Anfängen bis zum hohen Mittelalter', *Zeitschrift für Kunstgeschichte*, 35, 1972, pp.1-68. I am grateful to Professor Kauffmann for providing me with this reference.

49. Dublin, Trinity College, MS 53, fols. 4r and 4v. A. Heimann, 'A twelfth-century manuscript from Winchcombe and its illustrations, Dublin Trinity College MS 5.3', *JWCI*, 28, 1965, pp.86-106.

50. 'But in the cloister, under the eyes of the Brethren who read there, what profit is there in those ridiculous monsters, in that marvellous and deformed comeliness, that comely deformity? To what purpose are those unclean apes, those fierce lions, those monstrous centaurs, those half-men, those striped tigers, those fighting knights, those hunters winding their horns?...'. For this translation of St Bernard's *Apologia*, see C. Davis-Weyer, *Early Medieval Art 300-1150*, Medieval Academy of America, Toronto, 1986, p.170. For the Latin text, see *Apologia ad Guillelmum*, Migne, *PL*, CLXXXII, col.916.

51. For the use of this motif on Roman imposts see for instance E. von Merklin, *Antike Figuralkapitelle*, Berlin, 1962, pp.261-266.

52. T.F.C. Blagg, *Roman Architectural Ornament in Britain*, Ph.D. thesis, University of London, 1981, pp.195-199, shows that the motif may derive from bundles of laurel leaves. It was relatively common throughout Roman Britain, though in Kent only one fragment of the motif survives at Springhead.

53. J.C. Higgitt, 'The Roman background to medieval England', *JBAA*, XXXVI, 3rd series, 1973, pp.1-15; Adhémar, op. cit., see note 45

54. See R.W. Scheller, *A Survey of Medieval Model Books*, Haarlem, 1963, pp.53-63.

55. E. Vergnolle, 'Un carnet de modèles de l'an mil originaire de Saint-Benoît-sur-Loire', *Arte Medievale*, II, 1984, pp.1-34, 23-56; id., *Saint-Benoît-sur-Loire et la sculpture du XIe siècle*, Paris, 1985, pp.118-122.

56. Only the engaged semi-columns have cushion capitals, which are plain, though no doubt they were originally painted.

57. Certainly we cannot be expected to believe Gervase's statement that at the time of Anselm's choir, axes were the sole tools of sculptors; Gervase, I, p.27.

58. M.R. James was the first to draw attention to Master Hugo's interdisciplinary activities (*On the Abbey of St Edmunds at Bury*, Cambridge, 1895, especially pp.7, 134, 199). Cf. also C.M. Kauffmann, 'The Bury Bible (Cambridge, Corpus Christi College, MS 2)', *JWCI*, XXIX, 1966, pp.60-81; G. Zarnecki, *English Romanesque Lead Fonts: Lead Fonts of the Twelfth Century*, London, 1957, pp.7, 28-29.

59. For Ely see G. Zarnecki, *Early Sculpture of Ely*, London, 1958, pp.10-13, pls.2-12; for Hereford see G. Zarnecki, *ERA*, p.157; M. Thurlby, 'A note on the Romanesque sculpture at Hereford Cathedral and the Herefordshire school of sculpture', *Burlington Magazine*, CXXVI, April 1984, pp.233-234; for Durham and Gloucester see G. Zarnecki, *English Romanesque Sculpture 1066-1140*, London, 1951, pp.12-13, pls.3-9; for Westminster see G. Zarnecki, *ERA*, pp.154-155; for Winchester, ibid., pp.150-151.

60. Zarnecki, op. cit. note 21, pp.38-42.

61. The chronology of Romsey Abbey is still very uncertain, but see M.F. Hearne, 'A note on the chronology of Romsey Abbey', *JBAA*, XXXII, 1969, pp.29-37, and id., 'Romsey Abbey, a progenitor of the English national tradition', *Gesta*, XIV/i, 1975, pp.27-40.

62. See G. Zarnecki, *ERA*, p.186. For the Westminster capital see W.R. Lethaby, *Westminster Abbey Re-examined*, London, 1925, p.35, fig.20. The capital was already broken when Zarnecki photographed it in 1948 (Zarnecki, *Regional Schools*, p.78, n.1). It has since been lost altogether.

63. For Worcester see C.M. Kauffmann, 'Manuscript illumination at Worcester in the eleventh and twelfth centuries', *BAA CT*, Worcester, 1978, pp.45-46; for other links between the two communities, see A. Gransden, 'Cultural transition at Worcester in the Anglo-Norman period', *BAA CT*, Worcester, 1978, p.9.
For Durham: A. Lawrence, 'The influence of Canterbury on the collection and production of manuscripts at Durham in the Anglo-Norman period', *The Vanishing Past. Studies in Medieval Art, Liturgy and Metrology presented to Christopher Hohler*, British Archaeological Report, III, 1981, pp.94-104; and M. Baker, 'Bede's Life of St Cuthbert', *JWCI*, 41, 1978, p.19. R.A.B. Mynors, *Durham Cathedral Manuscripts to the end of the Twelfth Century*, Durham, 1939.

64. Ernulf 'fecit dormitorium, capitulum (et) refectorium'; see J. Thorpe, *Registrum Roffense*, London, 1769, p.120. These buildings must have been destroyed in the fire of 1137 which consumed the offices of the bishop, the monks and the entire town, forcing the temporary transfer of the monks to other communities (Gervase, I, p.100, and *VCH, Kent*, II, ed. W. Page, 1926, p.121). For the monastic buildings at Rochester Cathedral, see Kahn, pp.57-70.

65. The chapter house doorway is badly eroded, but see Thorpe, op. cit. note 64, pl.XXXVIII, for a clear engraving. The motif also entered the ornamental repertoire of local illuminators where it is sometimes specifically identifiable (Cambridge, St John's College, MS 8, f.91).

66. A local Canterbury example of this motif is London, B.L., MS Arundel 91, f.206v, initial B; see C.M. Kauffmann, *ERA*, p.156.
For the most extensive treatment of sculpture from St Augustine's, see Zarnecki, *Regional Schools*, pp.70-76. For new discoveries, see J. Geddes, 'Recently discovered Romanesque sculpture in South-east England', *SAOP*, 1983, pp.95-96; D. Sherlock and H. Woods, 'St Augustine's Abbey: Report on Excavations', *Kent Archaeological Society*, Maidstone, 1988, especially pp.89-99. See also J.P. McAleer, 'The Ethelbert tower, St Augustine's, Canterbury', *JBAA*, CXL, 1987, pp.88-111.

67. S.E. Rigold in 'The demesne of Christ Church at Brook', *Proceedings of the Royal Archaeological Institute*, 1969, p.96, argues that the church at Brook may have been used by Anselm for his private devotions.

68. Fernie (op. cit. note 19, pp.27-38) was the first to call attention to this point; see also id., 'The spiral piers of Durham Cathedral', *BAA CT*, III, 1980, pp.49-58.

69. J. Toynbee and J.W. Ward-Perkins, *The Shrine of St Peter*, London, 1956, p.205. J.W. Ward-Perkins, 'The shrine of St Peter and its twelve spiral columns', *Journal of Roman Studies*, XLII, 1952, pp.21-33.

70. A. Blunt, 'The Temple of Solomon with special reference to South Italian Baroque art', *Kunsthistorische Forschungen: Otto Pächt zu seinem 70 Geburtstag*, ed. A. Rosenauer and G. Weber, Vienna, 1972, pp.258-265. Cf. also E. Bertaux, *L'art dans l'Italie méridionale*, I, Paris, 1904, p.75, for the inscribed columns in Otranto crypt.

71. P. Kidson (P. Murray and P. Thompson), *A History of English Architecture*, Harmondsworth, 1965, p.31. Spiral columns used in manuscripts sometimes had associations with St Peter's; see E. Rosenbaum, 'The vine columns of Old St

Peter's in Carolingian canon tables', *JWCI*, XVIII, 1955, pp.1-15.

72. '... ex quadam parte ad imitationem ecclesiae beati apostolorum principis Petri in qua sacratissimae reliquiae illius totius orbis veneratione celebrantur, decenter composita', '... cripta quam confessionem Romani vocant. Subtus erat ad instar confessionis sancti Petri fabricata'; *Anglia Sacra*, II, p.206. See Gem, 'Towards an iconography of Anglo-Saxon architecture', *JWCI*, 48, 1983, pp.5-6.

73. Southern, *St Anselm*, p.165.

74. Ibid., pp.135-136.

75. Gervase, I, p.6; Willis (1845), pp.35-36.
The new choir had an aisled presbytery of nine bays with an apse and ambulatory of seven bays. It had eastern transepts each with two apsidal chapels and three radiating chapels (A.W. Clapham, *English Romanesque Architecture After the Conquest*, Oxford, 1934, p.48). For an analysis of the appearance of the choir, see F. Woodman, *The Architectural History of Canterbury Cathedral*, London, 1981, pp.45-76. The cathedral was planned with a double transept. The only other church at that time with a double transept was Cluny. Southern, *St Anselm*, p.260, attributes this to the visit Archbishop Anselm made to Cluny in 1099, but the Cluny plan must have been known in Canterbury some years before and surely before 1095 when the east end was consecrated by Pope Urban II. By this date the plans for the Canterbury choir must have been well advanced.

76. G.T. Rivoira, *Lombardic Architecture. Its Origin, Development and Derivatives*, London, 1910, pp.167-168.

77. For the most recent views on the issue, see E. Fernie, 'Reconstructing Edward's abbey at Westminster', *Romanesque and Gothic*, pp.63-67. Capitals similar to those at Jumièges were used at Ste-Marie-de-la-Charité (later known as Ronceray) in Angers, which was founded in 1028. J. Mallet, *L'art roman de l'ancien Anjou*, Paris, 1984, fig.27.
See also G. Zarnecki, 'Romanesque sculpture in Normandy and England in the eleventh century', *PBC*, 1979, pp.176-177. Zarnecki speculated that William the Conqueror shifted the Westminster masons to work on his important new keep in London, and this would account for the appearance of the capital type in St John's chapel in the Tower. R. Gem, in 'The Romanesque rebuilding of Westminster Abbey', *PBC*, 1981, p.60, argues that the dorter at Westminster Abbey dates to 1070. If he is correct, then the tau-cross capitals in the abbey dorter pre-date those of the Tower (1077-87).

78. T.M.C. Crum and M.M. Crum, 'The tau-cross capitals in the undercroft of Canterbury Cathedral', *AC*, 45, 1933, pp.193-200.

79. See Chapter II, note 16.

80. Most of the arcade on the north side (east of the transept) was replaced during the 19th century. Unfortunately there are no records concerning the 19th-century restoration of the outside of the choir.

81. Mr Durnan carried out the conservation work and I undertook the art historical recording. All our documentation is stored in Canterbury Cathedral Library.

82. Eadmer (*Hist. Nov.*, pp.107-110) goes into great detail about his visit with Archbishop Anselm to Bari in 1098.

83. Nor did the Canterbury sculptures serve as an inspiration for Continental art. There are faint echoes in Scandinavia (e.g. Trondheim Cathedral), but Continental sculpture is mute of all direct reference to Canterbury; see E.B. Hohler, 'The capitals of Urnes church and their background', *Acta Archaeologia*, 1976, pp.1-46. Such parallels as exist (e.g. the doorway capitals of Goult Priory in Normandy, the choir chapel capitals at Fécamp Abbey, the Marmoutier Abbey crypt capitals, and the apse capitals of La Trinité at Caen) are the result of similar manuscript models rather than of direct English influence. For Goult see L. Grodecki, 'Le prieuré de Goult', *CA*, CXI, 1953, pp.350-353; for Fécamp see J. Vallery-Radot, *CA*, LXXXIX, 1927, pp.431-433; G. Zarnecki (op. cit. note 32, p.102), demonstrated that the use of 'Winchester acanthus' in the church of Guillaume de Ros (1082-1108) at Fécamp, derived from manuscripts rather than sculpture; C. Lelong, 'Recherches sur l'abbatiale de Marmoutier à l'époque romane', *Comptes rendus de l'Académie des Inscriptions et Belles-Lettres*, Paris, 1976, pp.732-733, and id., 'L'abbatiale romane de Marmoutier (1066-1096)', *BM*, 145/ii, 1987, pp.173-204.

84. It is worth remembering here that this period witnessed a revival of the Anglo-Saxon past; see F. Wormald, 'The survival of Anglo-Saxon illumination after the Norman Conquest', *Proceedings of the British Academy*, XXX, 1944, pp.1-19; T.D. Kendrick, 'Instances of Saxon survival in post-Conquest sculpture', *Proceedings of the Cambridgeshire Antiquarian Society*, XXXIX, 1940, pp.78-84; G. Zarnecki, op. cit. note 58, pp.10-12, 32-33.

Notes to III : Theobald

1. *The Letters of John of Salisbury*, I, ed. and transl. W.J. Millor, H.E. Butler and C.N.L. Brooke, London 1955, p.161, letter 101.

2. J. le Patourel, *The Norman Empire*, Oxford, 1976, especially Ch.4; J. Boussard, *Le gouvernement d'Henri Plantagenet*, Paris, 1956.

3. *The Historical Works of Master Ralph de Diceto, Dean of London*, ed. W. Stubbs, *Rolls Series*, LXVIII, i, London, 1876, p.351.

4. In fact, Theobald headed the list recorded by Abbot Suger of those at the consecration of the twenty-six altars at Saint-Denis; see *Abbot Suger. On the Abbey Church of St.-Denis and its Art Treasures*, ed. and transl. E. Panofsky, Princeton, 1946, p.119.

5. C.H. Haskins, *The Renaissance of the Twelfth Century*, New York, 1970, pp.49-51. For Nigel Wireker see Knowles, pp.677-678.
   The evidence for John of Salisbury's early arrival in Theobald's household is provided in Saltman, *Theobald*, p.171. See also R.L. Poole, 'The early correspondence of John of Salisbury', *Proceedings of the British Academy*, XI, 1924-1925, pp.27-53; H. Liebeschütz, *Medieval Humanism in the Life and Writings of John of Salisbury*, London, 1950.

6. A charter records Archbishop Theobald's donation of this property to the monks. Saltman (*Theobald*, p.273, charter no.46) published the charter, and dated it to between 1154 and 1160 on the basis of the witnesses present.

7. 'Hic inter multa bona opera quae fecit isti ecclesiae aqueductum cum stagnis et lavatoriis et piscinis suis fieri fecit, quam aquam fere milliario ab urbe intra curiam, et sic per omnes ipsius curiae officinas, mirabiliter transduxit'; see Willis (1869), pp.182-183. Gervase, I, p.146 describes Wibert as 'virum commendabilem et in operibus bonis mirabilem'.

8. 'licet etiam bene litteratus esset et eloquentiae studens, erat tamen in exterioribus insufficiens procurator'; Gervase, I, p.143.
   For Wibert as subprior see Gervase, I, p.146. There is disagreement about the date at which Wibert became prior and the deposition of his predecessor, Walter Parvus; see Urry (1967), p.6, n.1; D. Knowles, C.N.L. Brooke and V. London, *Heads of Religious Houses, England and Wales*, Cambridge, 1972, p.34.

9. Gervase, I, pp.144 and 146. For the lavish meals served to guests at the prior's table in the late 12th century, see Knowles, p.463. Monks presumably ate a more modest diet.

10. Urry (1967), pp.206, 221-225. Urry believed that Wibert's two primary objectives in making these acquisitions were to establish a strategic boundary for the cathedral precinct and to build up the endowments of the monastery. For more on this point see W. Urry, 'Saint Anselm and his cult at Canterbury', *Spicilegium Beccense*, I, 1959, pp.571-593.

11. Two wells from the previous water system at Canterbury Cathedral are shown on the water-works plan. Presumably they were retained as a precaution, in case the new system failed.

12. The excavations at St Augustine's have been incompletely published, but for the cloister laver see P. Bennett, 'Rescue excavations in the outer court of St Augustine's Abbey 1983-1984', *AC*, CIII, 1986, pp.79-117, especially pp.98-99.

13. H. Brakspear, *Waverley Abbey. The Surrey Archaeological Society*, London, 1905, pp.89-90; for Churchdown, *Materials*, I, p.253, II, p.263; *Memorials of St Edmund's Abbey*, ed. T. Arnold, *Rolls Series*, LXLVI, ii, London, 1892, p.292. For the above references and many later examples of water systems see L.F. Salzman, *Building in England Down to 1540*, Oxford, 1952, pp.266-276; see also W.H. St John Hope, 'The London Charterhouse and its old water supply', *Archaeologia*, LVIII, 1902, pp.293-312.
    For Durham see W.H. Hope and J.T. Fowler, 'Recent discoveries in the cloister of Durham Abbey', *Archaeologia*, vol. LVIII (1902), especially pp.444-457. For Lewes see W.H. St John Hope, 'The Cluniac priory of St Pancras at Lewes', *Sussex Archaeological Collections*, XLIX, 1906, pp.72-73. Also, see W.H. Godfrey, 'English cloister lavatories as independent structures', *Arch Jnl*, CVI, suppl., 1949, pp.91-97.

14. Gervase, I, p.146. Walter Durdent was Bishop of Lichfield 1149-1159; see J. Gould, 'The twelfth century water-supply to Lichfield close', *Antiquaries Journal*, LVI, 1976, pp.75-79. Another ambitious water-supply system of the late 12th century was installed at Dover Castle; see A.W. Clapham, 'Dover Castle', *Arch Jnl*, LXXXVI, 1929, pp.254-255.
    The model on which the water system at Canterbury was based is no longer known. The obvious written sources to consult would have been Vitruvius or Frontinus; see Vitruvius, *De architectura*, ed. and transl. F. Granger, II, Cambridge, 1962, book VIII; C. Herschel, *The Two Books on the Water-Supply of the City of Rome by Sextus Julius Frontinus*, London, 1913. For Roman engineering skills see T. Ashby, *Aqueducts of Ancient Rome*, Oxford, 1935. Frontinus would have been the better source for technical information, but if either was used it is more

likely to have been Vitruvius, for there was a copy of his manuscript at St Augustine's (London, B.L., MS Cotton Cleopatra D.I). Vitruvius devoted one of his ten books to water, explaining not only how to locate a good spring but also the construction of aqueducts, wells and cisterns.

15. Both drawings are bound with the Eadwine Psalter, which is now in Trinity College, Cambridge, MS R.17.I, fols.284v to 286; see M.R. James, *The Canterbury Psalter*, London, 1935. The drawings were first published by the Society of Antiquaries of London in *Vetusta Monumenta*, II, 1755, pl.XV. The psalter has traditionally been dated to 1147; see Dodwell, pp.41-47; C.M. Kauffmann (*ERA*, p.119) dates it *c*.1150-1160. The portrait of the scribe Eadwine which is contained in the psalter has recently been dated on stylistic grounds to around 1170; see G. Zarnecki, 'The Eadwine portrait', *Etudes d'art médiéval offertes à Louis Grodecki*, eds. S. McKnight Crosby *et al.*, Paris, 1981, pp.93-104. A forthcoming publication of the psalter to be edited by M. Gibson and T.A. Heslop will no doubt cast light on many unsolved problems concerning the manuscript and put to rest the claims of D. Verfaille-Markey, 'Le dernier cahier du Psautier d'Eadwine', *Scriptorium*, XXXVII, 1983, pp.245-258.
For Wibert's donations to Canterbury see J.W. Legg and W.H. St John Hope, *Inventories of Christchurch Canterbury*, London, 1902, p.44.

16. It would take an entire volume to do justice to the plans. For a recent treatment with a current bibliography see W. Urry, 'Canterbury, Kent', *Local Maps and Plans from Medieval England*, eds. R.A. Skelton and P.D.A. Harvey, Oxford, 1986, pp.43-58.

17. See A. Gransden, 'Realistic observation in twelfth-century England', *Speculum*, XLVII/4, October, 1972, pp.29-51. For St Gall see W. Horn and E. Born, *The Plan of St Gall*, Berkeley, 1979.

18. See Willis (1869), p.4. Urry (op. cit. note 16, pp.47-49) believed that the drawings were earlier because the almonry, which is absent from the plan, was constructed by 1161 when its 'new wall' is referred to in a charter. But Urry argues that the plan cannot date from much before that year, because the *aula nova* is shown as complete and the site was still in private hands in the 1150s. His dating assumes that the 'Canterbury plan is a view of developments which had actually taken place'; however, it is hard to imagine how such an enormous project which included not only a great number of new monastic buildings but also additions to the church and the laying of great lengths of pipes

and drains could have taken place in so short a time.

19. W. Gostling (*A Walk in and Around the City of Canterbury*, Canterbury, 1825, pp.203-206, first published in 1777) calls the building a 'baptistry', no doubt because of its shape. S. Denne, 'Evidence of a lavatory appertaining to the Benedictine priory of Canterbury Cathedral and observations on fonts', *Archaeologia*, XI, 1794, p.108, was the first author to refute this, though the building continued to be called a 'baptistry' for some time.

20. It has been calculated that with the use of two and a half inch lead pipes, the monastery was able to obtain 2000 gallons of water an hour; see J. Hayes, 'Prior Wibert's waterworks', *The Canterbury Chronicle*, LXXI, 1977, p.25. Urry (op. cit. note 16, p.54) records that the primary pipes had a circular bore of 55-60mm. and the secondary pipes of 35mm.
Professor Cesar Mendoza-Cabrales of the Civil Engineering and Engineering Mechanics Department of Columbia University was most generous with his time and his help in interpreting the functioning of the water system at Christ Church.

21. At ground level, external buttresses were added to counter the outward thrust of the vault, and the central drum was restored. Work on the upper storey was also undertaken in the later Middle Ages when the walls were heightened and Gothic windows were inserted.
For a fuller architectural description see D. Caröe, 'The water tower', *Friends of Canterbury Cathedral*, January, 1929, pp.25-37. Urry's view (op. cit. note 16, p.56) that the structure was built in two stages in the 12th century is most unlikely.

22. The only roughly contemporary building in England with dogtooth is the north doorway on the west front of Lincoln Cathedral; see G. Zarnecki, *Romanesque Lincoln*, Lincoln, 1987, p.26, fig.16. For the use of dogtooth in France, see note 69.

23. The lobed shape was the common form for fountains and basins across Europe; see G. Zarnecki, 'A late Romanesque fountain from Campania', *Minneapolis Institute of Arts Bulletin*, 1973, pp.1-10 (reprinted in Zarnecki, *Studies*). It is even found in fonts, e.g. Stafford; see F. Bond, *Fonts and Font Covers*, London, 1908, p.110.
See also B. Davidson, 'A carved fragment of Purbeck marble from a late twelfth-century fountain in the Palace of Westminster', *Antiquaries Journal*, LV, 1975, p.399, pl.LXXXIII; G. Zarnecki, *ERA*, pp.200-202.
For Durham laver see *Rites of Durham*, ed. J.T.

Fowler, Surtees Society, CVII, 1902, pp.82-83; see also W.H. Hope and J.T. Fowler, 'Recent discoveries in the cloister of Durham Abbey', *Archaeologia*, LVIII, 1902, pp.437-460.

24. H. Brakspear, 'Purbeck marble capitals and bases from St Nicholas priory, Exeter', *Proceedings of the Society of Antiquaries*, 1915-1916, pp.245-250; F. Anderson 'The Tournai marble sculptures from Lewes Priory', *Sussex Archaeological Collections*, 122, 1984, p.86.
See also Caröe (op. cit. note 21); cf. also G.D. Drury, 'The use of Purbeck marble in medieval times', *Proceedings of the Dorset Natural History and Archaeological Society*, LXX, 1948, pp.1-28.

25. The building appears in abbreviated form on the plan with only one arch to the south of the stairway and two to the north, but excavations have revealed that originally there was a total of nine bays. Those on the north side of the staircase were dismantled in 1730, and only three bays now remain on the south side. The structure was extensively restored in the 19th century. The first floor and the entire west wall are modern. The interior of the substructure was partitioned by a row of columns which supported groin vaults. Two of these columns remain, both with round scallop-shaped capitals. The sawtooth chevron arches of the east wall are primarily original; these are supported by piers with angle shafts. Two 12th-century bases with prominent almond-shaped spurs also remain. For a complete structural analysis see J. Bowen, 'The architecture of the *aula nova*', and D. Kahn, 'The sculpture of the *aula nova*', *Canterbury Archaeological Trust* (forthcoming).
For the function of the *aula nova* see Willis (1869), pp.15, 148; M. Sparks, 'The *aula nova* documentary evidence', *Canterbury Archaeological Trust Report* (forthcoming); W. Braufels, *The Monasteries of Western Europe*, Princeton, 1972, p.61, suggested that it was modelled on the great guest house at Cluny, but this seems a long shot.

26. For the bases see S.E. Rigold, 'Romanesque bases in and south-east of the limestone belt', *Ancient Monuments and their Interpretations. Essays Presented to A.J. Taylor*, ed. M.R. Apted *et al.*, London, 1977, pp.99-137.
Willis (1869), p.147, postulated that a redirecting of funds following the fire of 1174 delayed completion of the *aula nova* until the early 13th century.

27. The outside walls have been restored, but there are areas of original sculpture, including deeply cut x-in-square, pipeline billet, sawtooth chevron and cable roll. Just below the original roof line is a row of stones carved with pinwheel

motif. In the later Middle Ages an additional room with flint walls was added on the top. Willis (1869), p.79, called this building the treasury. It may be significant that between 1163 and 1167 the financial system of the monastery was centralized by the introduction of a new obedientiary, a *dispensator* or *thesaurarius*. It was his duty to receive the rents of the cellarer, chamberlain and sacrist. There is a remote possibility that the *vestiarium* could have been built in connection with the creation of this new office; see R.A.L. Smith, *Canterbury Cathedral Priory*, Cambridge, 1969, p.14; F.R.H. Du Boulay, *The Lordship of Canterbury*, London, 1966, p.252. Three bays of the south transept at Winchester Cathedral were used as a 'treasury' or 'sacristy'; see Y.L. Kusaba, 'The function, date and stylistic sources of the treasury of Henry of Blois in the south transept of Winchester Cathedral', *Winchester Cathedral Record*, 57, 1988, pp.38-49.

28. Beaded interlacing similar to that in the *vestiarium* decorates the font at St Martin's church, a short distance from the cathedral (ill. 207). This font is composed of separate blocks of Caen stone. The blocks are slightly curved and were clearly intended for a round object, but the interlacing pattern does not match across the joints. T. Tatton-Brown, 'The font in St Martin's church', *Historical Essays in Memory of James Hobbs*, ed. M. Sparks, Canterbury, 1980, pp.19-20, argues that the font is in fact made up of reused stones from the well-head shown on the Canterbury plan in the infirmary cloister and labelled *puteus*; see also F. Bond, op. cit. note 23, p.91.
For carved key-stones see C.J.P. Cave, 'The roof-bosses in Canterbury Cathedral', *Archaeologia*, LXXXIV, 1935, pp.41-42.

29. I am grateful to Mr Dimes, formerly of the Geological Museum, London, for identifying the stone. There are other onyx shafts at Canterbury, in the infirmary cloister and north crypt doorway at Canterbury. This is not the first time that the unusual appearance of the stone has been noted. F. Woodman, *The Architectural History of Canterbury Cathedral*, London, 1981, pp.79-80, suggests that the shafts are of jasper. For a general discussion of *en délit* shafts see J. Bony, 'Origines des piles gothiques à fûts en délit', *Gedenkschrift Ernst Gall*, Berlin/Munich, 1965, pp.95-122.

30. By the second half of the 12th century, this type of stylized scallop capital, with pleated shields, had fully evolved and was relatively widespread in England, as can be seens at Bridlington (Yorkshire), Ivychurch (Wiltshire), Shaftesbury (Dorset) and St Albans (ills. 165-166). The scallop capitals of the so-called Pudsey

doorway at Durham Castle (Bishop Pudsey's years of office were 1154-1195), with their projecting cones and beaded shields (ill. 167), are perhaps the closest in type to the *vestiarium* capital. See J. Bilson, 'Le chapiteau à godrons en Angleterre', *CA*, LXXVII, 1908, pp.645-646.

31. For the implications of this on the date of the wall-paintings in St Gabriel's chapel, see D. Kahn, 'The structural evidence for the dating of the St Gabriel chapel wall-paintings at Christ Church Cathedral, Canterbury', *Burlington Magazine*, CXXVI, April 1984, pp.225-229; M. Caviness, 'Romanesque "belles verrières" in Canterbury?', *Romanesque and Gothic*, pp.35-38.

32. For a different view see Woodman (op. cit. note 29, p.53) who argued that the columns were inserted in the apse openings around 1100.

33. Gervase, I, p.27.

34. T.A. Heslop, 'The conventual seals of Canterbury Cathedral, 1066-1232', *BAA CT*, Canterbury, 1982, p.94. The seal first appears on London, B.L., Additional Charter 67, f.123, which is dated 4 July 1158. Urry (1967), p.384, gives the first use of the seal a wider berth, between 1152 and 1161.

35. These views were expressed in an unpublished paper by G. Zarnecki, 'The St Paul fresco in St Anselm's chapel', read at the Anselm Society Conference in May 1979. Similar conclusions were reached independently by U. Nilgen, 'Thomas Becket as a patron of the arts', *Art History*, III/4, December 1980, pp.357-374. In a private letter Sir Richard Southern calculated that the translation took place either in 1163 or 1168, and in view of the sculpture's similarity with the water tower and *vestiarium* the earlier year is more likely. Moreover, Archbishop Becket (a strong supporter of Anselm's canonization) was in exile by 1168, and this adds weight to the argument that 1163 was the year of the translation. Against this, however, stands the view that Anselm's body was translated in 1146, expressed by R. Foreville in 'Canterbury et la canonisation des saints', *Tradition and Change. Essays in Honour of Marjorie Chibnall*, eds. D. Greenway, C. Holdsworth and J. Sayers, Cambridge, 1985, p.68.
For Anselm's cult at Canterbury see Urry (op. cit. note 10) and Southern, *St Anselm*, pp.337-341.
On the reinforcement of the chapels see W.A. Scott Robertson, 'St Anselm's chapel, Canterbury Cathedral, *AC*, XVIII, 1889, pp.169-173; J.B. Sheppard, 'Discoveries in St Anselm's chapel, Canterbury Cathedral', *AC*, XVIII, 1889, pp.174-176.

36. J. Britton, *Historical and Descriptive Account of the Metropolitan Cathedrals of Canterbury and York*, I, London, 1836, pl.XXII.
The only other church in the region at which a similar moulding occurs is Patrixbourne (c.1170). It was also used at Hyde Abbey, where it survives among the fragments left after the church was burnt in 1141 on the orders of Bishop Henry of Blois during his siege of Empress Matilda.
For the origins of the unusual sunken roundels on the tower see G. Zarnecki, 'The carved stones from Newark Castle', *Transactions of the Thornton Society of Nottinghamshire*, XL, 1955, pp.23-28.

37. C. Dudley, 'The transept towers: a reappraisal', *Canterbury Cathedral Chronicle*, LXXI, 1977, pp.27-34. The argument given here, that the towers were actually moved by William of Sens, is impossible to accept. The burn marks match exactly across the masonry joints, proving that the masonry was never disturbed.

38. A. Borg, 'The development of chevron ornament', *JBAA*, third series, XXX, 1967, pp.122-140, argues that chevron came into use in England during the early 12th century. It has since been shown that it was already in use in the last two decades of the 11th century in Normandy; see G. Zarnecki, 'Romanesque sculpture in Normandy and England in the eleventh century', *PBC*, I, 1978, p.181.

39. The engraving is reproduced in F.W. Cross and J.R. Hall, *Rambles Round Old Canterbury*, London, 1884, p.78. Hackington lies roughly a mile from the centre of Canterbury and was the property of the Archdeacon of Canterbury; see W. Dugdale, *Monasticon Anglicanum*, I, London, 1817, p.89. For the great controversy that surrounded Hackington later in the twelfth century see C.R. Cheney, *Hubert Walter*, London, 1967, p.135; Knowles, pp.319-329.

40. This was formerly assumed to be Tournai stone, but recent tests have proved that it is actually onyx. Tournai shafts were used nearby at about the same period, however, in the cloister at Rochester. For the export of Tournai stone see J.-C. Ghislain, 'Dalles funéraires romanes tournaisiennes en Belgique', *Revue des historiens d'art, des archéologiques, des musicologues et des orientalistes de l'etat à Liège*, II, 1983, pp.53-71. See also note 29.

41. Both the lattice pattern and the *opus reticulatum* have parallels in 12th-century works in Kent, the first on the west wall of the chapter house at Rochester Cathedral, presumably near the middle of the 12th century and the latter on the façade of Rochester Cathedral, also well into

the 12th century; see D. Kahn, 'The west door-way at Rochester Cathedral', *Romanesque and Gothic*, pp.129-134.

42. W.D. Carőe, 'The three towers of Canterbury Cathedral', *Architectural Review*, XVII, 1905, p.3, notes that the walls of the Anglo-Norman tower still exist as high as the second gallery of the lantern. Carőe thought that this masonry dated to Anselm's archiepiscopate and so, according to him, it proved that Anselm had heightened the tower. If the central tower were indeed raised, the gilt cherub with which Lanfranc had crowned the steeple (see Gervase, I, p.9) was saved and moved up to its new position. It is illustrated on the plan, and the name of the central tower, 'the angel steeple', recalls it today.

43. R. Willis, 'The architectural history of Winchester Cathedral', *Proceedings of the Archaeological Institute*, 1846, p.27; for Exeter see A.W. Clapham, *English Romanesque Architecture After the Conquest*, Oxford, 1934, p.48.
The Low Countries and Germany: K.J. Conant, *Carolingian and Romanesque Architecture 800-1200*, Harmondsworth, 1959, p.266. For towers see P. Rolland, 'Chronologie de la cathédrale de Tournai', *RB*, IV, 1934, pp.103-137; for the chronology of the buildings see P. Héliot, 'Les parties romanes de la cathédrale de Tournai', *RB*, XXV, 1956, pp.68-69.

44. J. Bilson, 'The Norman school and the beginnings of Gothic architecture. Two octopartite vaults: Montivilliers and Canterbury', *Arch Jnl*, LXXIV, 1917, pp.1-25. J. Vallery-Radot, 'Montivilliers, église abbatiale', *CA*, LXXXIX, 1926, pp.492-499, argues that the vault at Montivilliers is entirely Norman and bears no trace of influence from the Ile-de-France. He dates them to around 1150-1160. (There are other filiations between Canterbury and Montivilliers too, notably the keystones carved with similar rosettes.) See also J. Bony, 'Diagonality and centrality in early rib-vaulted architecture', *Gesta*, XV, 1976, pp.15-25.

45. M. Baylé, *La Trinité de Caen*, Paris, 1979, p.67. See also the vaults at Saint-Etienne, Caen, Bernières (19th-century copies) and New Shoreham.

46. For La Trinité see Baylé (op. cit. note 45, pp.65-67) and for Saint-Etienne see E. Carlson, *The Abbey Church of Saint-Etienne at Caen*, Ph.D. thesis, Yale University, 1968, pp.110-114, and M. Baylé, 'Les ateliers de sculpture de Saint-Etienne de Caen au XIe et XIIe siècles', *PBC*, X, 1987, pp.1-25. See also R. Fage, 'La décoration géométrique', *CA*, LXXV, ii, 1909, pp.622-623.

47. For the occurence of fret-ornament in Anglo-Saxon times, see 'The columns of Reculver

church', *AC*, III, 1860, pp.135-137. Also on the 9th-century sculptures at Breedon-on-the-Hill, see R.H.I. Jewell, 'The Anglo-Saxon friezes at Breedon-on-the-Hill, Leicestershire', *Archaeologia*, CVIII, 1986, pp. 95-115, especially p.103.
For Old Sarum see R. Stalley, 'A twelfth-century patron of architecture — a study of the buildings erected by Roger, Bishop of Salisbury 1102-1139', *JBAA*, XXXIV, 1971, pp.75-83; For Lincoln see G. Zarnecki, *Romanesque Lincoln*, Lincoln, 1988, pp.22, 99 n.42.

48. This is clear from pre-restoration engravings; see J.S. Cotman, *Architectural Antiquities of Normandy*, London, 1822, pls.28, 29, 31. It is confirmed by examination of the tooling, and by the existence of the same repertoire of motifs at other churches in Lower Normandy, notably Vieux-Saint-Sauveur (ill. 199) and Creuilly. The original vaults at La Trinité were destroyed in 1788 and replaced with oak copies in the following year. Although the supporting capitals may have been damaged during this operation, they do not appear to have been tampered with. Between 1854 and 1862 the vaults were rebuilt in stone by the architect V. Ruprich-Robert. Some capitals were replaced at that time, and many were retouched, but the compositions were largely unchanged. Baylé (op. cit. note 45, pp.171-174) has made a detailed study of the restoration.
There were also numerous scallop capitals. The capital type reached Normandy from England. Their first systematic use in Normandy was at Lessay; see M. Baylé, 'La sculpture romane en normandie à l'époque ducale', *Les siècles romans en basse normandie. Art de basse-normandie*, 92, Spring 1982, p.61. By the time the scallop capital appeared at La Trinité, the capital type had been assimilated as part of the local artistic vocabulary.

49. See L. Musset, *Normandie romane*, I, La-Pierre-qui-Vire, 1975, p.32, for Creuilly; and L. Serbat, 'Vieux-Saint-Sauveur, Caen', *CA*, LXXXV, i, 1908, pp.81-86, for Caen.

50. The great Norman abbey at Bec provided Canterbury with a succession of eminent archbishops : Lanfranc, Anselm and Theobald. After Becket's martyrdom, the archbishopric was offered to yet another abbot of Bec, Roger, but he refused it, see Saltman, *Theobald*, p.3; see also M. Gibson, 'History of Bec in the twelfth century', *The Writing of History in the Middle Ages. Essays Presented to R.W. Southern*, eds. R.H.C. Davis and J.M. Wallace-Hadrill, Oxford, 1981, pp.167-186. It would be interesting to know something of the abbey's physical appearance, but it was almost entirely destroyed during the

Revolution; see A.A. Porée, *Histoire de l'abbaye du Bec*, I, II, Evreux, 1901.

51. There is no good building stone in the region. For other building stones used at Canterbury see T. Tatton-Brown, 'The use of Quarr stone in London and East Kent', *Medieval Archaeology*, XXIV, 1980, pp.213-215.
    For the export of Caen stone see L.F. Salzman, *Building in England Down to 1540*, Oxford, 1952, pp.135-136; L. Gosselin, 'La pierre de Caen dans l'histoire', *Bulletin de la société des antiquaries de normandie*, LVII, 1963-1964, p.621. For the most complete and recent article on the subject see L. Musset, 'La pierre de Caen: extraction et commerce, XIe-XVe siècles', *Pierre et métal dans le bâtiment au moyen-âge*, eds. O. Châpelot and P. Benoît, Paris, 1985, pp.219-235.

52. There are various architectural fragments from St Augustine's Abbey with architectural mouldings which are related to those at Christ Church; see C. Miscampbell, 'A twelfth-century re-building at St Augustine's Abbey, Canterbury', *Collectanea Historica: Essays in Memory of Stuart Rigold*, ed. A. Detsicas, Maidstone, 1981, pp.63-65. The finds at Leeds Priory included architectural fragments related to those from Christ Church; P.J. Tester, 'Excavations on the site of Leeds Priory Part I — the church', *AC*, XCIII, 1977, pp.33-45; id., 'Excavations on the site of Leeds Priory Part II — the claustral buildings and other remains', *AC*, XCIV, 1978, pp.75-98. Much material has perished; see R.C. Jenkins, 'On some fragments of Norman building recently discovered at Great Woodlands in the parish of Lyminge', *AC*, IV, 1861, pp.123-126.

53. K.P. Whitney, *The Jutish Forest. A Study of the Weald of Kent from 450-1380 AD*, London, 1976, pp.104-154.

54. See the illustration of fragments (now lost) in W.R. Lethaby, *Westminster Abbey Re-examined*, London, 1925, p.33, fig.15. See also F. Slater, 'Chislet church', *AC*, XII, 1878, pp.106-112; C.E. Keyser, *Norman Tympana and Lintels*, London, 1927, p.12; and M. Livett, 'Notes on the church of St-Margaret-at-Cliffe', *AC*, XXIV, 1900, pp.175-180.

55. See J. Puckle, 'The ancient fabric of the church of St Mary the Virgin, Dover', *AC*, XX, 1893, pp.119-127. L.S. Stone, *Sculpture in Britain: The Middle Ages*, Harmondsworth, 1955, p.85, noted the general influence of Normandy at St-Margaret-at-Cliffe and Sandwich.

56. The *aula nova* provides a *terminus ante quem* of *c*.1160. Land purchases provide the *terminus post quem* of *c*.1152. Thus the architectural evidence clearly pin-points the date around 1155,

which is contemporary with the style of the water tower, *aula nova*, *vestiarium*, etc.

57. Fairly exact manuscript parallels can also be found. There is a close similarity between the alternating lozenge and circular frames of the gateway and London B.L., MS Arundel 60, f.85v; see Kauffmann, p.53.

58. The style which relies so heavily on geometric ornament, associated with the hydraulic system, played a relatively small role: the pipeline billet and chevron of the side niches and the sunken roundels are the only evidence of its influence. The same motifs appear in the roundels in the upper walls. This was heavily restored by Austin.

59. F. Spurell, 'Architectural relics of Lewes Priory', *Sussex Archaeological Collections*, VI, 1853, p.258, fig.11.

60. The same image also occurs on an oak casket from Canterbury of around 1150-1160; see G. Zarnecki, 'A Romanesque casket from Canterbury in Florence', *Canterbury Cathedral Chronicles*, 64, 1969, pp.37-43.

61. M.M. Postan, *The Medieval Economy and Society*, Harmondsworth, 1978, p.213; T.H. Lloyd, *The English Wool Trade in the Middle Ages*, Cambridge, 1977, Ch. 1. For trade with the Flemings see C. Brooke and G. Keir, *London 800-1216: the Shaping of a City*, London, 1975, pp.268, 275; for Flemings in the town of Canterbury, see Urry (1967), p.171.

62. See C. Enlart, *Monuments religieux de l'architecture romane et de transition dans la région Picardie*, Amiens/Paris, 1895; P. Héliot, *Les églises du moyen-âge dans le Pas-de-Calais*, Arras, 1951-1953. For Arras and Cambrai see J. Vanuxem, 'Les portails détruits de la cathédrale de Cambrai et de Saint Nicolas d'Amiens', *BM*, CIII, 1945, pp.89-102; id., 'La sculpture du XIIe à Cambrai et à Arras', *BM*, CXIII, 1955, pp.1-35; L. Serbat, 'Quelques églises anciennes détruites du nord de la France', *BM*, 1929, pp.365-435.

63. Exh. cat., *Sculptures romanes et gothiques du Nord de la France*, Musée des Beaux-Arts de Lille, 1978-1979, 89, no.18. The fragments are deposited in the Musée de l'Hôtel Sandelin at Saint-Omer.

64. Saltman, *Theobald*, pp.25-28. See also C. Kelleher, *Illumination of Saint-Bertin at Saint-Omer under Odbert*, Ph.D. thesis, Courtauld Institute, 1968; P. Grierson, 'The relations between England and Flanders before the Norman Conquest', *Essays in Medieval History*, ed R.W. Southern, London, 1968, pp.61-92.

65. Gervase, I, pp.99-100; Knowles, p.365. N.E. Toke, 'The opus Alexandrinum and sculpted stone roundels in the retro-choir of Canterbury Cathedral', *AC*, XLII, 1930, pp.189-221, especially p.194, believed that the pavement in the choir of Canterbury was produced by craftsmen from St Bertin. For the most recent assessment of the pavement see E. Eames, 'Notes on the decorated stone roundels in the Corona and Trinity Chapel in Canterbury Cathedral', *BAA CT*, Canterbury, 1982, pp.67-70. For the re-paving see E.C. Norton and M.C. Horton, 'A Parisian workshop at Canterbury. The late thirteenth century tile pavement in the Corona Chapel, and the origins of Tyler Hill', *JBAA*, CXXXIV, 1981, pp.58-80.

66. R. Eales, 'Local loyalties in Norman England: Kent in Stephen's reign', *PBC*, 1986, pp.88-108. William of Ypres contributed to building campaigns both in Kent and in Flanders, for instance he donated money for the rebuilding of Saint-Bertin after the fire there in 1152. He also made gifts of Kentish property to the Flemish abbey, and as a result of these gifts an alien cell of Saint-Bertin was established at Throwley, near Canterbury; see *VCH, Kent*, II, ed. W. Page, London, 1926, p.239.

67. R. Branner, 'Gothic architecture 1160-1180 and its Romanesque sources', *Romanesque and Gothic Studies in Western Art. Acts of the Twentieth International Congress of the History of Art*, I, New York, 1963, pp.92-104. For metalwork see G. Zarnecki, *English Romanesque Lead Sculpture: Lead Fonts of the Twelfth Century*, London, 1957, p.12, and N. Stratford, 'Niello in England in the twelfth century', *SAOP*, 1986, pp.31-45. For manuscripts see C.R. Dodwell, *The Great Lambeth Bible*, London, 1959, pp.16-19. R.M. Thomson, *Manuscripts from St Albans Abbey 1066-1235*, Woodbridge, 1985, pp.31-33, has recently argued that the Lambeth Bible was made not for Canterbury, but for St Albans Abbey. See also M.-R. Lapiere, *La lettre ornée dans les manuscrits mosans d'origine bénédictines (XIe-XIIe siècle)*, Bibliothèque de la faculté de philosophie et lettres de l'université de Liège, CCXXIX, Paris, 1981.

68. It was during this period that Swalon, subdeacon of Saint-Amand from 1143, was active as an illuminator as proved by his signature in the five-volume bible at Valenciennes (MS 1-5 and 186). The elongated dragon was a favorite motif of this artist; see A. Boutemy, 'Quelques aspects de l'oeuvre de Swalon, decorateur de manuscrits à l'abbaye de Saint-Amand', *RB*, IX, 1939, pp.299-316. For the Floreffe Bible (London, B.L., Add. MS 17737) and its *terminus ante quem* of 1139, see G. Chapman, 'The Bible of Floreffe: redating of a Romanesque manuscript', *Gesta*, X/2, 1971, pp.49-62. See for example f.13v, initial P. These blossoms also occur in local Canterbury manuscripts, but they and other decorative features probably signify artistic exchange between England and Flanders, see T.A. Heslop, 'Dunstan Archiepiscopus and painting in Kent around 1120', *Burlington Magazine*, CXXVI, April 1984, pp.195-204. See Douai, Bibl. Communale, MS 232, f.2r, for the connection with Anchin Abbey.

69. For the use of dogstooth in the Soissonais and in Picardy, see J. Bony, 'French influences on English Gothic architecture', *JWCI*, XXII, 1949, p.8. There are other parallels, such as the lion masks of the *vestiarium* boss and the similar masks of the keystones at Saint-Germer-en-Fly; see J. Henriet, 'Une édifice de la première génération gothique: L'abbatiale de Saint-Germer-en-Fly', *BM*, 143/ii, 1985, fig.21. The rich carving on the vault ribs at Saint-Germer-en-Fly is also similar to the archivolts of the *porta curie* (see ibid., pp.125-126).

70. M.M. Postan, *Medieval Trade and Finance*, Cambridge, 1973, pp.150-157.

71. There are numerous examples as illustrated in J.J.M. Timmers' survey *De Kunst van het Maasland*, Essen, 1971, pl.304 (Tongres), pl.339 (Maastricht), pl.335 (Hakendover); for Utrecht see L. Tollenaere, *La sculpture sur pierre de l'ancien diocèse de Liège à l'époque roman*, Namur, 1957, pl.II; for further comparative illustrations, see H.A. Dieppen, *Die Romanische Bauornamentik in Klosterrath*, The Hague, 1931, pls.LXVI, LXXXVI.

72. D. Radocsay, 'Vier verlorengegangene romanische Kapitelle aus der Sammlung Schnütgen', *Westfalen*, XLII, 1964, pp.225-233, especially p.230.

Notes to IV : Becket

1. For relations between Henry II and Becket, see W.L. Warren, *Henry II*, London, 1977, pp.447-517; R. Foreville, *L'église et la royauté en Angleterre sous Henri II Plantagenet (1154-1189)*, Paris, 1943.

2. R.W. Southern 'The monks of Canterbury and the murder of Archbishop Becket', *Friends of Canterbury Cathedral*, 1985, p.12. Becket's administrative *acta* are far less copious than his diplomatic correspondence; see *English Episcopal Acta, Canterbury 1162-1190*, ed. C.R. Cheney and B.E.A. Jones, London, 1986, p.xxiii.

3. This was despite the fact that Becket had a reputation for loving splendour. M.D. Knowles, 'Archbishop Thomas Becket. A character study', *Proceedings of the British Academy*, XXXV, 1949, pp.11-12; U. Nilgen, 'Intellectuality and splendour: Thomas Becket as a patron of the arts', *SAOP*, 1986, pp.145-158; id., 'Becket as a patron of the arts', *Art History*, III/4, December, 1980, pp.357-374.

4. If Prior Eastry's early 14th-century catalogue can be relied upon, the *Libri Sancti Thome* included a complete set of glossed books of the Bible as well as other glossed texts; see James, pp.82, 510. They are referred to as Becket's *bibliotheca*; see *Materials*, p.87. This group of books have been attributed to Pontigny, which is in the diocese of Sens where Becket spent some of his exile. But C. de Hamel (*Glossed Books of the Bible and the Origins of the Paris Booktrade*, Woodbridge, 1984, pp.53-54) has suggested that they were produced in Paris where Herbert Bosham was working *c.*1174-78. For manuscripts at Canterbury during the second half of the twelfth century and their links with Northern France, especially with Sens, Pontigny and Saint-Bertin at Saint-Omer, see Dodwell, pp.104-113.

5. Gervase, I, p.248; II, pp.395-396. E. Walberg, *La tradition hagiographique de Saint Thomas Becket avant la fin du XIIe siècle*, Paris, 1929.

6. Gervase, I, p.293. His son Philip was to be crowned on his fourteenth birthday in 1179. The ceremony had to be cancelled because the boy became seriously ill. Louis was advised in a dream to seek help from St Thomas. He did so and his son recovered. But the pilgrimage made by King Louis was tinged with tragedy for, on his return from Canterbury, Louis himself had a stroke and was unable to attend his son's coronation.

7. W. Urry, 'Some notes on the resting places of St Thomas Becket at Canterbury', *Thomas Becket actes du colloque international de Sédières*, ed. R. Foreville, Paris, 1975, pp.195-208. Becket's cult was of great financial benefit to the Christ Church community; see C.E. Woodruff, 'The financial aspect of the cult of St Thomas of Canterbury', *AC*, XLIV, 1932, pp.13-32.

8. Gervase, I, pp.244-247 and 249. For Richard see *The Heads of Religious Houses: England and Wales 940-1216*, eds. D. Knowles, C.N.L. Brooke and V. London, Cambridge, 1972, p.88. Richard had previously been chaplain to Archbishop Theobald.

9. Gervase, I, pp.3-4. For the translation see Willis (1845), p.32. According to Urry (1967), p.115,

10. This hypothesis is not new. It was put forward by George Zarnecki in a public lecture entitled 'Canterbury Cathedral', delivered at the University of Manchester in 1962. A similar conclusion was also reached by P. Kidson, 'The Gothic choir', *Arch Jnl*, CXXVI, 1969, pp.244-246.

11. Gervase, I, p.5. For the translation see Willis (1845), p.34. Portions of the infirmary chapel and hall remain, and both are wholly Romanesque (see Appendix I). The fabric is streaked with scorch marks from the fire, but Gervase's statement that they were consumed is clearly an exaggeration.

12. Gervase, I, p.6; Willis (1845), p.5.

13. For a clear summary of the architecture of the choir, see P. Kidson, 'The Gothic choir', *Arch Jnl*, CXXVI, 1969, pp.244-246. The new building had a significant and lasting effect on the country as a whole. In the last two decades of the 12th century almost all major buildings erected in England bear the imprint of the Early Gothic style.

14. Gervase, I, pp.6-7; Willis (1845), pp.35-36. For the most recent surveys of Early Gothic architecture in France see D. Kimpel and R. Suckale, *Die gotische Architektur in Frankreich 1130-1270*, Munich, 1985; J. Bony, *French Gothic Architecture of the 12th and 13th Centuries*, Berkeley, 1983.

15. Gervase, I, pp.48-49. The columns of the external choir arcade of Anselm's church alternate round and octagonal, and this arrangement might also suggest the pattern used in the choir. Gervase, II, pp.414-415, gives an astute comparison of the different appearances of the two choirs.

16. J. Bony, 'French influences on the origins of English Gothic architecture', *JWCI*, XII, 1949, pp.1-16, especially p.7.

17. Gervase, I, pp.22-23; Willis (1845), pp.52-55. For what might have been, see P. Draper, 'William of Sens and the original design of the choir termination of Canterbury Cathedral 1175-1179', *Journal of the Society of Architectural Historians*, XLII/3, October 1983, pp.238-247.

18. K. Severens 'William of Sens and the double columns at Sens and Canterbury', *JWCI*, XXXIII, 1970, pp.307-313. For Sens Cathedral itself see J. Henriet, 'La cathédrale Saint-Etienne de Sens: le parti du premier maître et les campagnes du XIIe siècle', *BM*, CXL, 1982, pp.155-168.

19. The choir capitals, however, had little impact in England. The only really convincing copies are

the fire began in the workshop of the minter Lambin Frese.

at Oakham Castle; see R. Emmerson, 'Twelfth century sculpture at Oakham Castle', *Leicestershire Museums, Art Galleries and Records Service*, 1981. The other sculptures at Oakham, including animals playing musical instruments, may reflect other sculptures in the Canterbury choir which are now lost.

20. R. Mair, 'The choir capitals of Canterbury Cathedral 1174-1184', *BAA CT*, Canterbury, 1982, pp.56-66. Kidson (op. cit. note 13, p.246) stresses the links between the choir capitals and those of Reims.
    For the architectural links between Cambrai and Canterbury see R. Branner, 'The transept of Cambrai Cathedral', *Gedenkschrift Ernst Gall*, Berlin/Munich, 1965, p.74. For sculpture at Cambrai and Arras see J. Vanuxem, 'Les portails détruits de la cathédrale de Cambrai et de St Nicolas d'Amiens', *BM*, CIII, 1945, pp.89-102; id., 'La sculpture du XIIeme siècle a Cambrai et Arras', *BM*, CXIII, 1955, pp.9-15. Nearly all of the sculpture from the destroyed church of Notre-Dame at Valenciennes has vanished; see L. Serbat, 'L'église Notre-Dame de la Grande à Valenciennes', *Revue de l'art chrétien*, XIV, 1903, p.370.

21. C.J.P. Cave, 'The roof-bosses in Canterbury Cathedral', *Archaeologia*, LXXXIV, 1935, p.45. Animal forms are only introduced on two of the choir capitals; see Mair (op. cit. note 20, p.60).

22. Gervase, I, p.7.

23. J. Bony, 'Origines de piles gothiques anglaises à fûts en délit', *Gedenkschrift Ernst Gall*, Berlin/Munich, 1965, pp.95-98; and Mair (op. cit. note 20, p.66). For the Faversham capital see D. Kahn, *ERA*, p.182. For Henry of Blois and the use of marbles in mid 12th-century England see G. Zarnecki, 'Henry of Blois as a patron of sculpture', *SAOP*, 1986, pp.159-172.

24. It must have been truly splendid: 'the King's receiver confessed that gold and silver and precious stones and sacred vestments taken away from the shrine filled six-and-twenty carts' (A. Gasquet, *Henry VIII and the English Monasteries*, London, 1906, p.409, n.3).

25. Some were reproduced in *Canterbury. Romanesque Work*, ed. G. Zarnecki, Courtauld Institute Archives, London, 1978, 1/8/131-1/8/154, and in G. Zarnecki, *ERA*, pp.195-198. Photographs of some of the stones are appended to G. Zarnecki, 'The Faussett Pavilion: The King Canute relief', *AC*, LXVI, 1953, pp.1-14 (reprinted in Zarnecki, *Studies*). They were also discussed by M. Thurlby, *Transitional Sculpture in England*, unpublished Ph.D. thesis, University of East Anglia, 1976, pp. 1-92. For other contemporary

carving in England, see G. Zarnecki, 'The transition from Romanesque to Gothic in English sculpture', *Acts of the Twentieth International Congress of the History of Art*, I, New York, 1963, pp.152-158 (reprinted in Zarnecki, *Studies*).
For the York figures see G. Zarnecki, *ERA*, pp.204-209; for Glastonbury see Thurlby, op. cit. above, pp. 190-201.

26. Faussett's garden pavilion was specially built to display antiquities, near his house at Heppington in Kent. He believed that the relief represented King Cnut, but there is no evidence to support this claim.

27. The pieces were found in the second bay (third and fourth buttress) of the west walk where they had been reused as masonry, with the carved side facing in. In addition to the four panels, the incomplete remains of a fifth panel were found, completely smashed.

28. See for instance the fragments with grotesques from the tomb of Raoul le Vert at Saint-Rémi, Reims; F. Saxl, *English Sculptures of the Twelfth Century*, ed. H. Swarzenski, London, 1954, pp.26-27.

29. E. Panofsky, *Tomb Sculpture*, London, 1964; K. Bauch, *Das Mittelalterliche Grabbild*, Berlin/New York, 1976. See also P. Tudor-Craig, 'The tomb', *BAA CT*, Canterbury, 1982, pp.72-75; and *La Estorie de Seint Aedward le Rei*, intro. M.R. James, Roxburghe Club, Oxford, 1920 (Cambridge, University Library, Ee.3.59, f.65). The picture shows the deposition of Edward in his new shrine on 13 October 1163.

30. F. Woodman, *The Architectural History of Canterbury Cathedral*, London, 1981, pp.83-84.

31. S. Pressouyre, *Images d'un cloître disparu*, Paris, 1976; L. Pressouyre, 'St Bernard to St Francis: Monastic ideals and iconographic programmes in the cloister', *Gesta*, XII, 1973, pp.71-92.

32. Ternay - sur - Vienne (Isère), Saint - Donat -sur-L'Herbasse (Drôme), and Aix-en-Provence. I am grateful to Neil Stratford for drawing my attention to these examples.

33. In addition, there is evidence that the main cloister had been newly completed some ten to twenty years earlier by Prior Wibert, so there was hardly an incentive to rebuild so soon; see p. 135.

34. Gervase, I, p.6; Willis (1845), p.52.

35. Gervase, I, p.22: 'Murum igitur qui chorum circuit et presbiterium cum summa festinatione construxit'.

36. Gervase, I, p.13; Willis (1845), p.43.

37. Gervase, I, p.13; Willis (1845), pp.44-45.

38. The figure sculpture of the screen is among the finest from the early 15th century (aside from tomb sculpture) to remain in England. Left and right of the doorway are Ethelbert and Edward the Confessor, with other kings flanking them; see J. Newman, *North East and East Kent, B/E*, Harmondsworth, 1976, pp.203, 215.

39. Willis (1845), p.110.

40. Sir G. G. Scott, 'The choir screen in Canterbury Cathedral', *Arch Jnl*, XXXII, 1875, pp.86-88.

41. A.W. Pugin, *A Treatise on Chancel Screens and Rood Lofts*, London, 1851; F. Bond, *Screens and Galleries in English Churches*, London, 1908; A. Vallance, *Greater English Church Screens*, London, 1947; F.B. Bond and D. Camm, *Roodscreens and Roodlofts*, London, 1909.

42. *Royal Commission on Historical Monuments, City of Salisbury*, I, London, 1980, p.20.

43. For Chichester see G. Zarnecki, 'The Chichester reliefs', *Arch Jnl*, 110, 1954, pp.106-120 (reprinted in Zarnecki, *Studies*); for Durham see G. Zarnecki, *ERA*, pp.188-189; for Barking see F. Saxl, (op. cit. note 28) p.56, pls.xxx-xxxi; for Ely see W.H. St John Hope, 'Quire screens in English churches with special reference to the twelfth-century quire screen formerly in the cathedral church of Ely', *Archaeologia*, LXVIII, 1916-1917, pp.43-110; for Southwick Priory see G. Soffe, 'Southwick Priory and its late Romanesque sculpted lavabo', *Hampshire Field Club and Archaeological Society*, New Series, III, Spring 1985, pp.27-29.

44. E. Viollet-le-Duc, *Dictionnaire raisonné de l'architecture française XI-XVI siècle*, VI, Paris, 1863, pp.47-50. For Chartres see J. Maillon, *Chartres. La jubé de la cathédrale*, Paris, 1964.

45. E. Kirchner-Doberer, *Die deutschen Lettner bis 1300*, Vienna/Linz, 1946.
The pieces from the Mariengraden church in Cologne were moved to the church at Gustdorf and are now housed in the Landesmuseum, Bonn; see F. Rademacher, *Die Gustorfer Chorschranken*, Bonn, 1975. At Trier Cathedral portions of the screen remain *in situ*, with Christ flanked by the Virgin and St John, St Peter and St Paul; F.J. Ronig, *Der Trierer Dom*, 1980, pp.238-239, pl.75.
See also H. Beenken, Romanische Skulptur in Deutschland 11. und 12. Jahrhundert, Leipzig, 1924; for Halberstadt see pp.228-237. For Hildesheim see C. Schulz-Mons, *Die Chorschrankenreliefs der Michaeliskirche zu Hildesheim. Schriftenreihe des Stadtarchivs und der Stadtbibliothek Hildesheim*, 7, Hildesheim, 1979. For the screen at Bamberg of *c*.1230 see D.V. Winterfeld, *Der Dom in Bamberg*, Berlin, 1979, pp.76-84; for the screen

at Naumburg of *c*.1250 see W. Pinder, *Der Naumburger Dom und seine Bildwerke*, Berlin, 1933, pl.24.

46. The bottom edge of three others were trimmed so the original shape of these blocks is uncertain, but the general concept appears to have been similar to the *pulpitum* at Halberstadt; even the trefoil frames that terminate the arms of the Halberstadt Crucifix suggest comparison with the frames of the quatrefoils at Christ Church.

47. This roundel may have been a pair with the defaced roundel on which traces of a similar headband and similar ears are still just evident.

48. G. Zarnecki, 'English twelfth-century sculpture and its resistance to St Denis', *Tribute to an Antiquary: Essays Presented to Mark Fitch*, London, 1976, p.91, argues that the figure is *Synagoga*.
For the iconography of *Synagoga* see L. Grodecki, 'Les vitraux allégoriques de Saint-Denis, *Art de France*, I, 1961, pp.32-34. For the use of the image in France see B. Blumenkranz, 'Géographie historique d'un thème de l'iconographie religieuse: les representations de Synagoga en France', *Mélanges René Crozet*, II, Poitiers, 1966, pp.1141-1157. See P. Lasko, *ERA*, pp.224-225 for figure on the Cloisters ivory cross.

49. See Rademacher (op. cit. note 45, pp.69-112) for *Luna* from Mariengraden.

50. *Rites of Durham* (1593), ed. T.J. Fowler, Surtees Society, CVII, 1902, pp.32-34.

51. This hypothetical arrangement is given further weight by the portion of a 14th-century wooden screen from Christ Church that survives in Adisham, Kent. This is arranged in three registers: at the bottom are the four Evangelists under trefoil arches; in the middle zone are blank quatrefoils and foliage; and at the top are standing figures, again under trefoil arches. The arrangement of tiers of alternating figures and quatrefoils might reflect the disposition of sculpture of the main choir screen; see H.M. Villers 'Adisham Church', *AC*, XIV, 1882, p.159.

52. H. Omont, *Psautier illustré XIIIe siècle*, Paris, 1906 (for facsimile edition) and A. Heimann, 'The last copy of the Utrecht Psalter', *The Year 1200: A Symposium*, New York, 1975, pp.313-329. For the most recent views and bibliography see N. Morgan, *Early Gothic Manuscripts*, I, London, 1982, pp.47-49. Attention has already been drawn to the links between Canterbury glass and manuscripts; see L. Grodecki, 'The ancient glass of Canterbury Cathedral', *Burlington Magazine*, XCII, 1950, pp.294-297. Despite their damaged condition, the paintings

in the nave of St Gabriel's chapel at Canterbury, with foliage scrolls enclosing busts of prophets, can be seen to have been in a style similar to the Paris Psalter.

The paintings, now destroyed, on the vaults of the Trinity chapel ambulatory where kings and local saints were depicted might have paralleled the screen. For these paintings see M.H. Caviness, 'A lost cycle of Canterbury paintings of 1220', *Antiquaries Journal*, LIV, 1974, pp.66-74.

53. M. Bieber, *The Sculpture of the Hellenistic Age*, New York, 1961, pp.62, 175, fig.197. Aside from a male figure on a voussoir at Barfreston church, the only other piece to assume this pose in the 12th century to my knowledge is the bronze Bacchus *acquamanile* in the Aachen Minster Museum, see H. Swarzenski, *Monuments of Romanesque Art*, London, 1954, fig.358.

54. They appear, for instance, in the 6th-century water cistern in Constantinople. Later, they became purely decorative enrichments as, for example, on Carolingian ivories such as the 9th-century Lorsch Bible cover (now in the Victoria and Albert Museum) or Ottonian metal objects, such as the Basel antependium (now in the Musée de Cluny).

55. D. Kahn, 'The west doorway at Rochester Cathedral', *Romanesque and Gothic*, pp.129-134. There are other examples at Newlands Chapel, Charing, and at the churches of Selling and Hythe. Also see A.H. Collins, 'The sculptural ornament of the south doorway of Barfreston church', *AC*, XLV, 1933, pp.1-12. For useful notes on the pre-restoration appearance of the church see 'Barfreston', *A Report of the Proceedings of the British Archaeological Association*, I, 1844, pp.287-296.

56. Cave (op. cit. note 21), pp.44 and 45.

57. The description of these carvings is considerably complicated by the vagaries of traditional art historical terminology. In terms of traditional labelling, these sculptures perfectly exemplify that independent style, which overlapped with the close of the Romanesque and the emergence of the Early Gothic the so-called 'Transitional style'.

58. R.B. Green, 'Ex ungue leonem', *De Artibus Opuscula XL. Essays in Honour of Erwin Panofsky*, New York, 1961, pp.157-169.

59. *Abbot Suger on the Abbey Church of St.-Denis and its Art Treasures*, ed. and transl. E. Panofsky, Princeton, 1979, p.59. For Henry of Blois as a patron see G. Zarnecki (op. cit. note 23), pp.159-172.

60. This device is also used at Rochester, as on Christ's mandorla and on one of the roundels.

It is a frequent feature too in Canterbury glass; see M.H. Caviness, *The Windows of Christ Church Cathedral, Canterbury. Corpus Vitriarum Mediiaevi*, II, London, 1981, p.13.

Also see H. Schnitzler, *Der Schrein des Heiligen Heribert*, Monchengladbach, 1962; H. Fillitz and M. Pippal, *Schatzkunst*, Salzburg/Vienna, 1987, p.258.

61. In the restoration of the Saint-Rémi chapter house in 1953, a series of capitals were discovered in the arcades of the two walls; see M. Bouxin, *Les chapiteaux romans de la salle capitulaire de l'abbaye Saint-Rémi de Reims*, Reims, 1976. Apart from the early Gothic capitals and the chapter house capitals, Reims sculpture of the period is known only from a few pieces, such as the 'porte romane' of the cathedral, the 'Odo' tomb (now in the Musée Saint-Rémi) and the charming tympanum from a secular building of c.1160-1170. See W. Sauerländer, *Gothic Sculpture in France 1140-1210*, London, 1972, pp.415-416, pls.56-57, for the 'porte romane'; pp.394-395, pl.27, for the 'Odo' tomb; pp.414-415, pl.55, for the tympanum. Despite the fact that this is a little earlier than the Canterbury sculptures, the tender expressions of the figures on this tympanum are akin to those of the Canterbury sculptures, as is the graceful, meandering foliage and the delicate ruffled leaves.

62. This was first noted by M.H. Caviness, *The Early Stained Glass of Canterbury Cathedral circa 1175-1220*, Princeton, 1977, p.56.

63. Ibid., n.96, pl.106. For new light on the evolution of this foliage see the important note by K.E. Haney, 'A Norman antecedent for English floral ornament of the mid-twelfth century', *Scriptorium*, XXXVI, 1982, pp.84-86.

64. D. Kahn, *ERA*, p.198. An album in the Rochester Cathedral Library contains a photograph taken sometime before 1939 showing this roundel, together with a virtual twin which has since vanished. The Rochester roundel also shares physiognomical characteristics with classical masks, and recalls the illustrations of Terence manuscripts.

For the shaft fragment from St. Augustine's: W.S. Walford, 'On a remarkable sculpture lately found in Bobbing Church, Kent', *Arch Jnl*, XXI, 1864, pp.246-253. The 28cm. high shaft was reset in the sedilia of the parish church at Bobbing. Nothing else in the church pre-dates the 14th century, so the piece (which was joined to a 14th-century shaft and installed with the carving side inwards) must have been brought to Bobbing as building material.

65. F. Wormald, *English Benedictine Kalendars after 1100*, Henry Bradshaw Society, 77, 1939, p.49.

66. The 'stigmatum' in the left hand of the attendant figure must be the result of later tampering. The scene is not readily identifiable with the events recorded in the Life of St Martial. A 13th-century window in Tours Cathedral has three panels with the saint flanked by acolytes, and it is conceivable that the concealed side of the shaft was carved with a second companion; see E. Mâle, *Religious Art in France of the Thirteenth Century*, New York, 1958, p.221.

67. T.A. Heslop, 'The conventual seals of Canterbury Cathedral 1066-1232', *BAA CT*, Canterbury, 1982, p.98.

68. On this subject, see W. Sauerländer, 'L'art antique et la sculpture autour de 1200', *Art de France*, I, 1961, pp.47-56.

69. P. Tudor-Craig and L. Keen, 'A recently discovered Purbeck marble sculptured screen of the thirteenth century and the shrine of St Swithin', *BAA CT*, VI, 1983, pp.72-75. The tomb may not have been executed until the monks were able to return to Canterbury in 1213 after the Interdict, but in all likelihood it was produced soon after the archbishop's death.

Notes to Appendix I

1. Gervase, I, p.5; Willis (1845), p.34.

2. Ibid., p.53.

3. Willis (1869), p.54. Opinions as to the date of the infirmary hall vary; C.E. Woodruff and W. Danks, *Memorials of the Cathedral and Priory of Christ in Canterbury*, London, 1912, p.252, date it to Lanfranc's archiepiscopate.

4. Urry, pp.27, 30, map 1(b), large scale sheet 4, and p.206.

5. I am grateful to Mr J. Bowen for allowing me to see his excellent drawings of the capitals.

6. J. Raspi Serra, 'English decorative sculpture of the early twelfth century and the Como-Pavian tradition', *Art Bulletin*, LI, 1969, p.358. The author sees links between the infirmary chapel capitals and the decoration of Pavian churches, particularly San Michele.

7. For the casket see G. Zarnecki 'A Romanesque casket from Canterbury in Florence', *Canterbury Cathedral Chronicle*, 64, 1969, p.44.

8. I am grateful to Mr Tatton-Brown for his help in analyzing the phases of building.

9. For the wall paintings see D. Kahn, 'The structural evidence for the dating of the St Gabriel chapel wall-paintings at Christ Church Cathedral, Canterbury', *Burlington Magazine*, CXXVI, April 1984, pp.225-229.

Notes to Appendix II

1. For a compilation of many of the most important of these, see T. Borenius, *St Thomas Becket in Art*, London, 1932; id., 'The iconography of St Thomas of Canterbury', *Archaeologia*, LXXIX, 1929, pp.29-54; id., 'Addenda to the iconography of St Thomas of Canterbury', *Archaeologia*, LXXXI, 1931, pp.19-31.

2. *Materials*, I, p.423.

3. T. Borenius, 'Some further aspects of the iconography of St Thomas of Canterbury', *Archaeologia*, 1933, pp.171-186, for Godmersham, pp.173-175.

4. R. Mellinkoff, *The Horned Moses in Medieval Art and Thought*, Berkeley and London, 1978.

5. J. Bowen, 'Domus Hospitum', *Canterbury Archaeological Trust, 11th Annual Report*, Canterbury, 1987, pp.26-27. The doorway is now in the Archdeacon of Canterbury's garden.

6. Willis (1845), p.133.

7. Borenius (op. cit. note 1), p.20, n.1.

List of Archbishops and Priors

ARCHBISHOPS *from the mid eleventh century to the end of the twelfth century*

Robert of Jumièges   1051-1052
Stigand   1052-1070
Lanfranc   1070-1089
Anselm   1093-1109
Ralph d'Escures   1114-1122
William de Corbeil   1123-1136

Theobald   1139-1161
Thomas Becket   1162-1170
Richard   1174-1184
Baldwin   1185-1190
Hubert Walter   1193-1205

PRIORS

Henry   *c.*1074-1096
Ernulf   1096-1107
Conrad   1108/9-1126
Geoffrey   1126-1128
Elmer   1128-1137
Jeremiah   1137-*c.*1143
Walter Durdent   *c.*1143-1149
Walter Parvus   1149-1152/3
Wibert   1152/3-1167

Odo   1167/8-1175
Benedict   1175-1177
Herlewin   1177-1179
Alan   1179-1186
Honorius   1186-1188
Roger Norreis   1189
Osbert de Bruto   1189-1191
Geoffrey   1191-1213
Walter   1213-1222

277. Capital from Canterbury, found in Chartham.
Canterbury Heritage Museum.

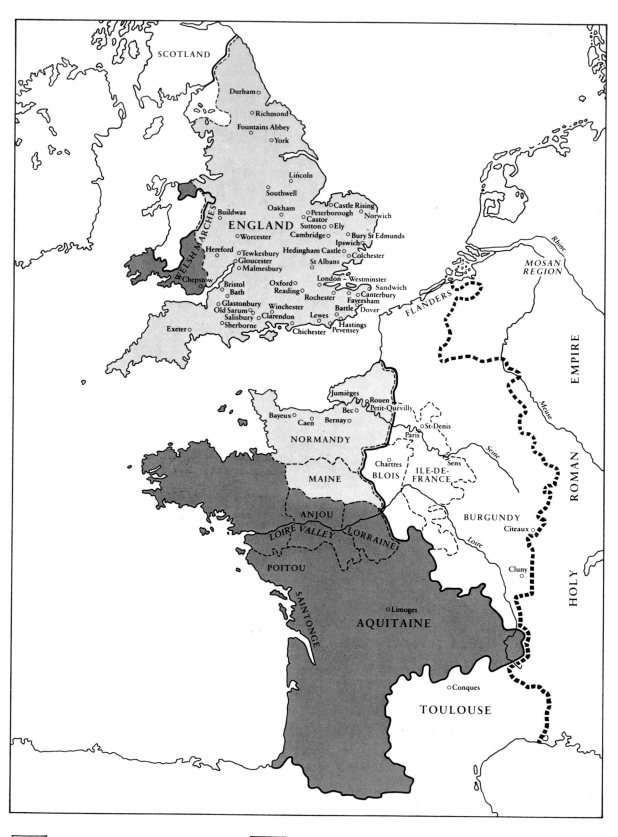

SCOTLAND

Durham

Richmond
Fountains Abbey
York

Lincoln
Southwell
Buildwas   Oakham   Castle Rising
                          Peterborough   Norwich
ENGLAND   Castor
                  Sutton   Ely
Worcester   Cambridge   Bury St Edmunds
Hereford   Hedingham Castle   Ipswich
Tewkesbury   Colchester
Gloucester   St Albans
Malmesbury   London — Westminster
Bristol   Oxford   Sandwich
Bath   Reading   Rochester   Canterbury
Glastonbury   Faversham
Old Sarum   Winchester   Battle   Dover
Salisbury   Clarendon   Lewes
Sherborne   Hastings
Exeter   Chichester   Pevensey

WELSH MARCHES
Chepstow

MOSAN
REGION

Rhine

FLANDERS

EMPIRE

Jumièges
Bayeux   Bec   Rouen
         Caen   Bernay   Petit-Quevilly
NORMANDY   St-Denis
                  Paris
MAINE   Chartres   Sens
               BLOIS   ILE-DE-
                        FRANCE
ANJOU
LOIRE VALLEY   LORRAINE   BURGUNDY
POITOU   Cîteaux
SAINTONGE   Loire   Cluny
               Limoges
          AQUITAINE
                              Conques
          TOULOUSE

Meuse
Seine

ROMAN

HOLY

■ Territories ruled by William I   ■ Territories ruled by Henry II in 1154

Abbreviations

AC	*Archaeologia Cantiana*
Anglia Sacra	H. Wharton, *Anglia Sacra*, London, 1691
Anglo-Saxon Art	*The Golden Age of Anglo-Saxon Art 966-1066*, eds. J. Backhouse, D.H. Turner and L. Webster, London, 1984
Arch Jnl	*Archaeological Journal*
BAA CT	*British Archaeological Conference Transactions*
B/E	*The Buildings of England*
BM	*Bulletin Monumental*
CA	*Congrès Archéologique*
Dodwell	C.R. Dodwell, *The Canterbury School of Illumination, 1066-1200*, Cambridge, 1954
Eadmer, Hist. Nov.	Eadmer, *Historia Novorum in Anglia*, ed. M. Rule, *Rolls Series*, LXXXI, 1884
ERA	*English Romanesque Art 1066-1200*, ed. G. Zarnecki, Arts Council of Great Britain Exhibition, London, 1984
Gervase I or II	Gervase of Canterbury, *Opera Historica*, I, II, ed. W. Stubbs, *Rolls Series*, LXXIII, London, 1879-1880
Gibson, *Lanfranc*	M. Gibson, *Lanfranc of Bec*, Oxford, 1978.
James	M.R. James, *The Ancient Libraries of Canterbury and Dover*, Cambridge, 1903
JBAA	*Journal of the British Archaeological Association*
JWCI	*Journal of the Warburg and Courtauld Institutes*
Kahn	D. Kahn, *Romanesque Architectural Sculpture in Kent*, unpublished Ph.D. thesis, Courtauld Institute of Art, 1982
Kauffmann	C.M. Kauffmann, *Romanesque Manuscripts 1066-1190*, London, 1975
Knowles	Dom D. Knowles, *The Monastic Order in England*, Cambridge, 1978
Materials	*Materials for the History of Thomas Becket*, ed. J.C. Robertson, *Rolls Series*, LXVII (in 7 vols.), London, 1875-1885
Migne, *PL*	*Patrologie cursus completus, series Latina*, ed. J.P. Migne, Paris, 1852-1904

PBC	*Proceedings of the Battle Abbey Conference*
RAI	*Royal Archaeological Institute Journal*
RB	*Revue belge d'archéologie et d'histoire de l'art*
Romanesque and Gothic	*Romanesque and Gothic. Essays for George Zarnecki*, Woodbridge, 1987
Saltman, *Theobald*	A. Saltman, *Theobald, Archbishop of Canterbury*, London, 1956
SAOP	*Society of Antiquaries Occasional Paper*
Somner (1640)	W. Somner, *The Antiquities of Canterbury*, London, 1640
Southern, *St Anselm*	R.W. Southern, *St Anselm and His Biographer. A Study of Monastic Life and Thought 1059-c.1130*, Cambridge, 1966
Urry	W. Urry, *Canterbury under the Angevin Kings*, London, 1967
VCH	*Victoria Histories of the Counties of England*
Willis (1845)	R. Willis, *The Architectural History of Canterbury Cathedral*, London, 1845
Willis (1869)	R. Willis, *The Architectural History of the Conventual Buildings of the Monastery of Christ Church Canterbury*, London, 1869 (also in *AC*, VII, 1868, pp.1-206)
Zarnecki, *Regional Schools*	G. Zarnecki, *Regional Schools of English Romanesque Sculpture in the Twelfth Century. The Southern School and the Herefordshire School*, unpublished Ph.D. thesis, Courtauld Institute of Art, 1950
Zarnecki, *Studies*	G. Zarnecki, *Studies in Romanesque Sculpture*, London, 1979

Bibliography

For the convenience of the general reader, a number of titles of interest for further reading have been marked □

Abbot, E., *St. Thomas of Canterbury, his Death and Miracles*, 2 vols., London, 1898.

Abbot Suger on the Abbey Church of St. Denis and its Art Treasures, ed. and transl. E. Panofsky, Princeton, 1979.

Adhémar, J., *Influences antiques dans l'art du moyen âge français*, London, 1939.

Adolf, H., 'The ass and the harp', *Speculum*, XXV, 1950, pp. 49-57.

Alexander, J.J.G., *Norman Illumination at Mont St Michel 966-1100*, Oxford, 1970.

Alexander, J.J.G., *Insular Manuscripts 6th-9th Century*, London, 1978.

Anglo-Saxon Chronicle, transl. G.N. Garmonsway, London, 1953.

Anselmi, Opera Omnia, ed. F.S. Schmitt, 6 vols., Edinburgh, 1940-1961.

Ashby, T., *Aqueducts of Ancient Rome*, Oxford, 1935.

Ayres, L.M., 'The role of an Angevin style in English Romanesque painting', *Zeitschrift für Kunstgeschichte*, 36, 1974, pp. 193-223.

Balt, H., ' Zur Romanischen Löwensymbolik', *Festschrift für Andreas Posch*, Graz, 1963.

Baltrusaitis, J., *Art sumerien, art roman*, Paris, 1934.

Barlow, F., 'A view of Archbishop Lanfranc', *Journal of Ecclesiastical History*, XVI/II, 1965, pp. 163-177.

Barlow, F., *The English Church 1000-1066*, London, 1979.

Barlow, F., *William Rufus*, London, 1983.

□ Barlow, F., *Thomas Becket*, London, 1986.

Barrow, G.W.S., 'David I of Scotland 1124-1153. The balance of new and old', *Stenton Lecture*, Reading, 1984.

The Bayeux Tapestry, ed. Sir F. Stenton, London, 2nd edition, 1965.

Baylé, M., *La Trinité de Caen; sa place dans l'histoire de l'architecture et du décor romane*, Paris, 1979.

Baylé, M., 'Les chapiteaux de Stogursey (Somerset) ancien prioré de Lonlay l'Abbaye', *BM*, CXXXVII, 1980, pp. 405-416.

Baylé, M., 'La sculpture romane en normandie à l'époque ducale', *Les siècles romans en basse normandie. Art de basse-normandie*, 1982, pp. 55-64.

Materials for the History of Thomas Becket, Archbishop of Canterbury, eds. J.C. Robertson and J.B. Sheppard, 7 vols., Rolls Series, London, 1875-1885.

Beckwith, J., *Ivory Carving in Early Medieval England*, London, 1972.

Beenken, H., *Romanische Skulptur in Deutschland 11. und 12. Jahrhundert*, Leipzig, 1924.

Bégule, L. and Bertaux, E., 'Les chapiteaux byzantins à figures d'animaux', *BM*, 1911, pp. 199-211.

Bennett, P., 'Rescue excavations in the outer court of St. Augustine's Abbey 1983-1984', *AC*, CIII, 1986, pp. 79-117.

Bennett, P., Frere, S.S. and Stow, S., *Excavations at Canterbury Castle; The Archaeology of Canterbury*, I, Canterbury, 1982.

Bernstein, D.J., *The Mystery of the Bayeux Tapestry*, Chicago, 1986.

Bertaux, E., *L'art dans l'Italie méridionale*, Paris, 1904.

Bilson, J., 'The Norman school and the beginnings of Gothic architecture. Two octopartite vaults: Montivillers and Canterbury', *Arch Jnl*, LXXIV, 1917, pp. 1-25.

Bishop, E., *Liturgica Historica*, Oxford, 1918.

Blagg, T.F.C., *Roman Architectural Ornament in Britain*, University of London, Ph.D. thesis, 1981.

Blumenkranz, B., 'Geographie historique d'un thème de l'iconographie religieuse: les representations de Synagoga en France', *Mélanges René Crozet*, II, Poitiers, 1966, pp. 1141-1157.

Blunt, A., 'The Temple of Solomon with special reference to south Italian Baroque art', *Kunsthistorische Forschungen: Otto Pächt zu seinem 70 Geburtstag*, ed. A. Rosenauer and G. Webster, Vienna, 1972, pp. 258-265.

Boase, T.S.R., *English Art, 1100-1216*, Oxford, 1953.

Bond, F., *Fonts and Font Covers*, London, 1908.

Bond, F., *Screens and Galleries in English Churches*, London, 1908.

Bond, F. and Camm, D., *Roodscreens and Roodlofts*, London, 1909.

Bony, J., 'French influence on the origins of English Gothic architecture', *JWCI*, 12, 1949, pp. 1-15.

Bony, J., 'Origines des piles gothique anglaises à fûts en délit', *Gedenkschrift Ernst Gall*, Berlin/Munich, 1965, pp. 95-122.

Bony, J., 'Diagonality and centrality in early ribvaulted architecture', *Gesta*, XV, 1976, pp. 15-25.

Bony, J., 'Durham et la tradition saxonne', *Etudes d'art médiéval offerts à Louis Grodecki*, eds. S. McKnight Crosby, A. Chastel and A. Prache, Paris, 1981, pp. 79-92.

Bony, J., *French Gothic Architecture of the 12th and 13th Century*, Berkeley, 1983.

Borenius, T., 'The iconography of St Thomas of Canterbury', *Archaeologia*, LXXIX, 1929, pp. 29-54.

Borenius, T., 'Addenda to the iconography of St Thomas of Canterbury', *Archaeologia*, LXXXI, 1931, pp. 19-31.

Borenius, T., *St Thomas Becket in Art*, London, 1932.

Borenius, T., 'Some further aspects of the iconography of St Thomas of Canterbury', *Archaeologia*, 1933, pp. 171-186.

Borg, A., 'The development of chevron ornament', *JBAA*, 3rd series, XXX, 1967, pp. 122-140.

Bosanquet, G., *Eadmer's History of Recent Events in England*, London, 1964.

Boussard, J., *Le gouvernement d'Henri II Plantagenet*, Paris, 1956.

Boutemy, A., 'Quelques aspects de l'oeuvre de Swalon, decorateur de manuscrits à l'abbaye de Saint-Amand', *RB*, IX, 1939, pp. 299-316.

Bouxin, M., *Les chapiteaux romans de la salle capitulaire de l'abbaye Saint-Remi de Reims*, Reims, 1976.

Brakspear, H., *Waverley Abbey*, The Surrey Archaeological Society, London, 1905.

Branner, R., 'Gothic architecture 1160-1180 and its Romanesque sources', *Romanesque and Gothic in Western Art, Acts of the Twentieth International Congress of the History of Art*, I, New York, 1963, pp. 92-104.

Braunfels, W., *The Monasteries of Western Europe*, Princeton, 1972.

Brett, M., *The English Church under Henry I*, Oxford, 1975.

Britton, J., *Historical and Descriptive Account of the Metropolitan Cathedrals of Canterbury and York*, I, London, 1836.

Brønsted, J. *Early English Ornament*, London/Copenhagen, 1924.

Brooke, C., 'John of Salisbury and his world', *The World of John of Salisbury*, ed. M. Wilks, Oxford, 1984, pp. 1-20.

Brooke, C. and Keir, G., *London 800-1216: The Shaping of a City*, London, 1975.

Brooke, Z.N., *The English Church and the Papacy from the Conquest to the Reign of John*, Cambridge, 1931.

☐ Brooks, N., *The Early History of the Church of Canterbury*, Leicester, 1984.

Brooks, N.P., and Walker, H.E., 'The authority and interpretation of the Bayeux Tapestry', *PBC*, I, 1979, pp. 1-34.

Brown, B.G., *The Arts in Early England, Anglo-Saxon Architecture*, II, London, 1925.

Brown, R.A., 'The Norman Conquest and the genesis of English castles', *Château Gaillard...European Castle Studies Conference at Battle, Sussex*, (1966), ed. A.J. Taylor, London/Chichester, 1969, pp. 1-15.

Cahn, W., 'St. Albans and the Channel style in England', *The Year 1200: A Symposium*, New York, 1975, pp. 187-211.

Cahn, W., *Romanesque Bible Decoration*, Cornell, 1982.

Camden, W., *Camden's Britannia, Kent*, London, 1586.

Camille, M., 'Seeing and reading: some visual implications of medieval literacy and illiteracy', *Art History*, VIII/i, 1985, pp. 26-49.

Camille, M., 'The language of images in medieval England, 1200-1400', *Age of Chivalry*, eds. J. Alexander and P. Binski, London, 1987, pp. 33-40.

Campbell, E.M.J., 'Kent', *The Domesday Geography of South-east England*, eds. H.C. Darby and E.M.J. Campbell, Cambridge, 1962.

Campbell, J., 'Some Twelfth-century Views of the Anglo-Saxon Past', *Essays in Anglo-Saxon History*, London, 1986, pp. 209-228.

Carlson, E., *The Abbey Church of Saint-Etienne at Caen*, Ph.D. thesis, Yale University, 1968.

Caröe, W.D., 'Three towers of Canterbury', *Architectural Review*, XVII, 1905, pp. 3-12.

Caröe, W.D., 'Wall paintings in the infirmary chapel, Canterbury Cathedral', *Archaeologia*, LXIII, 1912, pp. 51-56.

Cave, C.J.P., 'The roof-bosses in Canterbury Cathedral', *Archaeologia*, 84, 1934, pp. 41-61.

Caviness, M.H., 'A lost cycle of Canterbury paintings of 1220', *Antiquaries Journal*, LIV, 1974, pp. 66-74.

☐ Caviness, M.H., *The Early Stained Glass of Canterbury Cathedral*, Princeton, 1977.

Caviness, M.H., *The Windows of Christ Church Cathedral Canterbury, Corpus Vitriarum Mediiaevi*, II, London, 1981.

Caviness, M.H., 'Canterbury Cathedral clerestory: the glazing programme in relation to the campaigns of construction', *BAA CT*, 1982, pp. 46-55.

Chamot, M., *English Medieval Enamels*, London, 1930.

Chapman, G., 'The bible of Floreffe: redating of a Romanesque manuscript', *Gesta*, X/2, 1971, pp. 49-62.

Cheney, C.R., *From Becket to Langton. English Church Government 1170-1213*, Manchester, 1956.

Cheney, C.R., *Hubert Walter*, London, 1967.

Chronicle of Battle Abbey, ed. E. Searle, Oxford, 1980.

Churchill, J., *Canterbury Administration*, London, 1933.

Clapham, A., 'Dover Castle', *Arch Jnl*, LXXXVI, 1929, pp. 245-255.

Clapham, A., *English Romanesque Architecture Before the Conquest*, I, Oxford, 1930.

Clapham, A., *English Romanesque Architecture After the Conquest*, II, Oxford, 1934.

Clapham, A., *St Augustine's Abbey*, London, 1955.

Cobban, A.B., *The Medieval English Universities: Oxford and Cambridge to c.1500*, Cambridge, 1988.

Colling, J.K., *English Medieval Foliage*, London, 1874.

Collins, A.H., 'The sculptural ornament of the south doorway of Barfreston church', *AC*, XLV, 1933, pp. 1-12.

Cotman, J.S., *Architectural Antiquities of Normandy*, London, 1822.

Cotton, C., *The Saxon Cathedral at Canterbury and the Saxon Saints Buried Therein*, Manchester, 1929.

Courtauld Institute Illustration Archives; Cathedrals and Monastic Buildings in the British Isles, part 8, Canterbury, ed. G. Zarnecki, 1978.

Cronne, H.A., *The Reign of Stephen*, London, 1970.

Cross, F.W. and Hall, J.R., *Rambles Round Old Canterbury*, London, 1884.

Crum, T.M.C. and M.M., 'The tau-cross capitals in the undercroft of Canterbury Cathedral', *AC*, 45, 1933, pp. 193-200.

Dale, W., 'An English Crozier of the Transitional Period', *Art Bulletin*, XXXVIII, 1956, pp. 138-141.

Dart, J., *The History and Antiquities of the Cathedral Church of Canterbury*, London, 1726.

'De Miraculis Sancti Dunstani, Memorials of St Dunstan', ed. W. Stubbs, *Rolls Series*, LXIII, London, 1874.

Demus, O., *Romanesque Mural Painting*, London, 1970.

Demus, O., 'European Wall Painting around 1200', *The Year 1200: A Symposium*, New York, 1975, pp. 95-118.

Denne, S., 'Evidence of a lavatory appertaining to the Benedictine priory of Canterbury Cathedral and observations on fonts', *Archaeologia*, XI, 1794.

Deuchler, F., *Der Ingeborgpsalter*, Berlin, 1967.

Dieppen, H.A., *Die Romanische Bauornamentik in Klosterrath*, The Hague, 1931.

☐ Dodwell C.R., *The Canterbury School of Illumination 1066-1200*, Cambridge, 1954.

Dodwell, C.R., *The Great Lambeth Bible*, London, 1959.

Douglas, D.C., *The 'Domesday Monachorum' of Christ Church Canterbury*, London, 1944.

Douglas, D.C., *William the Conquerer*, London, 1977.

Draper, P., 'William of Sens and the original design of the choir termination of Canterbury Cathedral 1175-1179', *Journal of the Society of Architectural Historians*, XLII/3, 1983, pp. 238-247.

Drury, G.D., 'The use of Purbeck marble in medieval times', *Proceedings of the Dorset Natural History and Archaeological Society*, LXX, 1948, pp. 1-28.

Du Boulay, F.R.H., *The Lordship of Canterbury*, London, 1966.

Dugan, A., *Thomas Becket. A Textual History of his Letters*, Oxford, 1980.

Dugdale, W., *Monasticon Anglicanum*, eds J. Caley, H. Ellis and B. Bandinel, 6 vols., London, 1817-1830.

Dunbabin, J., *France in the Making, 843-1180*, Oxford, 1985.

Eadmer, *Historia Novorum in Anglia*, ed. M. Rule, *Rolls Series*, LXXXI, London, 1884.

Eadmer, *Vita Sancti Dunstani*, ed. W. Stubbs, *Rolls Series*, LXIII, London, 1874, pp. 162-223.

Eadmer, *Liber Miraculorum*, ed. W. Stubbs, *Rolls Series*, LXIII, London, 1874, pp. 223-251.

Eadmer, *The Life of St Anselm, Archbishop of Canterbury*, ed. & transl. R.W. Southern, Oxford Medieval Texts, Oxford, 1962.

Eadmer, *Vita Bregwini*, Migne *PL*, CLIX, pp. 757-758.

Eales, R., 'Local loyalties in Norman England; Kent in Stephen's reign', *PBC*, VIII, 1986, pp. 88-108.

Eames, E., 'Notes on the decorated stone roundels in the Corona and Trinity Chapel in Canterbury Cathedral', *BAA CT*, V, 1982, pp. 67-70.

The Ecclesiastical History of Orderic Vitalis, ed. M. Chibnall, Oxford, 1973.

Thomas of Elmham, *Historia Monasterii S. Augustini Cantuariensis*, ed. C. Hardwick, *Rolls Series*, VIII, London, 1858.

English Episcopal Acta, Canterbury 1162-1190, ed. C.R. Cheney and B.E.A. Jones, London, 1986.

☐ *English Romanesque Art, 1066-1200*, Arts Council Exhibition Catalogue, London, 1984.

Enlart, C., *Monuments religieux de l'architecture romane et de transition dans la région Picardie*, Amiens/Paris, 1895.

La Estoire de Seint Aedward le Rei, intro. M.R. James, Roxburghe Club, Oxford, 1920.

Fage, R., 'La décoration géométrique', *CA*, LXXV, ii, 1909, pp. 622-623.

Falke, O. von, *Decorative Silks*, London, 3rd edition, 1936.

Fernie, E., 'The spiral piers of Durham Cathedral', *BAA CT*, III, 1980, pp. 49-58.

Fernie, E., 'St. Anselm's crypt', *BAA CT*, V, 1982, pp. 27-38.

Fernie, E., 'The effect of the Conquest on Norman architectural patronage', *PBC*, IX, 1986, pp. 71-86.

Foreville, R., *L'église et la royauté en Angleterre sous Henri II Platagenet, 1154-1189*, Paris, 1943.

Foreville, R., *Le jubilé de Saint Thomas Becket du XIIIe au XVe siècle (1220-1470): Etude et documents*, Paris, 1958.

Foreville, R., 'Canterbury et la canonisation des saints', *Tradition and Change. Essays in Honour of Marjorie Chibnall*, eds. D. Greenway, C. Holdsworth and J. Sayers, Cambridge, 1985, pp. 63-75.

Francovich, G. de, 'La corrente comasca nella scultura romanica europea', *Revista del R. Istituo d'Archeologia e Storia dell'Arte*, V, 1935-1936, pp. 267-305.

Francovich, G. de, 'La diffusione', *Revista del R. Istituto d'Archeologia e Storia dell'Arte*, VI, 1937-1938, pp. 47-129.

Frank, P., *The Gothic: Its Interpretation through Eight Centuries*, Princeton, 1960.

Franklin, J., 'The twelfth century: The building of a cloister', *Medieval Sculpture from Norwich Cathedral*, ed. A. Borg, Norwich, 1980.

Freedberg, D., *The Power of Images. Studies in the History and Theory of Response*, Chicago/London, 1989.

Frere, S.S., 'The Roman theatre at Canterbury', *Britannia*, I, 1970, pp. 83-113, and VIII, 1977, pp. 423-425.

Fröhlich, W., 'St Anselm's special relationship with the Conqueror', *PBC*, X, 1987, pp. 101-110.

Gaborit-Chopin, D., *Ivoires du moyen age*, Fribourg, 1978.

Gasquet, A., *Henry VIII and the English Monasteries*, London, 1906.

Gasquet, A. and Bishop, E., *The Bosworth Psalter*, London, 1908.

Geddes, J., 'Recently discovered Romanesque sculpture in south-east England', *SAOP*, 1983, pp. 95-96.

Gem, R., 'The Romanesque rebuilding of Westminster Abbey', *PBC*, III, 1980, pp. 33-60.

Gem, R., 'The significance of the 11th century rebuilding of Christ Church and St. Augustine's Canterbury, in the development of Romanesque architecture', *BAA CT*, V, 1982, pp. 1-19.

Gem, R., 'Canterbury and the cushion capital: a commentary on passages from Goscelin's De Miraculis Sancti Augustini', *Romanesque and Gothic*, pp. 83-97.

Gem, R., 'Towards an iconography of Anglo-Saxon architecture', *JWCI*, 48, 1983, pp. 1-18.

Gervase, *Actus Pontificum*, ed. W. Stubbs, *Rolls Series*, LXXIII, London, 1880, pp. 325-413.

Gervase, *Gesta Regum*, ed. W. Stubbs, *Rolls Series*, LXXIII, London, 1880.

Gervase of Canterbury, *Opera Historica*, ed. W. Stubbs, *Rolls Series*, LXXIII, I, London, 1879.

Gervase, *Tractatus de Combustione et Reparatione Cantuariensis Ecclesiae*, ed. W. Stubbs, *Rolls Series*, LXXIII, I, London, 1879, pp. 4-29.

Gesta Stephani, transl. K.R. Potter, Oxford Medieval Texts, London, 1955.

☐ Gibson, M., *Lanfranc of Bec*, Oxford, 1978.

Ghislain, J.-C., 'Dalles funéraires romanes touraisiennes en Belgique', *Revue des historiens d'art, des archéologiques, des musicoloques et des orientalistes de l'état à Liège*, II, 1983, pp. 53-71.

Gillingham, J., *The Angevin Empire*, London, 1984.

Gilyard-Beer, R., 'The eastern arm of the abbey church of Bury-St-Edmunds', *Proceedings of the Suffolk Institute of Archaeology*, XXXI, 1969, pp. 256-262.

Godfrey, W.H., 'English cloister lavatories as independent structures', *Arch Jnl*, CVI, suppl., 1949, pp. 91-97.

Goldschmidt, A., *Die Elfenbeinskulpturen aus der Romanischen Zeit XI-XIII Jahrhunderts*, 2 vols., Berlin, 1923-1926.

Goldschmidt, A., *An Early Manuscript of the Aesop Fables of Avianus*, Princeton, 1947.

Gostling, W., *A Walk in and about the City of Canterbury*, Canterbury, 1777.

Gould, J., 'The twelfth century water-supply to Lichfield close', *Antiquaries Journal*, LVI, 1976, pp. 75-79.

Gransden, A., 'Realistic observation in twelfth century England', *Speculum*, 47, 1972, pp. 29-51.

☐ Gransden, A., *Historical Writings in England, c.550-1307*, Ithaca, 1974.

Grant, L., *Gothic Architecture in Normandy*, Ph.D. thesis, Courtauld Institute of Art, 1987.

Grierson, P., 'The relations between England and Flanders before the Norman Conquest', *Essays in Medieval History*, ed. R.W. Southern, London, 1968, pp. 61-92.

Grodecki, L., 'Le prieuré de Goult', *CA*, CXI, 1953, pp. 350-353.

Grodecki, L., 'The ancient glass of Canterbury Cathedral', *Burlington Magazine*, 92, 1950, pp. 294-297.

Grodecki, L., 'Les débuts de la sculpture romane en Normandie', *BM*, CVIII, 1950, pp. 7-67.

Grodecki, L., 'Les vitraux allégoriques de Saint-Denis', *Art de France*, I, 1961, pp. 32-34.

Grodecki, L., 'Problèmes de la peinture en Champagne pendant la seconde moitié du douzième siècle', *Romanesque and Gothic Art; Studies in Western Art*, Princeton, 1963, pp. 129-141.

Grodecki, L., 'Les chapiteaux cubiques de l'église de Vignory', *Le Moyen Age Retrouvé*, Paris, 1986, pp. 115-118.

Haines, C.R., *Dover Priory*, Cambridge, 1930.

Hamann, R., *Deutsche und Französische Kunst im Mittelalter II. Die Baugeschichte der Klosterkirche zu Lehnin und die Normannische Invasion in der Deutschen Architektur des 13.Jahrhunderts*, Marburg, 1923.

Hamel, C. de, *The Manuscripts of Herbert of Bosham*, R.W. Hunt Memorial Exhibition, Oxford, 1980.

Hamel, C. de, *Glossed Books of the Bible and the Origins of the Paris Book Trade*, Woodbridge, 1984.

Haney, K.E., 'A Norman antecedent for English floral ornament of the mid-twelfth century', *Scriptorium*, XXXVI, 1982, pp. 84-86.

Hare, J.N., 'The buildings of Battle Abbey: a preliminary survey', *PBC*, III, 1980, pp. 78-95.

Harnischfeger, E., *Die Bamberger Apokalypse*, Stuttgart, 1981.

Harris, A., 'A Romanesque candlestick in London', *JBAA*, XXVII, 1964, pp. 32-52.

Haseloff, A., *La scultura preromanica in Italia*, Florence, 1930.

Haskins, C.H., *The Renaissance of the Twelfth Century*, Cambridge, MA, 1927.

Hasted, E., *The History and Topographical Survey of the County of Kent*, 4 vols., Canterbury, 1778-1799.

The Heads of Religious Houses: England and Wales 940-1216, eds. D. Knowles, C.N.L. Brooke and V. London, Cambridge, 1972.

Hearne, M.F., 'A note on the chronology of Romsey Abbey', *JBAA*, XXXII, 1969, pp. 29-37.

Hearne, M.F., 'Romsey Abbey, a progenitor of the English national tradition', *Gesta*, XIV/i, 1975, pp. 27-40.

Heimann, A., 'A twelfth century manuscript from Winchcombe and its illustrations: Dublin, Trinity College, MS 53', *JWCI*, 28, 1965, pp. 86-109.

Heimann, A., 'The last copy of the Utrecht Psalter', *The Year 1200: A Symposium*, New York, 1975, pp. 313-338.

Héliot, P., *Les églises du moyen âge dans le Pas-de-Calais*, Arras, 1951-1953.

Héliot, P., 'Les parties romanes de la cathédrale de Tournai', *RB*, XXV, 1956, pp. 3-76.

Henderson, G., 'Narrative illustration and theological exposition in medieval art', *Studies in Church History*, XVII, 1981, pp. 19-31.

Henriet, J., 'La cathédrale Saint-Etienne de Sens: le parti du premier maître et les campaignes du XIIe siècle', *BM*, CXL, 1982, pp. 155-168.

Henriet, J., 'Une édifice de la première génération gothique; L'abbatiale de Saint-Germer-en-Fly', *BM*, 143/ii, 1985, pp. 7-142.

Henry, F. and Zarnecki, G., 'Romanesque arches decorated with human and animal heads', *JBAA*, XX-XXI, 1957-1958, pp. 1-35.

Henwood-Reverdot, A., *L'Eglise Saint-Etienne de Beauvais; histoire et architecture*, Beauvais, 1982.

Herschel, C., *The Two Books on the Water-Supply of the City of Rome by Sextus Julius Frontinus*, London, 1913.

Hervieux, L., *Les fabulistes latins depuis le siècle d'Auguste jusqu'à la fin du moyen âge*, 5 vols., Paris, 1884-1899.

Heslop, T.A., 'The conventual seals of Canterbury Cathedral, 1066-1232', *BAA CT*, V, 1982, pp. 94-100.

Heslop, T.A., 'Dunstanus Archiepiscopus and painting in Kent around 1120', *Burlington Magazine*, CXXVI, 1984, pp. 195-204.

Heslop, A. and Zarnecki, G., 'An ivory fragment from Battle Abbey', *Antiquaries Journal*, LX, 1980, pp. 341-342.

Higgitt, J.C., 'The Roman background to medieval England', *JBAA*, XXXVI, 3rd series, 1973, pp. 1-15.

Historia Monasterii S. Augustini Cantuariensis by Thomas of Elmham, ed. C. Hardwick, *Rolls Series*, VIII, 1858.

The Historical Works of Gervase of Canterbury, ed. W. Stubbs, *Rolls Series*, LXXIII, I-II, London, 1879-1880.

The Historical Works of Master Ralph de Diceto, Dean of London, ed. W. Stubbs, I, 1876.

The History of the King's Works, eds. R.A. Brown, H.M. Colvin and A.J. Taylor, London, 1963.

A History of York Minster, ed. G.E. Aylmer and R. Cant, Oxford, 1977.

Hohler, E.B., 'The capitals of Urnes church and their background', *Acta Archaeologia*, 1976, pp. 1-46.

Hollister, C.W., 'St Anselm on lay investiture', *PBC*, X, 1987, pp. 145-158.

Homburger, O., *Die Anfänge der Malschule von Winchester im X. Jahrhundert*, Leipzig, 1912.

Homburger, O., 'Zur Stilbestimmung der Figurlichen Kunst Deutschlands und des Westlichen Europas im Zeitraum zwischen 1190 und 1250', *Formositas Romanica. Festschrift J. Ganter*, Frauenfeldt, 1958, pp. 31-45.

Hope, St John W., *The Architectural History of the Cathedral Church and Monastery of St Andrew Rochester*, London, 1900.

Hope, W. St. John, 'The London Charterhouse and its old water supply', *Archaeologia*, vol. LVIII, 1902, pp. 293-312.

Hope, St John W., 'Quire screens in English churches, with special reference to the twelfth-century quire screen formerly in the cathedral church of Ely', *Archaeologia*, LXVIII, 1916-1917, pp. 43-110

Hope, W.H. and Fowler, J.T., 'Recent discoveries in the cloister of Durham Abbey', *Archaeologia*, LVIII, 1902, pp. 437-460.

Horn, W. and Born, E., *The Plan of St Gall*, Berkeley, 1979.

Hoyt, R.S., 'A pre-Domesday Kentish assessment list', *A Medieval Miscellany for D. M. Stenton*, eds. P.M. Barnes and C.F. Slade, *Pipe Roll Society*, new series, XXXVI, London, 1962, pp. 189-202.

☐ James, M.R., *The Ancient Libraries of Canterbury and Dover: the Catalogue of the Libraries of Christ Church Priory and St Augustine's Abbey at Canterbury and of St Martin's Priory at Dover*, Cambridge, 1903.

James, M.R., *A Bestiary of the Twelfth Century*, Roxburghe Club, 1928.

James, M.R., *The Canterbury Psalter*, London, 1935.

Jenkins, R.C., 'On some fragments of Norman building recently discovered at Great Woodlands in the parish of Lyminge', *AC*, IV, 1861, pp. 123-126.

Jewell, R.H.I., 'The Anglo-Saxon friezes at Breedon-on-the-Hill, Leicestershire', *Archaeologia*, CVIII, 1986, pp. 95-115.

Jullian, M., 'L'image de la musique dans la sculpture romane en France', *Cahiers de civilisation médiévale*, XXX, 1987, pp. 33-44.

Kahn, D., 'The structural evidence for the dating of the St Gabriel chapel wall-painting at Christ Church Cathedral, Canterbury', *Burlington Magazine*, CXXVI, 1984, pp. 225-229.

Kahn, D., 'The west doorway at Rochester Cathedral', *Romanesque and Gothic*, pp. 129-134.

Kahn, D., 'La sculpture romane en Angleterre: état des questions', *BM*, 146/iv, 1988, pp. 307-340.

Katzenellenbogen, A., *Allegories of Virtue and Vice in Medieval Art*, London, 1939.

Kauffmann, C.M., 'The Bury Bible (Cambridge, Corpus Christi College, M.S. 2)', *JWCI*, XXIX, 1966, pp. 60-81.

Kauffmann, C.M., *Romanesque Manuscripts 1066-1190*, London, 1975.

Kautzsch, R., 'Oberitalien und der Mittelrhein im 12. Jahrhundert', *Atti del X Congresso Internationale di Storia dell'Arte in Roma; L'Italia e l'arte straniera*, 1922, pp. 123-130.

Kautzsch, R., *Kapitellstudien. Beiträge zu einer Geschichte des spätantiken Kapitelles im Osten vom vierten bis ins siebente Jahrhundert*, Berlin/Leipzig, 1936.

Kelleher, C., *Illumination of Saint-Bertin at Saint-Omer under Odbert*, Ph.D. thesis, Courtauld Institute of Art, 1968.

Kendrick, T.D., *Anglo-Saxon Art*, London, 1938.

Kendrick, T.D., 'Instances of Saxon survival in post-Conquest sculpture', *Proceedings of the Cambridgeshire Antiquarian Society*, XXXIX, 1940, pp. 78-84.

Kendrick, T.D., *Late Saxon and Viking Art*, London, 1949.

Kepinski, Z., 'La symbolique de la porte de Gniezno', *Drzwi Gnie'znie'nskie*, ed. M. Walicki, II, Warsaw, 1959, pp. 161-283.

Ker, N.R., *Medieval Libraries of Great Britain*, London, 1941.

Ker, N.R., *English Manuscripts in the Century After the Conquest*, Oxford, 1960.

Keyser, C., *Norman Tympana and Lintels*, London, 1927.

Kidson, P., 'The Gothic choir', *Arch Jnl*, CXXVI, 1969, pp. 244-246.

Kiesow, G., *Romanik in Hessen*, Stuttgart, 1984.

Kimpel, D. and Suckale, R., *Die gotische Architektur in Frankreich 1130-1270*, Munich, 1985.

Kirchner-Doberer, E., *Die deutschen Lettner bis 1300*, Vienna/Linz, 1946.

☐ Knowles D., *The Monastic Order in England, 940-1216*, Cambridge, 1940.

Knowles, D., *The Monastic Constitutions of Lanfranc*, Cambridge, 1949.

Knowles, D., Brooke, C.N.L. and London, V., *The Heads of Religious Houses: England and Wales, 940-1216*, Cambridge, 1972.

Knowles M.D., 'Archbishop Thomas Becket. A character study', *Proceedings of the British Academy*, XXXV, 1949, pp. 3-31.

Kubach, H.W. and Haas, W., *Der Dom zu Speyer*, Berlin, 1972.

Lanfry, G., 'La crypte romane de l'onzième siècle de la cathédrale de Rouen', *BM*, 95, 1936, pp. 181-201.

Lapiere, M., *La lettre ornée dans les manuscrits mosans d'origine bénédictine (XIe-XIIe siècles)*, Bibliothèque de la Faculté de Philosophie et Lettres de l'Université de Liège, CCXXIX, Paris, 1981.

Lasko, P., *Ars Sacra*, Harmondsworth, 1972.

Lasteyrie, R. de, *L'architecture religieuse en France à l'époque romane*, Paris, 1929.

Lawrence, A., 'Manuscripts in Canterbury 1060-1090', M. A. thesis, Courtauld Institute of Art, 1977.

Lawrence, A., 'The influence of Canterbury on the collection and production of manuscripts at Durham in the Anglo-Norman period', *The Vanishing Past. Studies in Medieval Art, Liturgy and Metrology presented to Christopher Hohler*, eds. A. Borg and A. Martindale, British International Report, International Series, III, 1981.

Ledwich, E., 'Observations on ancient churches', *Archaeologia*, VIII, 1787.

☐ Legg, J.W. and St John Hope, W.H., *Inventories of Christ Church, Canterbury*, London, 1902.

Le Goff, J., *Time, Work and Culture in the Middle Ages*, transl. A. Goldhammer, Chicago, 1980.

Lehmann-Brockhaus, O., *Lateinische Schriftquellen zur Kunst in England, Wales, und Schottland vom Jahre 901 bis zum Jahre 1307*, I-V, Munich, 1955-1960.

Lelong, C., 'L'abbatiale romane de Marmoutier (1066-1096)', *BM*, 145/ii, 1987, pp. 173-204.

Lethaby, W.R., *Westminster Abbey Re-examined*, London, 1925.

W. Levison, *England and the Continent in the Eighth Century*, Oxford, 1946.

Leyser, K.J., *Medieval Germany and its Neighbours, 900-1250*, London, 1982.

Licht, E., *Ottonische und frühromanische Kapitelle in Deutschland*, Marburg, 1935.

Liebeschutz, H., *Medieval Humanism in the Life and Writings of John of Salisbury*, London, 1950.

Livett, G.M., 'Notes on the church of St-Margaret-at-Cliffe', *AC*, XXIV, 1900, pp. 175-180.

Lloyd, T.H., *The English Wool Trade in the Middle Ages*, Cambridge, 1977.

Magni, M., 'Cryptes du haut moyen âge en Italie: problèmes de typologie du IXe jusqu'au début du XIe siècle', *Cahiers archéologiques*, XXVIII, 1979, pp. 41-85.

Maillon, J., *Chartres. Le jubé de la cathédrale*, Paris, 1964.

Mair, R., 'The choir capitals of Canterbury Cathedral, 1174-84', *BAA CT*, V, 1982, pp. 56-66.

Mâle, E., *L'Art religieux du XIIe siècle en France. Etude sur l'origine de l'iconographie du moyen âge*, Paris, 1922.

William of Malmesbury, *De Gestis Pontificum Anglorum*, ed. N.E.S.A. Hamilton, *Rolls Series*, LII, London, 1870.

Mallet, J., *L'art roman de l'ancien Anjou*, Paris, 1984.

Materials for the History of Thomas Becket, ed. J.C. Robertson, *Rolls Series*, LXVII, 7 vols., London, 1875-1885.

McAleer, J.P., 'The Ethelbert tower, St Augustine, Canterbury', *JBAA*, CXL, 1987, pp. 88-111.

McKnight Crosby, S., *The Royal Abbey of Saint Denis from its Beginnings to the death of Suger; 475-1151*, New Haven, 1987.

Mellinkoff, R., *The Horned Moses in Medieval Art, and Thought*, Berkeley, 1978.

Memorials of St Dunstan, Archbishop of Canterbury, ed. W. Stubbs, *Rolls Series*, LXIII, London, 1874.

Mende, U., *Die Bronzetüren des Mittelalters*, Munich, 1983.

Mercklin, E. von, *Antike Figuralkapitelle*, Berlin, 1962.

Meredith, J., *The impact of Italy on the Romanesque architectural sculpture of England*, Yale University, Ph.D. thesis, 1980.

Miscampbell, C., 'A twelfth-century re-building at St Augustine's Abbey, Canterbury', *Collectanea Historica: Essays in Memory of Stuart Rigold*, ed. A. Detsicas, Maidstone, 1981, pp. 63-65.

Morgan, N., *Early Gothic Manuscripts, 1190-1250*, I, London, 1982.

Musset, L., 'La pierre de Caen: extraction et commerce, XIe-XVe siècles', *Pierre et métal dans le bâtiment au moyen âge*, eds. O. Chapelot and P. Benoît, Paris, 1985, pp. 219-235.

Mynors, R.A.B., *Durham Cathedral Manuscripts from the Sixth to the Twelfth Centuries*, Oxford, 1939.

Newman, J., *West Kent and the Weald, B/E*, Harmondsworth, 1969.

Newman, J., *North East and East Kent, B/E*, Harmondsworth, 1976.

Nicholl, D., *Thurstan of York, 1114-1140*, York, 1964.

Nilgen, U., 'Thomas Becket as a patron of the arts', *Art History*, III/4, 1980, pp. 357-374.

Nilgen, U., 'Intellectuality and splendour: Thomas Becket as a patron of the arts', *SAOP*, VIII, 1986, pp. 145-158.

Nortier, G., 'Les bibliothèques médiévales des abbayes bénédictines de Normandie', *Revue Mabillion*, 1957, pp. 57-83.

Norton, E.C., 'A Parisian workshop at Canterbury. A late thirteenth century tile pavement in the Corona Chapel, and the origins of Tyler Hill', *JBAA*, CXXXIV, 1981, pp. 58-80.

Omont, H., *Psautier illustré XIIIe siècle*, Paris, 1906.

The Ecclesiastical History of Orderic Vitalis, I-VI, ed. M. Chibnall, Oxford, 1980.

Osbern, *Vita Sancti Dunstani*, ed. W. Stubbs, *Rolls Series*, LXIII, London, 1874, pp. 69-128.

Osbern, *Liber Miraculorum*, ed. W. Stubbs, *Rolls Series*, LXIII, London, 1874, pp. 129-161.

Osbern, *Vita S. Elphegi, Anglia Sacra*, II, pp. 122-142.

Pächt, O., 'Hugo Pictor', *Bodleian Library Record*, III, no. 30, Oxford, 1950.

Pächt, O., *The Rise of Pictorial Narrative in Twelfth Century England*, Oxford, 1962.

Pächt, O., 'The pre-Carolingian roots of early Romanesque art', *Congrès International d'Histoire de l'art, Studies in Western Art*, I, 1963, pp. 67-75.

Panofsky, E. and Saxl, F., 'Classical Mythology in Medieval Art', *Metropolitan Museum Studies*, IV, 1933, pp. 228-280.

Papsturkunden in England, II, ed. W. Holtzmann, Göttingen, 1935.

Patourel, J. le, 'The report of the trial on Penenden Heath', *Studies in Medieval History presented to F.M. Powicke*, ed. R. Hunt et al., Oxford, 1948.

Patourel, J. le, *The Norman Empire*, Oxford, 1976.

Phillips, D., *Excavations at York Minster*, II, London, 1985.

Philp, B., 'Excavations at Faversham', *Kent Archaeological Research Groups Council*, Crawley, 1968.

Plât, A.G., *L'architecture religieuse en Touraine, des origines au XIIe siècle. L'art de bâtir en France des romains à l'an 1100*, Paris, 1939.

Pinder, W., *Der Naumburger Dom und seine Bildwerke*, Berlin, 1933.

Poole, A.L., *From Domesday Book to Magna Carta, 1087-1216*, 2nd ed., Oxford, 1955.

Poole, R.L., 'The early correspondence of John of Salisbury', *Proceedings of the British Academy*, XI, 1925, pp. 27-53.

Porée, A.A., *Histoire de l'abbaye de Bec*, Evreux, 1901.

Porter, A.K., *Lombard Architecture*, 2 vols., New York, 1917.

Postan, M.M., *Medieval Trade and Finance*, Cambridge, 1973.

Postan, M.M., *The Medieval Economy and Society*, Harmondsworth, 1978.

Powicke, F.M., *The Loss of Normandy (1189-1204) Studies in the History of the Angevin Empire*, Manchester, 1913.

Pressouyre, L., 'St. Bernard to St. Francis: Monastic ideals and iconographic programs in the cloister', *Gesta*, XII, 1973, pp. 71-92.

Pressouyre, S., *Images d'un cloître disparu*, Paris, 1976.

Prior, E.S., and Gardner, A., *An Account of Medieval Figure-Sculpture in England*, Cambridge, 1912.

Pugin, A.W., *A Treatise on Chancel Screens and Rood Lofts*, London, 1851.

Rademacher, F., *Die Gustorfer Chorschranken*, Bonn, 1975.

Radocsay, D., 'Vier verlorengegangene romanische Kapitelle aus der Sammlung Schnütgen', *Westfalen*, vol. XLII, 1964, pp. 225-233.

Raspi Serra, J., 'English decorative sculpture of the early twelfth-century and the Como-Pavian tradition', *AB*, vol. LI/4, 1966, pp. 352-362.

Renn, D., 'The decoration of Canterbury Castle keep', *BAA CT*, vol. V, 1982, pp. 125-128.

Rickert, M., *Painting in Britain in the Middle Ages*, Harmondsworth, 1954.

Rigold, S.E., 'The demesne of Christ Chruch at Brook', *Arch Jnl*, vol. CXXVI, 1970, pp. 270-272.

Rigold, S.E., 'Romanesque bases in and south-east of the limestone belt', *Ancient Monuments and their Interpretations. Essays Presented to A.J. Taylor*, ed. M.R. Apted, L.P. Gilard-Beer, A.D. Saunders, London, 1977, pp. 99-137.

Rites of Durham (1593), ed. J.T. Fowler, *Surtees Society*, vol. CVII, 1902.

Rivoira, G.T., *Lombardic Architecture. Its Origins, Development and Derivatives*, London, 1910.

Robertson, W.A. Scott, 'The crypt of Canterbury Cathedral', *AC*, vol. XIII, 1880, pp. 17-80, 500-52.

Robertson, W.A. Scott, *The Crypt of Canterbury Cathedral: Its Architecture, its History and its Frescos*, London, 1880.

Robertson, W.A. Scott, 'St Anselm's chapel, Canterbury Cathedral', *AC*, XVIII, 1889, pp. 169-173.

Robinson, G., and Urquart, H., 'Seal bags in the treasury of the cathedral church of Canterbury', *Archaeologia*, vol. 84, 1934, pp. 163-211.

Robinson, J.A., *The Times of St Dunstan*, Oxford, 1923.

Rolland, R., 'Chronologie de la cathédrale de Tournai', *RB*, vol. IV, 1934, pp. 103-137.

Routledge, C.F.; Robertson, W.A.S. and Sheppard, J.B., 'On discoveries in the crypt of Canterbury Cathedral', *AC*, vol. XVIII, 1889, pp. 254.

Ruprich-Robert, V., *L'architecture normande aux XIe et XIIe siècle en normandie et en angleterre*, 2 vols., Paris, 1884.

The Letters of John of Salisbury. The Early Letters (1153-1161), I, eds. W.J. Millor and H.E. Butler, revised by C.N.L. Brooke, London, 1955.

The Letters of John of Salisbury. The Later Letters (1163-1180), eds. W.J. Millor and C.N.L. Brooke, Oxford, 1979.

☐ Saltman, A., *Theobald, Archbishop of Canterbury*, London,1956.

Salzman, F., *Building in England down to 1540*, Oxford, 1952.

Sauerländer, W., 'L'art antique et la sculpture autour de 1200', *Art de France*, vol. I, 1961, pp. 98.

Sauerländer, W., 'Architecture and the Figurative Arts: The North', *Renaissance and Renewal in the Twelfth Century*, ed. R.Benson, and G.Constable, Cambridge, 1982.

Sauerländer, W., *Von Sens bis Strassburg: Ein Beitrag zur Kunstgeschichtlichen Stellung der Strassburger Querhausskulpturen*, Berlin, 1966.

Sauerländer, W., *Gothic Sculpture in France 1140-1210*, London, 1972.

☐ Saxl, F., *English Romanesque Sculptures of the Twelfth Century*, ed. H. Swarzenski, London, 1954.

Saxl, F., 'Illuminated science manuscripts in England', *Lectures*, London, 1957, pp. 96-110.

Saxl, F., *Lectures*, 2 vols., Warburg Institute, London, 1957.

Saxl, F., and Wittkower, R., *British Art and the Mediterranean*, Oxford, 1948.

Scheller, R.W., *A Survey of Medieval Model Books*, Haarlem, 1963.

Schiller, G., *Iconography of Christian Art*, 2 vols., London, 1971.

Schnitzler, H., *Rheinische Schatzkammer*, vol. I & II, Düsseldorf, 1959.

Schnitzler, H., *Der Schrein des Heiligen Heribert*, Monchengladbach, 1962.

Schulz-Mons, C., 'Die Chorschrankenreliefs der Michaeliskirche zu Hildesheim', *Schriftenreihe des Stadtarchivs und der Stadtbibliothek Hildesheim*, vol. 7, Hildesheim, 1979.

Scott, Sir. G.G., 'The choir screen in Canterbury Cathedral', *Arch Jnl*, vol. XXXII, pp. 86-88.

Sculptures Romanes et Gothiques du Nord de la France, Musée es Beaux-Arts de Lille, 1978-1979.

Serbat, L., 'Vieux-Saint-Sauveur, Caen', *CA*, vol. LXXXV, i, 1908, pp. 81-86.

Serbat, L., 'Quelques églises anciennement détruites du nord de la France', *BM*, 1929, pp. 365-435.

Severens, K., 'William of Sens and the double columns at Sens and Canterbury', *JWCI*, vol. XXXIII, 1970, pp. 307-313.

Sheppard, J.B., 'On discoveries in St Anselm's chapel, Canterbury Cathedral', *AC*, vol. XVIII, 1889, pp. 174-176.

Slater, F., 'Chislet church', *AC*, vol. XII, 1878, pp. 106-112.

Slomann, V., *Bicorporate, Studies in Revivals and Migrations of Art Motifs*, Copenhagen, 1967.

Smith, R.A.L., 'The central financial system of Christ Church, Canterbury, 1186-1512', *English Historical Review*, vol. 55, 1940, pp. 353-369.

Smith, R.A.L., 'The place of Gundulf in the Anglo-Norman Church', *English Historical Review*, vol. LVIII, 1943.

Smith, R.A.L., *Collected Papers*, London, 1947.

Smith, R.A.L., *Canterbury Cathedral Priory*, Cambridge, 1969.

Somner, W., *The Antiquities of Canterbury*, London, 1703.

Southern, R.W., *The Making of the Middle Ages*, London, 1953.

Southern, R.W., 'The English origins of the miracles of the Virgin', *Medieval and Renaissance Studies*, vol. IV, 1958, pp. 176-216.

☐ Southern, R.W., *St Anselm and his Biographer*, Cambridge, 1966.

Southern, R.W., 'The monks of Canterbury and the murder of Archbishop Becket', *Friends of Canterbury Cathedral and the William Urry Trust*, 1985.

Stalley, R., 'A twelfth-century patron of architecture; a study of the buildings erected by Roger, Bishop of Salisbury 1102-1139', *JBAA*, vol. XXXIV, 1971, p. 75-83.

Stanley, A., *Historical Memorials of Canterbury*, London, 1904.

☐ Stone, L., *Sculpture in Britain: The Middle Ages*, Harmondsworth, 1955.

Stratford, N., Tudor-Craig, P. and Muthesius, A.M. 'Archbishop Hubert Walter's tomb and its furnishings', *BAA CT*, vol. V, 1982, pp. 71-93.

Stratford, N. 'The 'Henry of Blois plaques' in the British Museum', *BAA CT*, vol. VI, 1983, pp. 28-37.

Strik, H.J. A., 'Remains of the Lanfranc building in the great central tower and the northwest choir/transept area', *BAA CT*, vol. V, 1982, pp. 20-26.

Strzygowski, J., *The Origins of Christian Church Art*, Oxford, 1923.

Sumption, J., *Pilgrimage, an Image of Medieval Religion*, London, 1975.

Swarzenski, H., *Monuments of Romanesque Art, the Art of Church Treasures in North-Western Europe*, London, 1954.

Tatton-Brown, T., 'Researches and discoveries in Kent', *AC*, vol. XCV, 1979, pp. 276-278.

Tatton-Brown, T., 'The font in St. Martin's church', *Historical Essays in Memory of James Hobbs*, ed. M. Spark, Canterbury, 1980, pp. 19-20.

Tatton-Brown, T., 'The use of Quarr stone in London and East Kent', *Medieval Archaeology*, vol. XXIV, 1980, pp. 213-215.

Taylor, H.M., *Anglo-Saxon Architecture*, vol. III, Cambridge, 1978.

Taylor, J., and Taylor, H.M., *Anglo-Saxon Architecture*, vol. I, Cambridge, 1965.

Taylor, J., and Taylor, H.M., 'Architectural sculpture in pre-Norman England', *JBAA*, vol. XXIX, 3rd series, 1966, pp. 47-49.

Tester, P.J., 'Excavations on the site of Leeds Priory', *AC*, vol. XCIII, 1977, pp. 33-45, and XCIV, 1978, pp. 75-98.

Tester, P.J., 'Excavations at Boxley Abbley', *AC*, vol. LXXXVIII, 1973, pp. 129-158.

Thomson, R.M., *Manuscripts from St. Albans Abbey 1066-1235*, Woodbridge, 1985.

Thorne, W., *Chronicle of St Augustine's Abbey*, ed. and transl. A.H. Davis, Oxford, 1934.

Thorpe, J., *Registrum Roffense*, London, 1769.

Thorpe, J., *Custumale Roffense*, London, 1788.

Thurlby, M., *Transitional Sculpture in England*, Ph.D. thesis, University of East Anglia, 1976.

Thurlby, M., 'A note on the Romanesque sculpture at Hereford Cathedral and the Hereford school of sculpture', *Burlington Magazine*, vol. CXXVI, 1984, pp. 233-234.

Timmers. J.J.M., *De Kunst van het Maasland*, Essen, 1971.

Toke, N.E., 'The opus Alexandrinum and sculptured stone roundels in the retro-choir of Canterbury Cathedral', *BAA CT*, vol. V, 1982, pp. 67-70.

Tollenaere, L., *La sculpture sur pierre de l'ancien diocèse de Liège à l'époque Roman*, Namur, 1957.

Toynbee, J., and Ward-Perkins, J.W., *The Shrine of St. Peter*, London, 1956.

Trésors des Abbayes Normandes, Rouen, 1979.

Tristram, E., ' The Paintings of Canterbury Cathedral', *Canterbury Papers*, 6, Canterbury, 1935.

Tristram, E., *English Medieval Wall Painting of the Twelfth Century*, London, 1944.

Tudor-Craig, P., 'The tomb', *BAA CT*, Canterbury, 1982, pp. 72-75.

Urry, W., 'Saint Anselm and his cult at Canterbury', *Spicilegium Beccense*, vol. I, 1959, pp. 571-593.

☐ Urry, W., *Canterbury under the Angevin Kings*, London, 1967.

Urry, W., 'Some notes on the resting places of St. Thomas Becket at Canterbury', *Thomas Becket Actes du Colloque International de Sédières*, ed. R. Foreville, Paris, 1975, pp. 195-208.

Urry, W., 'Canterbury, Kent', *Local Maps and Plans from Medieval England*, eds. R.A. Skelton and Ph.D. A. Harvey, Oxford, 1986, pp. 43-58.

Vallance, A., *Greater English Church Screens*, London, 1947.

Vallery-Radot, 'Motivilliers, église abbatiale', *CA*, vol. LXXXIX, 1926, pp. 492-499.

Vallery-Radot, J., *Églises romanes, filiation et échanges d'influences*, Paris, 1931.

Vanuxem, J., 'Les portails détruits de la cathédrale de Cambrai et de Saint Nicholas d'Amiens', *BM*, vol. CIII, 1945, pp. 89-102.

Vanuxem, J., 'La sculpture du XIIe à Cambrai et à Arras', *BM*, vol. CXIII, 1955, pp. 1-35.

Verfaille-Markey, D., 'Le dernier cahier du Psautier d'Eadwine', *Scriptorium*, vol. XXXVII, 1983, pp. 245-258.

Vergnolle, E., 'Un carnet de modèles de l'an mil originaire de Saint-Benoît sur-Loire', *Arte Medieval*, vol. II, 1985, pp. 1-34.

Vergnolle, E., *Saint-Benoît-sur-Loire et la Sculpture du XI siècle*, Paris, 1985.

Vetusta Monumenta, Society of Antiquaries of London, vol. II, London, 1755.

The Victoria History of the County of Kent, ed. W. Page, 3 vols., London, 1908-1932.

Vita Sancti Dunstani, ed. W. Stubbs, *Rolls Series*, vol. LXIII, London, 1874, pp. 69-128.

Vitruvius, *De Architectura*, ed. and transl. F. Granger, vol. II, Cambridge, 1962.

Walberg, E., *La tradition hagiographique de Saint Thomas Becket avant la fin du XIIe siècle*, Paris, 1929.

Walford, W.S., 'On a remarkable sculpture lately found in Bobbing church, Kent', *Arch Jln*, vol. XXI, 1864, pp. 246-253.

Ward, H.S., *The Canterbury Pilgrimage*, London, 1904.

Ward-Perkins, J.W.,'The shrine of St. Peter and its twelve spiral columns', *Journal of Roman Studies*, vol. XLII, 1952, pp. 21-33.

Warren, W.L., *Henry II*, London, 1977.

Warren, W.L., *King John*, London, 1978.

Watson, A., *The Early Iconography of the Tree of Jesse*, Oxford/London, 1934.

Webb, G., *Architecture in England: The Middle Ages*, Harmondsworth, 1954.

Webster, J.C., *The Labors of the Months in Antique and Medieval to the end of the Twelfth Century*, Chicago, 1938.

Wehrhahn-Staunch, L., 'Christliche Fischsymbolik von den Anfängen bis zum hohen Mittelalter', *Zeitschrift für Kunstgeschichte*, vol. 35, 1972, pp. 1-68.

Wentzel, H., 'Antiken-Imitationen des 12. und 13. Jahrhunderts in Italien', *Zeitschrift für Kunstwissenschaft*, Band vol. IX, Heft 1-2, 1955.

White, L., *Medieval Religion and Technology*, Los Angeles, 1978.

Whinney, M.D., *The Interrelation of the Fine Arts in England in the Early Middle Ages*, London, 1930.

Williamson, P., *An Introduction to Medieval Ivory Carvings*, London, 1982.

Williamson, P., *Catalogue of Romanesque Sculpture, Victoria and Albert Museum*, London 1983.

Willis, R., 'The architectural history of Winchester Cathedral', *Proceedings of the Archaeological Institute*, 1846.

☐ Willis, R., *The Architectural History of Canterbury Cathedral*, London, 1845.

☐ Willis, R., *The Architectural History of the Conventual Buildings of the Monastery of Christ Church in Canterbury*, London, 1869.

Wilson, D.M., 'Scandinavian settlement in the north and west of the British Isles', *Transactions of the Royal Historical Society*, fifth series, vol. XXVI, 1976, pp. 95-113.

Wilson, D.M., *The Bayeux Tapestry*, London, 1985.

Winterfeld, D.V., *Der Dom in Bamberg*, Berlin, 1979.

Withers, H., *The Cathedral Church of Canterbury; A Description of its Fabric and a brief History of the Archiepiscopal See*, Bell's Cathedral Series, London, 1899.

Witney, K.P., *The Jutish Forest, A Study of Weald of Kent from 450 to 1380 A.D.*, London,1976.

Wood, M., *Norman Domestic Architecture*, London, 1974.

Woodman, F., 'Lanfranc's cathedral at Canterbury', *Canterbury Cathedral Chronicle*, vol. LXXI, 1977, pp. 11-16.

☐ Woodman, F., *The Architectural History of Canterbury Cathedral*, London, 1981.

Woodruff, C., Danks, W., *Memorials of the Cathedral and Priory of Christ in Canterbury*, London,1912.

Woodruff, C.E., 'The Financial Aspect of the Cult of St. Thomas of Canterbury', *AC*, vol. 44, 1932, pp. 13-32.

Woolnoth, W., *A Graphical Illustration of the Metropolitan Cathedral Church of Canterbury*, London, 1816.

Wormald, F., *English Benedictine Kalendars after 1100*, Henry Bradshaw Society , London, 1939.

Wormald, F., 'Decorated Initials in English MSS. from A.D. 900 to 1100', *Archaeologia*, vol. XCI, (1941), repr. *Francis Wormald Collected Writings, Vol. I*, London, 1984, pp. 47-75.

Wormald, F., *English Drawing of the Tenth and Eleventh Centuries*, London, 1952.

Wormald, F., 'The survival of Anglo-Saxon Illumination after the Norman Conquest', *Proceedings of the British Academy*, vol. XXX (1944), repr. *Francis Wormald Collected Writings, Vol. I*, London, 1984, pp. 153-168.

Wormald, F., *Collected Writings, Vol. I*; eds. J.J.G. Alexander, T.J. Brown and J. Gibbs, *Studies in Medieval Art from the Sixth to the Twelfth Century*, London, 1984.

The Year 1200: A Centenial Exhibition at the Metropolitan Museum of Art, ed. K. Hoffmann, vol. I and II, New York, 1970.

☐ Zarnecki, G., *English Romanesque Sculpture, 1066-1140*, London, 1951.

Zarnecki, G., 'The Faussett Pavilion: the King Canute Relief', *Archeologia Cantiana*, vol. 66, 1953, pp. 1-8.

☐ Zarnecki, G., *Later English Romanesque Sculpture, 1140-1210*, London, 1953.

Zarnecki, G., 'The Winchester acanthus in Romanesque sculpture', *Wallraf-Richartz Jahrbuch*, vol. XVII, 1955, pp. 1-4.

Zarnecki, G., *English Romanesque Lead Sculpture: Lead Fonts of the Twelfth Century*, London, 1957.

Zarnecki, G., *The Early Sculpture of Ely Cathedral*, London, 1958.

Zarnecki, G., '1066 and architectural sculpture', *Proceedings of the British Academy*, vol. LII, 1966, pp. 87-104.

Zarnecki, G., 'A Romanesque casket from Canterbury in Florence', *Canterbury Cathedral Chronicles*, vol. LXIV, 1969, pp. 37-43.

Zarnecki, G., 'The capitals of the crypt', *Arch Jln*, vol. CXXVI, 1970, pp. 246-247.

Zarnecki, G., 'A Twelfth-Century Column-Figure of the Standing Virgin from Minister-in-Sheppey,' *Kunsthistorische Forschungen*, 1972, pp. 1-9.

Zarnecki, G., 'The Romanesque Capitals in the South Transept of Worcester Cathedral', *BAA CT*, vol.1, 1978, pp. 38-42.

Zarnecki, G., 'A Romanesque capital from Canterbury at Chartham', *AC*, vol. XCV, 1979, pp. 1-6.

Zarnecki, G., 'Romanesque sculpture in Normandy and England in the eleventh century', *PBC*, vol. I, 1979, pp. 168-189.

Zarnecki, G., *Studies in Romanesque Sculpture*, London, 1979.

Zarnecki, G., 'Sculpture in stone in the English Romanesque exhibition', *SAOP*, 1986, pp. 9-22.

Zarnecki, G. 'Henry of Blois as a patron of sculpture', *SAOP*, 1986, pp. 159-172.

Zarnecki, G., *Romanesque Lincoln, the Sculpture of the Cathedral*, Lincoln, 1988.

List of Illustrations

1. Cambridge, Trinity College, MS B.16.44., p. 405

2. Pen and ink drawing of Archbishop Lanfranc, Oxford, Bodleian Library 569 (S.C.2311) f.1.

3. Initial showing Archbishop Anselm seated on a throne. Rouen, MS 539, f.59.

4. Seal of Theobald, Archbishop of Canterbury (1139-1161)

5. The gabled end of a tomb showing an archbishop, presumably Thomas Becket.

6. Fragment presumably from the choir screen, c.1180, in Canterbury Cathedral.

7. The south doorway, c.1180, of the parish church of St Nicholas, Barfreston.

8. Capital of Purbeck marble, c.1150, from the royal abbey at Faversham.

9. The west doorway of Rochester Cathedral, c.1165.

10. The south doorway of St Mary's church, Patrixbourne, c.1170.

11. Eve hiding from the Lord in the Garden of Eden, c.1000. Detail from p.41 of Oxford, Bodleian Library, MS Junius 11.

12. St Luke from the Arenberg Gospels, c.990. New York, Pierpont Morgan Library, M 869, f.83v.

13. St John from the Eadui Psalter, c.1020. Hanover, Kestner Museum WM XXIa 36, f.147v.

14. The Gloucester Candlestick. London, Victoria and Albert Museum.

15. One of a pair of pierced bookcovers made of whalebone, c.1100. London, Victoria and Albert Museum.

16. Detail from the Bayeux Tapestry showing Westminster Abbey.

17. Watercolour by J.C. Buckler showing the elevation of the north-west tower of Canterbury Cathedral as it stood in 1832. London, Society of Antiquaries.

18. West front of Saint-Etienne, Caen.

19. Detail of watercolour by Buckler showing the cushion capitals of Lanfranc's western tower.

20. The west wall of Archbishop Lanfranc's crypt with its original cushion capitals, c.1071.

21-24. Four columns from the dark entry passage of Lanfranc's church, c.1080.

25-29. Five reliefs from Canterbury, carved with foliage and grotesques and pre-dating the crypt capitals. Canterbury Heritage Museum.

30. Two confronted grotesques from the border of the Bayeux Tapestry.

31. The south aisle of the crypt.

32. General view of the crypt.

33. Crypt shaft with unfinished capital.

34-35. Details of an unfinished cushion capital in ill. 33.

36. Unfinished crypt impost.

37. Crypt capital with unfinished scallop ornament.

38. Shaft with cushion capital and moulded base that has some additional foliage.

39. The Holy Innocents' Chapel in the crypt.

40. Cushion capital, carved with a winged dragon and twisted tail, in the Holy Innocents' Chapel.

41. Capital with dragon in the choir of Sant' Abondio, Como.

42. Capital with dragon from the chapter house at Hersfeld Abbey.

43. Cushion capital with a double-bodied lion in St Gabriel's Chapel.

44. Initial D with a double-bodied lion in London, BL, Royal MS 5.B.XV, f.3.

45. Cushion capital with a double-bodied grotesque in the choir of St. Margarethe, Weissendorf (Bavaria).

46. Initial O containing a double-bodied lion in Rouen, Bibl. Mun., MS A.85, f.36v.

47-48. Capitals in the crypt based on the Corinthian type.

49. Free-standing capital in the crypt based on the Corinthian type.

50. Crypt capital with elements of Corinthian and cushion forms.

51. Cushion capital in the crypt carved with foliage joined by a clasp.

52. Cushion capital in the crypt with animal head clasp and foliage.

53. Initial B with foliage joined by a clasp, in Cambridge, Trinity College, MS B.5.28, f.45v.

54. Initial D with animal head clasp and foliage, in Cambridge, Trinity College, MS B.4.26, f.2.

55. Cushion capital in the Innocents' Chapel with 'Winchester acanthus foliage'.

56. Initial I with 'Winchester acanthus'. Durham Cathedral Library, MS A.II.4, f.36v.

57. Block capital in the crypt, with angle masks and curling foliage.

58. Initial Q with curling foliage. Cambridge, Trinity College, MS 0.2.51, f.34.

59. Capital from the cloister of King Henry I's foundation (1121) at Reading Abbey with angle masks and foliage.

60. Block capital in the crypt carved with full-length bearded heads and foliage.

219

61. Detail of initial I in Baltimore, Walters Art Gallery, MS 10.18, f.29 showing a bearded head and foliage.

62. Block capital in the crypt showing a double-headed monster riding an amphisbaena.

63. Block capital in the crypt showing a winged monster spearing a running dog.

64. Initial F showing an amphisbaena. London, BL, Harley MS 624, f.128v.

65. Initial Q showing a double-headed monster. Baltimore, Walters Art Gallery, MS 10.18, f.152.

66. Block capital in St Gabriel's Chapel with animals standing on their hind legs playing musical instruments.

67. Initial F showing animals standing on their hind legs playing musical instruments. Cambridge, Trinity College, MS B.2.34, f.117.

68. Initial A with grotesques and an animal playing a harp. Cambridge, Trinity College, MS B.2.34, f.79v.

69. Detail of animal on hind legs playing a horn. London, BL, Cotton MS Claudius E.V, f.49.

70. Block capital in St Gabriel's Chapel with grotesques playing musical instruments.

71. Initial N with an animal blowing a horn. Cambridge, St John's College, MS A.8, f.64.

72. Initial with animals playing musical instruments. Canterbury Cathedral Library, MS E.42, f.36v

73-74. Man in cloak playing a fiddle; man playing a horn. Details of capitals on the external arcade on the south side of the choir.

75. Initial T with two men playing harps and a fiddle. London, BL, Arundel MS 91, f.218v.

76. Initial B with musicians and a knife thrower. Cambridge, Trinity College, MS B.5.26, f.1.

77. Block-shaped capital in St Gabriel's Chapel with two addorsed winged grotesques.

78. Initial O containing a pair of addorsed winged griffins. London, BL, MS Royal 6 B.VI, f.23.

79. Detail of Byzantine silk with addorsed winged griffins.

80. Addorsed winged griffins on the bronze doors of Trani Cathedral, 1180-1190.

81-82. Two sides of a block-shaped capital in the crypt, each with a lion raising his paw.

83. Marginal detail of a lion with raised paw. London, BL, Arundel MS 60, f.5.

84. Initial topped by a lion with raised paw. London, BL, Cotton MS Vit. CXII, f.134.

85. The zodiacal symbol for May. London, BL, Cotton MS Vit. CXII, f.127.

86. Cushion capital with a winged dragon with a twisted tail in the Holy Innocents' Chapel.

87. Image of the constellation Cetus. London, BL, Harley MS 647, f.10.

88. Initial with a monster and dog blowing a horn. London, BL, Cotton MS Claud. E.V, f.22v.

89. Pelican from Cambridge, Univ. Lib., MS Ii.4.26

90. Block capital in the crypt carved with a wolf biting its own foot.

91. Bestiary illustration. Cambridge, Univ. Lib., MS Ii.4.26, f. 12.

92-93. Block capitals in the crypt: a man wrestling with a lion, and a hooded rider.

94-95. Block capitals in the crypt: an pair of acrobats, and a two-headed monster.

96. Initial T with acrobat standing on a monster. London, BL, Arundel MS 91, f.156v.

97. Acrobats forming the initial L. London, BL, Arundel MS 91, f.40.

98. River God holding a fish and a flask. Mid 9th-century Carolingian ivory in the Bibliothèque Nationale in Paris.

99. Initial S with a two-headed monster. Florence, Bibl. Laurenziana, MS Plut. XII.17.

100. Cushion capital in the crypt with scallop pattern carved in low relief.

101-102. Details of carving on two imposts in the crypt.

103. Sarcophagus with scallop motif on the lid, early 12th century, Fordwich, near Canterbury.

104. Shaft with scallop decoration in the Holy Innocents' Chapel.

105. Cushion capital in St Gabriel's Chapel with a lion.

106. Double cushion capital with lions in the shields from the royal nunnery at Romsey Abbey.

107. Cushion capital on the north side of the entrance arch of the south-west transept of Worcester Cathedral.

108. Cushion capital presumed to come from Evesham Abbey.

109. Cushion capital with 'Winchester acanthus' in the Holy Innocents' Chapel.

110. Capital with 'Winchester acanthus' on the external arcade of the north-east transept.

111. Fragment from Westminster Abbey with 'Winchester acanthus' foliage.

112. Initial P with confronted dragons and foliage. Baltimore, Walters Art Gallery, MS 10.18, f.216v.

113. Impost of the chapter house doorway at Rochester Cathedral.

114. Voussoir with a bearded head flanked by dragons tugging its beard, from St.Augustine's Abbey.

115. Initial T with head flanked by dragons. London, BL, Harley MS 624, f.132.

116. Capital with foliage from St Augustine's Abbey.

117. Initial with foliage. London, BL, Cotton MS Tib. C.VI, f.72.

118. Fluted shaft and cushion capital carved in low relief, in the crypt.

119. Shaft carved in low relief and trefoil capital, in the crypt.

120. Detail of one of the spiral columns from the shrine of St Peter's in Rome.

121. One of a pair of columns with deeply cut spirals that flank the sanctuary.

122. The choir, Canterbury Cathedral.

123. Tau-cross capital from the choir of St Anselm, re-used in the crypt.

124. 9th-century tau-cross capital in the nave of San Vincenzo in Prato, Milan.

125. Tau-cross capital from the 9th-century dormitory at Westminster Abbey.

126. Tau-cross capital from the 11th-century ambulatory of St John's Chapel, White Tower, London

127. Capital with chamfered angles and a central projection, from the 11th-century nave of Jumièges Abbey.

128. Detail of window ornament in the apse of St Anselm's Chapel.

129. Detail of exterior window between the south-east transept and St Anselm's Chapel.

130. Capitals and arcading on the exterior of the north-east transept.

131. Capital on the external arcade of the north-east transept.

132. Detail of a hunting scene on a capital on the external arcade of the south-east transept.

133. Detail of a capital on the external arcade of the south-east transept.

134. Winged grotesques with whirling tail on the external arcade of the north-east transept.

135. Winged grotesques with whirling tails on a capital from the cloister of the royal abbey at Reading.

136. Detail of a cushion capital with foliage from the entrance-arch of the south transept of Worcester Cathedral.

137. Foliage capital on the external arcade of the south-east transept.

138. Cushion capital with foliage on the south doorway at the west end of the nave of Durham Cathedral.

139. Detail of foliage on the external arcade of the north-east transept.

140. Capital with bird-head from the external arcade of the south side of the choir.

141. Choir capital from Romsey Abbey.

142-143. Details of two of the carved shafts on the external arcade of the south-east transept.

144. Capital with falling figure on the external arcade of the south-east transept.

145-146. Capitals with grotesque masks on the external arcade of the south-east transept.

147. Capital of the external arcade of the north-east transept with a nude figure devoured by angle masks.

148. Capital with figure on horseback and another figure tumbling down, on the external arcade of the south-east transept.

149-150. Two sides of a capital on the external arcade of the north-east transept with a hunter stabbing a wild boar, and his foot bitten by a winged bird.

151. Exterior view of the main water tower, c.1155.

152. The ground storey of the water tower.

153. Diagramatic view of the buildings in the precinct at Christ Church Cathedral, Canterbury. Cambridge, Trinity College, MS R.17.1, f.286, c.1165.

154. The buildings and hydraulic system at Christ Church, Canterbury. Cambridge, Trinity College, MS R.17.1, ff.284v-285.

155. Decorated arch in the nave gallery at Rochester Cathedral.

156. Trumpet leaves and palmette ornament on the central pier of the water tower at Canterbury Cathedral.

157-159. Upper chamber of the water tower showing the geometric ornament used on the window heads.

160. Scallop capital from the ground storey of the water tower.

161. Aula nova staircase, south side.

162. Detail of the aula nova (guest house) and porta curie (main gate) from the waterworks drawing, ill. 154.

163. External view of the aula nova including the grand projecting 12th-century staircase.

164. External view of the west side of the treasury or vestiarium.

165. Stylized scallop capital with pleated shields from St Albans Abbey.

166. Scallop capital with pleated shields from Bridlington Abbey in Yorkshire.

167. Capitals with pleated shields from a doorway built by Bishop Pudsey (1154-1195) at Durham Castle.

168. Capital on the west wall of the vestiarium at ground level.

169. Central pillar of the vestiarium at ground level.

170. Boss from the ground storey of the vestiarium.

171. Boss from the upper chamber of the vestiarium with four lion's heads.

172. Vault boss from the ground storey of the water tower.

173. Vault boss carved with a flower from the ground storey of the water tower.

174. Mask capital in the vestiarium.

175. Bird capital in the vestiarium.

176. Capitals on the south side of St Anselm's Chapel.

177. St Andrew's Chapel.

178. The south-east transept tower of Canterbury Cathedral.

179. Engraving of the church tower of St Mary's Dover as it stood in 1814.

180. Detail of the north entrance to the crypt.

181. Volute capital and carved impost from Hackington, St Stephen's.

182. Engraving of 1822 of the south-east transept tower of Canterbury Cathedral.

183. North entrance to the crypt at Canterbury Cathedral.

184. Engraving of 1822 of the south-side capitals of the west doorway of Hackington, St Stephen's.

185. The vault of the first floor chamber in the church of Montivilliers.

186. The octopartite rib vault that crowns the spacious upper chamber of the vestiarium.

187-188. Two scallop capitals on the west side of the vestiarium.

189. A tower capital from St Clement's, Sandwich.

190. Scallop capital in the upper chamber of the vestiarium.

191. Scallop capital from the water tower.

192-193. Vault support capitals in the nave at La Trinité, Caen.

194. Capitals in St Anselm's Chapel.

195. Vault support capital from La Trinité, Caen.

196. Capital with angle masks and beaded intertwined stalks in St Anselm's Chapel.

197. Vault support capital from La Trinité, Caen.

198. Capital supporting the vaults of La Trinité, Caen.

199. Capital from Vieux Saint-Sauveur, Caen.

200-201. Two scallop capitals with masks from the nave of St Margaret-at-Cliffe.

202. Vault support capital from La Trinité, Caen.

203. The west face of the entrance arch to the vestiarium.

204. West doorway of St Michael's and All Angels, Throwley.

205. Doorway leading from the cloister to the dormitory in the precinct of Canterbury Cathedral.

206. Small tympanum from St Clement's, Sandwich.

207. Font in St Martin, Canterbury, decorated with beaded interlace.

208. Detail of a shaft from the dormitory doorway (ill.205) decorated with beaded interlace.

209. Small tympanum from the turret doorway at St Mary's, Chislet.

210. Upper part of the main gateway (porta curie) leading to the monastery at the north-west corner of the precinct.

211. Fragment of shaft from Saint-Bertin, now in the Musée de l'Hôtel Sandelin in Saint-Omer.

212-213. Decorative details from the main gate.

214. Carved head from the refectory at Dover Priory.

215. Page with foliage border. London, BL, Arundel MS 60, f.85v.

216. Capital on the main gateway of Canterbury Cathedral, with grotesque issuing foliage.

217. Capital with grotesque mask issuing foliage, on the east end of Sens Cathedral.

218-219. Capital from the Cathedral gateway with a central figure straddling two addorsed grotesques.

220. Initial P from London, BL, MS Add. 17738, f.13v.

221. Capital from the Cathedral gateway with a dragon in foliage.

222. Two capitals with headlong dragons on the main gateway.

223. Capital with a headlong dragon formerly in the Schnütgen Collection in Cologne.

224. Fragment of arch from the Infirmary cloister.

225. View of Canterbury from the south on a 12th-century seal.

226. Male head, presumably from the choir screen, c.1180, in Canterbury Cathedral.

227. Detail of choir aisle in Canterbury Cathedral.

228-230. Three bosses from the choir aisles at Canterbury Cathedral.

231. Female figure in quatrefoil frame presumably from the choir screen, c.1180, in Canterbury Cathedral.

232. Three-quarter length King pointing upward, in a quatrefoil frame, presumably from the choir screen, c.1180, in Canterbury Cathedral.

233. King pointing upward in a quatrefoil frame, presumably from the choir screen, c.1180, in Canterbury Cathedral.

234. Tomb of Bishop Hubert Walter (†1205) in Canterbury.

235. Reconstruction by James Essex of the 12th-century choir screen formerly at Ely Cathedral.

236-237. Screen and Rood at the Liebfraukirche, Halberstadt.

238-239. Bearded figures in quatrefoil frame presumably from the choir screen, c.1180, in Canterbury Cathedral.

240. Detail of the late 12th-century choir screen at St Michael, Hildesheim.

241. Roundel with a grotesque head presumably from the choir screen, c.1180, in Canterbury Cathedral.

242. Roundel with a three-quarter length figure holding a martyr's palm presumably from the choir screen, c.1180, in Canterbury Cathedral.

243-245. Roundels presumably from the choir screen, c.1180, in Canterbury Cathedral.

246. Roundel with a female head presumably from the choir screen, c.1180, in Canterbury Cathedral.

247. Detail from the font at Stanton Fitzwarren (Gloucestershire) showing figure of Synagoga with a blindfold.

248. Enthroned Christ with Luna in roundel on the right, from the 12th-century choir screen formerly in Mariengraden church, Cologne, now in Bonn, Landesmuseum.

249. Jesse page. Paris, BN, MS lat. 8846, f.4.

250-53. Figures with fingers emerging from within the cloak: Detail of f.66, Paris, BN, MS lat. 8846; an antique statue in the Vatican Museum, Rome; king from the choir screen at Canterbury; figures from the south doorway at Barfreston Church.

254. Label stop with a calf's head, presumably from the choir screen, c.1180, in Canterbury Cathedral.

255. Label stop in the form of a grotesque head presumably from the choir screen, c.1180, in Canterbury Cathedral.

256. Label stop grotesque holding a human head in its jaws presumably from the choir screen, c.1180, in Canterbury Cathedral.

257. Barfreston Church, chancel arch.

258. Annulet presumably from the choir screen, c.1180, in Canterbury Cathedral.

259. Annulet from the chancel arch at Barfreston Church.

260. Detail of the St Heribert shrine in Deutz showing a roundel with a cross-hatched background.

261. Fragment presumably from the Cathedral choir screen with cross-hatching similar to ill.260.

262-263. Two grotesque heads presumably from the choir screen, c.1180, Canterbury Cathedral.

264. Rochester Cathedral, grotesque head in a roundel.

265. St Bartholomew's, Bobbing. Small octagonal shaft with St Martial and an unidentified figure, probably from St Augustine's Abbey.

266. Second seal of St Augustine's Abbey, Canterbury.

267. Canterbury Cathedral, detail of a male head in a quatrefoil from the tomb of Bishop Hubert Walter.

268. Detail of the waterworks plan, Cambridge, Trinity College. R.17.1, f.284v (ill.154), showing the range of infirmary buildings in the precinct of Christ Church Canterbury.

269. Remains of the Infirmary Hall at Canterbury.

270. Remains of the Infirmary Chapel at Canterbury.

271. Capitals from the Infirmary Chapel with grotesque.

272. Capital from the Infirmary Chapel decorated with confronted grotesques.

273. Capital from the Infirmary Chapel decorated with a flower.

274. Infirmary cloister, Canterbury Cathedral.

275. Entrance to the *domus hospitum*, now in the Archdeacon's garden.

276. Gabled end of a scarcophagus now at St Lawrence, Godmersham, with the figure of an archbishop, presumably Thomas Becket.

277. Capital with confronted birds presumably from Canterbury, found in Chartham. Now Canterbury Heritage Museum.

278. St Paul and the Viper. Wall-painting in St Anselm's Chapel.

Page 11. General view of Canterbury Cathedral.

Page 34. Plan of the crypt.

Colour plates

I. St Gabriel's Chapel in the crypt of Canterbury Cathedral.

II. Capital in St Gabriel's Chapel with grotesques playing musical instruments.

III. Capital in St Gabriel's Chapel with animals playing musical instruments.

IV. Crypt capital with figure straddling two addorsed grotesques.

V. Crypt capital with winged monster spearing a dog.

VI. Crypt capital in St Gabriel's Chapel with two addorsed winged grotesques.

VII. Waterworks plan of Christ Church, Canterbury. Cambridge, Trinity College MS R.17.1, ff. 284v-285.

VIII. Capital in St Gabriel's Chapel with a lion.

IX. Capital in St Gabriel's Chapel with double-bodied lion.

X. Crypt capital with angle mask and foliage.

XI. Capital on the external arcade of the south-east transept.

XII. The south-east transept of Canterbury Cathedral.

Colour photography at Canterbury Cathedral
by Roger Musgrave

INDEX

Numbers in italics refer to illustrations

Aachen Museum, Bacchus *acquamanile*, 203 n.53
Adisham, Kent, screen from Christ Church, 202 n.51
Aix-en-Provence, 201 n.32
Anchin Abbey, 132, 133
Angers, Ste-Marie-de-la-Charité, 192 n.77
Angevin Empire, 17
Anselm, Archbishop of Canterbury, 14-15, 17, 33, 36,
    197 n.50; *3*
  Anselm's Cathedral *see* Chapter II *passim*
    enlargement, 174
  Cur Deus Homo, 15
  journey to Rome, 78-9
  seal of, 189 n.28
Anselm of Bury, 187 n.9
Anselm of Laon, 187 n.14
Aratus, *Phaenomena*, 60; *87*
Arenberg Gospels (New York, Pierpont Morgan Lib.,
    M.869), 23; *12*
Arras, 95
  Cathedral, 132
    capitals, 143
  St Vaast Abbey, 132
Augustine, St, 14, 20, 23
  Commentary on the Psalms (Cambridge, Trinity College
    MS B.5.28), 50; *53*
Austin Canons, 15
Auxerre, St Germain, 189 n.29

Baltimore, Walters Art Gallery
  MS 10.18, 52, 189 n.36; *61, 65, 112*
Barfreston, Kent, St Nicholas, 20, 162, 203 n.53; *257, 259*
  south doorway, 180; *7, 253*
Bari, Apulia, 88
Barisano da Trani, 189 n.37
Barking, Essex
  nunnery of All Hallows, choir screen, 151
Battle Abbey, water system, 98
Bayeux Tapestry, 25, 33; *16, 33*
Beauvais Abbey, 137
Bec, Abbey of, 13, 14, 15, 24, 95, 197 n.50
Becket, Thomas, 17-18, 57, 96, 139, 196 n.35, 197 n.50
  cult of, 139-40, 147
  images of, Appendix II, 180-181; *5, 276*
  Miracles of Thomas Becket, 98
  murder of, 25, 139
  sculpture at Canterbury after, Chapter IV, *passim*
  tomb of, 140, 145
Bellême, Robert, 187 n.13
Benedictine Houses, 73
Benedictines as Archbishops, 139
Benevento, Archbishop's cope, 184 n.20
Bernard of Clairvaux, St, 65
Bernay Abbey, Normandy, 49
Berteaucourt, Picardy, 158
Bertin, St, 132
Bestiaries, 61-2; *89, 91*
Bethersden 'marble', use of, 144

Bibury, Gloucestershire, 189 n.34
Birchington, Kent, 75
Bobbing, Kent, St Bartholomew's
    shaft in sedilia, 169, 203 n.64; *265*
Boethius, *De Consolatione Philosophiae*, 61
Bonn, Landesmuseum
    Luna from Cologne, Mariengraden choir screen; 151, 158;
      248
Bosham, Herbert, 200 n.4
Bourges Cathedral, choir screen, 151
Breedon-on-the-Hill, Leicestershire, 197 n.47
Bridlington, Yorkshire, capitals, 195 n.30; *166*
Brighton, St Nicholas, font, 130
Brito, Richard, 18
Britton, John, 114
    engraving of Canterbury Tower; *182*
Brook, Kent, 75
Brussels, Bibliothèque Royale
    MS 9987-91 (Prudentius, Psychomachia), 190 n.47
Buckler, J.C.
    Canterbury Cathedral, north-west tower (watercolour),
      29; *17, 19*
Bury St Edmunds Abbey, 98, 188 n.20
    Bury Bible (Cambridge, Corpus Christi College MS 2), 70
    Rood, 70
Byzantine silk, with griffins, 57; *79*
Byzantium, capitals from, 49

Caedmon poetry (Oxford Bodleian, MS Junius 11), 23; *11*
Caen, 115
    La Trinité, 28, 118, 120, 124, 127, 130, 192 n.83
      capitals, 31; *192, 193, 195, 197, 198, 202*
    quarries of, 17, 22, 123-4
    St Etienne, 13, 15, 28, 120; *18*
    Vieux Saint-Sauveur, capital, 123; *199*
Cambrai Cathedral, 132, 135
    capitals, 143
Cambridge
    Corpus Christi College
      MS 286 (Gospels of St Augustine), 184 n.16
    Pembroke College,
      MS 301 (Gospels), 189 n.34
    St John's
      MS 8 (Josephus), 191 n.65
    Trinity College
      MS B.2.34; *67, 68*
      MS B.4.26 (Passionale); *54*
      MS B.5.28 (St Augustine on Psalms), 50; *53*
      MS B.10.4, 189 n.34
      MS B.16.44, 13; *1*
      MS O.2.51 (Priscian), 50; *58*
      MS R.17.1 (Eadwine Psalter), 99, 101; *153, 154, 268,*
        col. pl. VII
    University Library
      Ee.3.59 (Life of St Edward), 148
      Ii.4.26 (Bestiary); *89, 91*

Canterbury Cathedral (Christ Church); *ill. p.11, 225*
  archdeacon's kitchen, 135
  aula nova (guest house), 98, 105, 117, 120, 173-4, 194 n.18;
        161, 162
     staircase, 135, 173-4; *163*
  Cellarer's Hall (*domus hospitum*), arch, 180; *275*
  cemetery gateway, 135
  choir, 79, 80, 101-2, 130-1, 141, 143, 144, 149; *122, 123, 227-
        230*
     bosses, 143, 164; *228-230*
  choir screen
     label stops; *254-6*
     sculptures, 145-50, 151, 154, 156, 158-9; *6, 226, 231-233,
           238, 239, 241-246, 252, 258, 261, 262, 263*
  cloister, 135
  corona, 143
     crypt under, 188 n.19
  crypt, 25, 37-79, 80, 86, 87-88, 114-15, 131; *20, 31-5, 37, 38,
        47-52, 60, 62, 63, 81-82, 90, 92-95, 100- 102,
        118-119, 180; col.pls.IV, V, X*
     entrance, 114, 115; *180, 183*
     Holy Innocent's Chapel, 37, 38, 44, 46, 51, 73, 84, 112-
           13; *39-40, 55, 86, 104 109*
     St Gabriel's Chapel, 37, 38, 46, 61, 69, 112-13, 203 n.52;
           43, 66, 105; col.pl.I, II, III, VI, VIII, IX
  dorter doorway, 135; *205*
     reconstruction, 149-50
  external arcade sculpture, 86, 87; *73-74, 130, 131, 133, 134,
        139, 142-143, 145-146; col. pls. XI, XII*
  Infirmary complex, Appendix I
     chapel, 135, 175, 177; *270-273*
     cloister, 135, 179, 180; *224, 268, 274*
     hall, 173-4; *269*
     Lanfranc's Infirmary, 174
  ivories, 25; *15*
  Jesus Chapel, 37
  library, 23-4, 57, 139
     MS E.42; *72*
     Lanfranc's additions to, 23-4
  porta curie (main gateway), 98, 128, 130-3, 135, 177; *210,
        212-13, 216, 218-19, 221, 222*
  prior's lodgings, 136
  St Andrew's Chapel, 107, 111, 114; *177*
  St Anselm's Chapel, 111-13, 114, 120, 123, 124; *176*
     figural sculpture, 117-18; *196*
     wall painting: *St Paul and the Viper, 278*
     window decoration; *128, 129*
  scriptorium, 23, 24, 50-1, 62, 87
  stained glass, 25, 203 n.60
  tomb of Thomas Becket, 140
  tomb of Bishop Hubert Walter, 147, 169; *234, 267*
  towers, 114, 117; *178*
  Trinity Chapel, 37, 143, 203 n.52
  vestiarium (treasury), 107, 111, 112, 117, 118, 120, 123, 124,
        130-1, 177; *168-169, 170-171, 174, 175, 186-188,
        190*
     entrance, *203*
  wall-paintings, 25 *see also* St Anselm's Chapel
  water resources, 98
     system, 98-9, 101; *153, 154, col.pl.VII*
  water-tower, 102, 120, 124, 135; *151, 152, 172, 173, 191*
  Wulfric's church, 189 n.29
Canterbury
  Heritage Museum
     capital found Chartham, 62; *277*
     reliefs; *25-29*

[Canterbury]
  Roman Theatre, 22
  St Augustine's Abbey, 19-20, 38-9, 49, 73, 75, 169,
        194 n.14; *114, 116, 265*
     crypt 38-9
     scriptorium, 44, 49-50
        Martyrology, 57
        Priscian, 50; 58
     second seal of, 169; *266*
  St Martin, font, 195 n.28; *207*
Carolingian manuscripts, 60, 62; *87*
  sources of decoration, 51
Châlons-sur-Marne
  cloister sculpture, 148
Chartham, capital found at *see* Canterbury Heritage
        Museum
Chartres Cathedral, 151
  John of Salisbury, Bishop of, 96
Chichester Cathedral, choir screen, 151
Chillenden, Prior of Christ Church, 149-50
Chislet, Kent
  St Mary's, 124; *209*
Choir screens, 150-151
Churchdown, Gloucestershire, 98
Clarendon, Council of, 17
Cluny Abbey III, 137, 192 n.75
Cnut, King, 22
Codex Aureus (Stockholm, Royal Library MS A.135), 23
Colchester Castle, capitals, 49
Cologne
  Mariengraden Church (formerly), 151, 158; *248*
  St Maria im Kapitol, 38
  Schnütgen Collection (formerly)
     capital, 135; *223*
  trade with, 135
Como, San Abondio, 44; *41*
Conrad, Prior of Canterbury, 19, 36
Constantinople, water cistern, 203 n.54
Creuilly nr Caen, capitals, 123

Danelaw, Viking, 13
David I, king of Scotland, 37, 187 n.15
Deutz, Shrine of St Heribert, 167; *260*
Deventer, Holland, spiral columns, 78
Domesday Book, 19
Domesday Monachorum, 183 n.8
Dover, Priory, 130; *214*
  St Mary's, 127
     engraving of tower; *179*
Dunstan, St, 23, 36, 151
  Life of (Osbern), 35
  Miracles of St Dunstan (Osbern), 35
Durdent, Walter, Bishop of Lichfield, 98-9
Durham Castle chapel
  capitals, 70, 196 n.30
  doorway, *167*
Durham Cathedral, 31, 73, 75
  capitals (nave and chapter house), 71; *138*
  choir screen, 151, 158
  laver, 103, 105
  spiral shafts, 78
  water system, 98
Durham Cathedral Library
  MS A.II.4 (Carilef Bible), 51; *56*

Eadmer, chronicler, 27, 29, 35, 36, 78
Eastry, Prior of Christ Church, 150, 200 n.4
Edward the Confessor, St, 27, 80; *16*
   Life of, (Cambridge Univ. Lib., Ee.3.59), 148
  sculpture of, 202 n.38
  shrine of, 148
Elphege, St, 35, 36, 151
  Life of (Osbern), 35
Ely Cathedral, 51, 183 n.8
  capitals, 70
  choir screen, 151
    drawings, 154; *235*
Enamel work, 166
Ernulf, Prior of Christ Church later Bishop of Rochester,
    19, 36, 73
Essex, James, 151
Ethelbert, king, sculpture, 202 n.38
Evesham Abbey
  crypt capital, 71; *108*
Exeter Cathedral, 117
  St Nicholas Priory, water system, 98, 105

Faussett, Rev. Bryan, 145
  Collection, 145
    relief sculpture, 145, 161, 169; *232*
Faversham Abbey, 20, 144
  capital; *8*
Fécamp Abbey, 192 n.83
FitzUrse, Reginald, 18
Flambard, Ranulf, 187 n.14
Flanders, books from, 23
  cushion capitals, 40, 47
  influence of, 136
  links with, 117, 131
  trading with (wool), 22, 135
Floreffe Bible (London, BL MS Add.17738), 133; *220*
Florence, Bibl. Laurenziana
  MS Plut.XII.17, 62; *99*
Fordwich, nr Canterbury, 123
  sarcophagus, 67; *103*
Frontinus, 193 n.14

Geoffrey, Prior of Christ Church, 172
Germany
  artistic developments, 47
  capitals from, 44, 47, 49
Gervase, chronicler, 35, 79, 96, 98, 114, 140, 141, 144, 149,
    150
Gesta Sacristarium, 70
Giffard, William, Bishop of Winchester, 15
Gilduinus, sculptor, 88
Glanville, Gilbert, Bishop of Rochester
  tomb of, 147, 169
Glastonbury, 51, 183 n.8
  Lady Chapel doorway, 145
Gloucester Candlestick, 25; *14*
Gloucester Cathedral, crypt capitals, 70-1
Gniezno, bronze doors, 190 n.41
Godmersham, Kent, St Lawrence
  tomb-slab showing Becket, 180; *5, 276*
Goult Priory, Normandy, 192 n.83
Gregory I, the Great, pope, 14, 78
Gregory III, pope, 78
Grimbald Gospels (London BL, MS Add. 34890), 23
Gundulf, Prior of Saint-Etienne, later Bishop of Rochester,
    28

Hackington, St Stephen
  capitals, 123; *181*
  doorway, 115; *184*
Halberstadt, Liebfrauenkirche
  choir screen, 151, 154; *236, 237*
Hanover, Kestner Museum
  MS WMXXIa 36 (Eadui Psalter), 23; *18*
Harley Psalter (London, BL MS Harley 603), 23
Henry I, king, 15, 18, 37, 86, 187 n.13
  foundation at Reading Abbey; *59*
Henry II, king, 17-18, 137, 139, 140, 186 n.2
Henry, Prior of Christ Church, 27, 36
Henry of Blois, Bishop of Winchester, 166, 196 n.36
Heppington, Kent
  Faussett Pavilion, 201 n.26
Herbert of Bosham, 139
Hereford Cathedral, capitals, 70
Heribert of Deutz, St, shrine of, 167; *260*
Hersfeld Abbey (Hesse)
  chapter house capitals, 44; *42*
Hildesheim, St Michael
  choir screen; *240*
Horfalde, Kent, 101, 102
Hugh II, Abbot of Saint-Amand, 133
Hugo Pictor, of Bury St Edmunds, 70; *3*
Hyginus, *Astronomicon*, 68
  Fables, 68

Ile de France, developments, 135
Innocent III, pope, 172
Italy, block capitals, 49
  sculptural styles, 44
Ivychurch, Wiltshire, 195 n.30

John, King, 172
John de Gray, Bishop of Norwich, 172
John of Salisbury, 17, 95, 96
  Metalogicon, Policratus, 96
Jumièges Abbey, capitals, 80; *127*

Kent, east, parish churches, 124
Kentish assessment list, 19

Lambeth Bible (Lambeth Palace MS 3), 133
Lanfranc, Archbishop of Canterbury, 13-14, 17, 19, 23,
    Chapter I *passim*, 39, 80, 87, 197 n.50; *2, 20,*
    21-24
Lanfranc's Constitutions, 35
Langton, Stephen, 172
Laon, 143, 144
Leeds Priory, Kent, 124
Lewes Priory, capitals, 130
  laver, 105
  water system, 98
Lichfield Cathedral, water system, 98-9
Liège, bronze font, 166, 189 n.28
Liessies Abbey (Hainault), 133
Limoges, Saint-Martial monastery, 68
Lincoln Cathedral, 120, 194 n.22
  capitals, 49
Loire Valley, pattern books, 68
Lombardy, cushion capitals, 44
London basin buildings, capitals, 80
London
  British Library
    MS Add. 17738 (Floreffe Bible) 133; *220*

[London, British Library]
  MS Add. 34890 (Grimbald Gospels), 23
  MS Arundel 60 (Psalter), 60, 198 n.57; *83, 215*
  MS Arundel 91 (Lives of Saints), 60, 75, 191 n.66; *75, 96, 97*
  MS Arundel 155 (Psalter), 189 n.34
  MS Cotton Claudius E.V (Canon Law), 51, 189 n.38; *6 9, 88*
  Cotton Cleopatra C.VIII (Prudentius), 62
  Cotton Cleopatra D.I (Vitruvius), 193-194 n.14
  MS Cotton Nero C.VII (Passionale), 75; *115*
  MS Cotton Tiberius C.VI (Psalter); *117*
  MS Cotton Vitellius C.XII, (Martyrology), 57; *85*
  MS Harley 603 (Utrecht Psalter copy), 23
  MS Harley 624 (Passionale), 189 n.36; *64, 115*
  MS Harley 647 (Aratus), 60; *87*
  MS Royal 5.B.XV, 47
  MS Royal 6.B.VI; *78*
  See of, 14
  Tower of London
    St John's Chapel, capitals, 49, 80; *126*
  Victoria & Albert Museum
    Gloucester Candlestick, 25; *14*
    ivory bookcovers from Canterbury, 25; *15*
    Lorsch Bible cover (ivory), 203 n.54
  Westminster Abbey, 27; *16*
    capitals, 73, 80; *111, 125*
  Westminster Hall, 71
    Palace, fluted basin from, 103, 105
Louis of France, king, 140, 200 n.6
Lund Cathedral, spiral columns, 78

Magna Carta, 1215, 172
Malmesbury Abbey, label stops, 161
Manuscript illumination, 24-5, 49-50, 87
Margaret of Scotland, Queen, 187 n.16
Marmoutier Abbey, crypt capitals, 192 n.83
Marian devotions, 36
Marquise, nr Boulogne, 186 n.12
Master Hugo, 70
Matilda, Queen, 37, 132, 187 n.15, 196 n.36
Metalwork, 135, 145, 166, 167, 203 n.54
Michael, St, 88
Milan
  San Vicenzo in Prato, capital, 80; *124*
  Sant' Ambrogio, choir screen, 151
  Santa Maria d'Ancona, 44
Milborne Port, Somerset, capitals, 189 n.32
Minster-in-Thanet, Kent, 124
Modena Cathedral, reliefs, 88, 151
Moissac, cloister capitals, 88
Mont-Saint-Michel, 38
Monte Gargano, Apulia, 88
Montivilliers Abbey, Normandy, 118; *185*
Morville, Hugh de, 18
Mosan art, 166, 189 n.28
Much Wenlock Abbey, Shropshire
  lobed bowl, 103, 105
  water system, 98

New York
  Cloisters, *Synagoga*, 158
  Pierpont Morgan Library
    M.689 (Arenberg Gospels), 23; *12*
Nicholas, St, 88

Nicholas of Verdun, 166
Norwich, Cathedral, spiral shafts, 78

Oakham Castle, Rutland, 20, 201 n.19
Oda, St, 36
  Life of (Osbern), 35
Odo, Prior of Christ Church, 139, 140
Old Sarum, 120
  plan of *pulpitum*, 151
Onyx, use of, 111, 117, 144
  shafts, 179
Opus reticulatum, 117
Osbern, chronicler, 35, 36
  Lives of St Dunstan, St Elphege and St Oda, 35
  Miracles of St Dunstan, 35
Oxford, Bodleian Library
  MS Bodley 569 (drawing of Lanfranc); *2*
  MS Junius 11 (Caedmon), 23; *11*
  Wadham College
    A.10.22 (Gospels), 189 n.34

Paris
  Bibliothèque Nationale
    ivory, Carolingian, 65; *98*
    MS lat.8846 (Utrecht Psalter copy), 160-1; *249, 250*
  Musée de Cluny, Basel Antependium, 203 n.54
  Notre-Dame, 144, 151
  region of, 143
  St Denis Abbey, 95
Paschal II, pope, 15
Patrixbourne, Kent
  St Mary's Church, chancel, 20, 196 n.36
    south doorway, 180; *10*
Pattern books, 68-9
Peckham, revenues from, 35
Penenden Heath, Trial of, 14
Peter, Abbot of Gloucester; *14*
Peter Lombard, glosses, 139
Phaedrus, fables, 61
Picardy, 132
Pontigny, 133, 200 n.4
Prudentius, *Psychomachia*, 62, 68
Pudsey, Bishop of Durham, 196 n.30
Purbeck Marble, use of, 103, 105, 135, 144, 170; *8*
  shafts, 179

Ralph d'Escures, Archbishop of Canterbury, 15, 36
Ravello Cathedral, S. Italy,
  doors with griffins, 57
Reading Abbey, 20, 86-7; *59, 135*
Regensburg, St Emmeram
  capitals, 46
Reginald, sub-prior of Christ Church, 172
Reims, 143
  Council of, 132
  Musée St-Remi, 'Odo' tomb, 203 n.61
  St Remi, chapter house, 167
    tomb of Raoul le Vert, 201 n.28
Relics, 36
Repton Derbyshire, St Wystan, 31
  crypt, 78
Rhine, Upper, trade with, 135
Rhineland, artistic developments, 47
  churches, 38, 135
  crypts, 188 n.19

Richard, Prior of Dover, 140
Richborough, triumphal monument, 22
Richmond Castle (N. Yorks.), capitals, 49
Robert of Winchelsey, Archbishop of Canterbury, 150
Rochester Castle, 187 n.14
Rochester Cathedral monastery, 20, 73, 75, 136, 187 n.14,
      196 n.41; *9, 113, 155, 264*
   capitals, 135
   chapter-house doorway, 196 n.41; *113*
   Christ's mandorla, 203 n.60
   crypt, 31
   manuscripts from, 52
   portal annulets, 162
   tomb of Bishop Gilbert de Glanville, 147, 169
Roger, Abbot of Bec, 197 n.50
Roger, Bishop of Old Sarum, 151
Rolduc, spiral columns, 78
Roman portraiture, 161; *251*
Rome
   St Peter's, 78-9
      spiral column from shrine, 75, 78, 79; *120*
   Vatican Museum
      antique statue, 161; *251*
Romsey Abbey, 71, 86; *106, 141*
Rouen, Bibliothèque Municipale
   MS A.85, 47; *46*
   MS 539; *3*
   Cathedral, 39
Ruprich-Robert, architect, 120

St Albans Abbey, capitals, 195 n.30; *165*
Saint-Amand Abbey, Normandy, 133
Saint-Donat-sur-l'Herbasse (Drome), 201 n.32
St Gall, Switzerland, 101
Saint-Germer-en-Fly, keystones, 199 n.69
Saint-Leu d'Esserent, 143
St Margaret-at-Cliffe, Kent, 124, 127; *200-201*
Saint-Omer, Normandy, 132
   Abbey of Saint-Bertin, 95, 132, 172, 199 n.66, 200 n.4
   Musée de l'Hôtel Sandelin
      fragment of shaft, 132; *211*
St Osyth, Essex, 15, 187 n.14
Saints, Anglo-Saxon, 15
   devotions to, 35 *see also* individual names:
      Augustine, Bernard of Clairvaux, Bertin, Dunstan,
         Edward the Confessor, Elphege, Heribert of
         Deutz, Michael, Nicholas, Oda
Salisbury Cathedral, choir screen, 151
Sandwich, Kent, 133
   St Clement's, 124, 127; *189, 206*
Santiago di Compostela, 88
Saxony, trade with, 135
Scotland, Abbot, 38
Sélincourt, font, *Synagoga*, 158
Sens, Normandy, 200 n.4 *see also* William of Sens
   Becket's flight to, 133
   Cathedral, 18, 133, 135, 144
      capitals, 135, 143; *217*
Shaftesbury, Dorset, capitals, 195 n.30
Sherborne Abbey, Dorset, 18
Smeeth, Kent, 75
Soissonais region, 133
Solomon, Temple of, 78
Southwick Priory, Hampshire
   choir screen, 151

Speyer, Rhineland, Imperial Cathedral, 38, 188 n.19
Spiral columns, 78
Springhead, Kent, laurel-leaf motif, 190 n.52
Stanton Fitzwarren, Gloucestershire
   Font with *Synagoga*, 158; *247*
Stephen, King, 95, 132
Steyning, Sussex
   St Andrew's, label-stops, 161
Stigand, Archbishop of Canterbury, 13, 14, 27
Stockholm, Royal Library
   MS A.135, Codex Aureus, 23
Stogersey, Somerset
   volute capitals, 49
Suger, Abbot of St Denis, 166, 193 n.4
Swalon, subdeacon of Saint-Amand, 199 n.68

Ternay-sur-Vienne (Isère), spandrels, 201 n.32
Thérouanne Cathedral, 132
Theobald, Archbishop of Canterbury, 16-17, 139, 197 n.50
   building and sculpture under, Chapter III *pasim*
   seal of, *4*
Thomas, Archbishop of York, 14
Throwley, Kent
   St Michael's and All Angels, 127; *204*
Tongres Abbey, Belgium, spiral columns, 78
Toulouse, St Sernin
   reliefs, 88
Tournai stone, 196 n.40
Tours Cathedral, Life of St Martial window, 204 n.66
Towers, multiple, 117, 135
Tracy, William dc, 18
Trani Cathedral, S. Italy
   doors with griffins, 57; *80*
Trier Cathedral, screen sculptures, 202 n.45
Trondheim Cathedral, 192 n.83

Urban II, pope, 192 n.75
Utrecht, spiral columns, crypt, 78
   University Library, MS 32 (Utrecht Psalter) 184 n.16

Vacarius, Master, 17, 96
Valenciennes
   Bibl. Mun., MS 1-5 and 186 (Bible), 199 n.68
   Notre-Dame-la-Grande, 132, 143, 200 n.20
   capitals, 143
Vezzolano, choir screen, 151
Via Emilia (route), 88
Villiers-Saint-Paul, 135
Vitruvius, 193 n.14

Walmer, Kent, 75
Walter de Banham, 98
Walter, Hubert, Archbishop, 172
   tomb of; *234, 267*
Walter Parvus, 96, 98, 102
Water systems, 98, 99, 101; *151-154, col.pl.VII*
Waverley Abbey, Surrey, 98
Weissendorf, Bavaria
   St Margarethe, 46; *45*
Wibert, Prior of Christchurch, 19, 96, 98, 99, 102, 113, 114,
      115, 117, 120, 128, 131, 139, 177, 201 n.33
Wiligelmo, sculptor, 88
William de Corbeil, Archbishop of Canterbury, 15, 37
William the Englishman, 37, 143
William of Malmesbury, 37, 82

William of Normandy (the Conqueror), 13, 14
William Rufus, 14, 15, 186 n.2
William of Sens, 69, 79, 114, 141, 143, 144, 162
  workshop of, 164
William of Ypres, 132
Winchcombe Psalter (Dublin, Trinity College MS 53), 65
Winchester Cathedral monastery, 19, 51, 73, 117, 195 n.27
  crypt, 188 n.19
  Hyde Abbey, 196 n.36

'Winchester School', acanthus decoration, 51; *55, 56, 109-111, 212-213*
Wireker, Nigel, 96
Worcester Cathedral monastery, 19, 20, 75, 188 n.20
  capital, 71; *107*
  crypt, 188 n.19

York, archbishopric of, 14, 15
  Minster, capitals, 49
  St Mary's Abbey, sculptures, 145

278. St Paul and the Viper.
Wall-painting in St Anselm's Chapel.